D0619754

PREPARING
TO BE A
Help Meet

DEBI PEARL
AUTHOR OF *CREATED TO BE HIS HELP MEET*

Preparing To Be A Help Meet®
Copyright © 2010 by Michael and Debi Pearl

ISBN: 978-1-61644-010-7
EBook: April 2010

ISBN: 978-1-61644-011-4
EPub: April 2010

ISBN: 978-1-61644-009-1
First printing: April 2010 - 20,000

All scripture quotations are taken from the King James Holy Bible.

Printed in the United States of America

Other books by Debi Pearl:
Created To Be His Help Meet
The Help Meet's Journey
Listen To My Dream
To Train Up A Child
The Last Publishers, *The Vision*

Visit www.NoGreaterJoy.org for information on this and other products produced by No Greater Joy Ministries.

Requests for information should be addressed to:
No Greater Joy Ministries Inc. *1000 Pearl Road, Pleasantville, TN 37033 USA*

Cover design by Clint Cearley
Interior design and layout by Clint Cearley, DesignForgeServices.com

Thanks Guys

Although my name is on the cover of this book, its pages contain the wisdom and insight of many people. To meet my splendid crew, go to: PreparingtobeaHelpMeet.com. There you can ask questions, post pictures of yourself or your Bible class and continue to learn.

Men were asked to add their comments on the contents of this book so throughout its pages you will see small call-outs (like the one below) containing statements from the men concerning the related underlined text.

Below is a breakdown of who the men are so you will better understand their viewpoints. The King/Command man profile is a combination of two men, one married and the other unmarried while the Priest and Prophet are both unmarried.

ICON			
TYPE	Visionary / Prophet	Steady / Priest	Command / Kingly
BIO.	Artist, age 27	Web Developer, age 26	Editors, age 29

 Example of the men's comments seen throughout the book. The icon at the left determines which man's comment it is. See the table above to recognize which icon belongs to whom.

You spend your time pining away for your one true love and suddenly…you're married, and it is a lot more than you bargained for. Now is the hour you should be preparing to be a wife—to be a help meet. God wants to make you become a lovely help meet, but to be a good one takes effort…*lots of effort*.

Teacher's Guide

A complete Teacher's Guide by Shalom (Pearl) Brand, starts on page 229.

There is a thread…
a bright thread running,
weaving, tying bows
and underlining our lives.
Sometimes the thread is narrow
and barely perceptible; other times it
is *flamboyant*, creating
showers of w i d e dashing
ribbons *falling* from every
corner of our lives, bringing
vibrant color
to our otherwise ordinary
existence.

AND SO YOUR THREAD BEGINS…

God Needs Our Prayers

MORAL TO THE STORY: God wants, no, he NEEDS us to pray.
A CAUTION: Don't pray amiss.

God did something totally different in my love story. When I
was just a child he told me who I would marry. He didn't tell
my future husband—just skinny little me. Why? God always has
a very good reason. I believe it was because my future husband
needed, really needed someone to pray for him. I prayed.

Is there a young man that you have met in passing that you
thought would be a good husband? Have you been praying for
him by name?

Maybe heaven waits on you.

CHAPTER 1

the

K ID

story one

I HAD JUST TURNED THIRTEEN when I first saw him and knew, just simply knew, he was my man. If he had glanced over and been able to read my mind he would have surely laughed. I almost laughed. It was preposterous to think that I, a scrawny little kid who had not even gone through puberty, would claim him. The whole community had been talking about the famous, young preacher who had been invited to speak at First Baptist Church's Teen Retreat. He was all man, plain and simple: at least 6 foot 4 inches, and a dark jaw shadow where he shaved away his beard. My young mind quickly assessed him. He seemed bigger than life, a super, in charge type man. He was old, very old, and way too big, outweighing me by over 100 pounds. I guessed that he must have been at least 21 years old. As far as I was concerned, he might as well have been 99. Anybody over fifteen seemed ancient to me.

Anyway, God had never talked to me before; why would he start now and tell me this? I was just a kid. Does God talk to kids? Furthermore, I was not particularly spiritually minded, and not looking for a supernatural epiphany or vision. To top it all off, I was a Baptist, and Baptists do not believe in gifts, words of knowledge or such. Don't misunderstand; I was very interested in the things of God. I liked to teach small children Bible stories; I enjoyed church and was highly entertained when preachers preached on end times, but I was never given to deep spiritual sensitivity. God had a big surprise for me that day. I discovered that God has his own sense of humor. He always does the unexpected. But even to this day, over 46 years later, this remains the biggest "unexpected" of my entire life. This is how it happened.

There was a serious storm warning that day. Tornadoes were expected. The church leaders almost decided to cancel the youth event due to the storm, but since the preacher was so important, they decided to take the chance. I sat at a lodge with about 30 other teenagers, all of whom seemed years older and way cooler than me.

The teenage girls were acting like they were afraid of the storm. Obviously they thought their twittering would make them appear more femininely attractive. The boys were playing macho, "Bring it on, we can handle a silly old tornado." Looking around, I groaned with disgust. All this teenage nonsense was so stupid. Horses, mud fights, BB guns, forts, and bikes were my life. I did not relate to the hormone-driven game. I was half mad that my mom made me come to this dumb meeting. Why should I have to go to the retreat with a bunch of old snobs? It wasn't even our church, so I didn't know many of the kids there. It was clear they dismissed me as a snotty kid not worthy of any notice.

Then the preacher and his little brother stood to play musical instruments and sing. They were pretty good and I found myself enjoying it. I even thought the little brother was kind of cute, even if he was old. I figured him to be about 17. Finally Michael, the big brother, began to preach. I don't remember if it happened at the beginning of his message or in the middle or maybe even toward the end, but sometime while he was preaching the gospel, God spoke to me. "He's the one you will marry."

Whoa, I thought, *I don't even need to wear a bra yet, and God is letting me know who I will marry?* I clearly remember thinking, *this is just too weird...he is too old and I am just a little kid.* But God's ways are not our ways. I'm sure glad about that.

To my knowledge I had never even thought of God leading me. Now that I am old, I look back over the many years and I can count on my hands the number of times I think God did speak to me. Not many. Anyway, like the child I was, I simply believed God. I was too young to realize what a monumental thing had just happened. Since he was going to be my husband, I figured I might as well deal with it and not fuss too bad, and besides, it seemed light years away, so I had time to adjust. At home that evening I told my mom about how stupid the older teenagers had acted at the meeting due to the storm. Then I casually told her that God had spoken to me and told me that, when I grew up, the preacher guy would be my husband. I handed her the flyer from the Teen Retreat. "Here's the preacher man's name." My mom acted like it was everyday fare. I think she really believed me. She was a new Christian, and I guess these things were as new to her as they were to me. She just said, "Well, you need to start praying for him. Being a preacher means he will need a lot of prayer."

I didn't see or hear of him for the next three years, but I prayed for him off and on when I saw the paper on the wall by the phone, which helped me remember his name. The spring I turned sixteen I finally went through puberty. About time! That summer I signed on to be a counselor and lifeguard at a Child Evangelism Fellowship Bible camp. Guess who was there? You got it: My future husband, Mr. King-in-Charge, Famous Preacher Man himself. He was the special speaker all week, so I had plenty of time to check him out. All the time I was checking him out, he was checking out one of the other girls at the camp. I didn't really care, as I had no emotional attachment to him. While

I was there at the camp one of the older women who was a head counselor came to me and said she thought God had spoken to her about something. She was a sober woman, a Baptist. Again, Baptists do not put words in God's mouth. Yet she said, "I think God wants you to know that Michael Pearl will someday be your husband." It was embarrassing for one of my mom's friends to tell me something like that. I went home and told my mom, but her friend had already called and informed her. Without a trace of emotion, Mom reminded me to pray for the preacher. She told me, "He will need a lot of prayer because he is in the ministry. You need to pray for him all the time."

That same summer our regular pastor left our church for greener pastures. My daddy was on the pulpit committee (the group of men responsible for finding a pastor). The men called several different preachers to try out. Some of the preachers were not KJV, so they were out; some did not like the rural area, so they decided not to come. A few were just too boring to tolerate, and so week after week our church had different preachers come and go. It was a tedious, time-consuming chore trying to find all those preachers and then to make arrangements for them to come each week, find a place for them to stay, etc.

Finally I said to my dad, "Hey, that preacher guy that was at camp was pretty good. He is still in Bible college, so maybe he could just fill in when you can't find someone else to preach." Since the men of the church were at their wits' end, they listened to the mature counsel of a 16 year-old girl. Did you know that sometimes God uses the unexpected? Anyway, my dad called the college and asked Michael to come to preach at our church for the next Sunday. Over the next year the young preacher filled in as the speaker on Sunday mornings or evenings several times a month. Finally, the men decided to ask him to come on as our regular pastor. So now I called my future husband "Brother Pearl." We became great friends, but he still treated me like I was a kid.

The way you meet your future spouse and the style of courtship used, pales to the importance of the person's character. Character can be refined by scripture, "*All scripture is given by inspiration of God, and is profitable for doctrine, for reproof, for correction, for instruction in righteousness*" (2 Tim. 3:16). I encourage you to search the scriptures to know whether the things said in this book are in accordance with the Word of God. Opinions are just opinions, learned or otherwise. Only scripture is absolute. Only scripture carries the power of God to salvation and effectually works in those that believe (1 Thess. 2:13).

At that time, our town hosted the largest inland naval training base in the USA, which also contained a huge hospital for soldiers coming back from the Vietnam War. Mike started a ministry for military where he needed a flunky, someone to carry out plans. We became running buddies. We worked side-by -side handing out tracts, sharing the gospel, setting up meetings, and cleaning up after the ministry was finished. And I prayed…really prayed that God would use him to minister to the lost.

Michael usually had a girl friend with him for all these events. Sometimes, I had a boy friend. It was truly strange. His girl friend would sit between us so he would have to lean forward to talk to me about the meetings or strategy or whatever we had going. There, right between us, sat his date with nothing to contribute. Sometimes we would pray together with some girl sitting there as if she were a non-being. I was his helper. He needed me. I jumped into any project he had going, not because I was after him, but because I was interested in the things he was interested in. We shared God's vision for winning the lost.

He never had a clue that I believed he would be my husband. He even laughingly told me of occasions when other girls approached him and told him that God wanted them to be his wife. The times he told me about the other girls, I was glad that I kept my mouth shut. I have to say, the other girls seemed much better candidates for his wife than I was. When I heard that some young woman had told him she was to be his wife, it always shook my confidence. I would ask myself, why would God choose me instead of her? Every one of those girls sang, played the piano, and looked what I called *fancified*. They all talked like dignified ladies. Queenly, that is the kind of girl he unconsciously always chose.

Once, one of the young ladies came to me and asked me, since I was such a close friend to Michael, if I would tell him that she was sure she was the one for him. I remember looking her in the eye and saying, "You'll have to grow your hair out first. He would never marry a woman with short hair." I didn't make up the short hair idea just to make her bug off. I knew he really was opinionated about long hair. Most young guys are.

I finished high school, went to a local Bible college until I grew bored of it, and then started working for one of my professors as a secretary in a large church. The years seemed to fly by. I was at school or work every day, then in the evenings we had prayer meetings, Bible studies, evangelistic meetings, street meetings, or meetings to plan other evangelistic outreaches. Michael and I came to know each other in a wholesome way. There was never any deep sharing of innermost feelings. We never confided, but he did see me as mad as a hornet a couple times. I saw him being pushy and demanding. Plus I knew he was the most prolific messer in history. His office always looked like someone broke into it and sought to tear it apart. But I knew he was genuine. I saw his heart for winning lost souls, and he saw my willingness to jump in and do the worst jobs for the gospel's sake, enjoying every minute of it.

When I turned 20 I knew the time was drawing near. Still, Mike had never seemed to notice that I was a female. After seven years, it was beginning to irritate me, so I played a trick on him. Every Sunday after church we loaded up a huge school bus with servicemen and took them to a lodge in the local forest. This, just by coincidence, was the very lodge where I first saw him when I was only 13 years old. Anyway, on this particular Sunday I asked a young serviceman, who was a cool guy and a good friend of Mike's, if he would help me play a trick on my pastor. With my arm tightly linked with this young man's arm, we walked up giggling to where Brother Pearl sat talking with some other men. I sweetly looked up at this guy's face then down to Michael and said, "Brother Pearl, I'm getting married." I don't really know what I expected him to say. His expression immediately sobered me, making me wish I had not played the trick. He looked aghast…horrified. Of course, I tried to laugh it off, saying it was a joke, but I knew at that moment something had changed. He did not think my trick was funny.

After we married, Michael told me that at that moment he suddenly saw me in a whole different light. He said he had always taken for granted that I would be there as his buddy, his friend, his helper. Now he knew I had grown up and would soon be gone. I would be another man's wife, another man's buddy and another man's helper. He decided he didn't like that idea. Can you believe how thick-headed this guy was? ***All those years, I was his right-hand man and he just never noticed.***

So, he still didn't give me the time of day…but I knew he was different. I often caught him looking at me like he was contemplating. When I looked back at him he just continued to stare as if trying to read my soul. Several weeks after my trick, he called me at work and asked if I would go with him that evening to a gospel meeting. He said he had been invited to give the gospel to a bunch of lost hippies (this was early '70s.) Over the years he had often called on me to be his female assistant. He needed to have a female helper because he had always been very careful not to allow himself to be in a compromising or tempting position with females. He always avoided any one-on-one counseling with the opposite sex, even to give the gospel. He has maintained this rule all his life.

He even told me where to meet him. He had always made a point to never give me the courtesy of going to my house to pick me up like a man would his date. It was his way of keeping our outing strictly ministry focused. So as I drove my little VW bug into the church parking lot where I was to meet him, I thought that this evening was no different from any other. It was ministry, plain and simple…at least that's what I thought.

That evening we crowded into a small upstairs apartment. There were about 40 young hippies, all intent on what Michael had to say. It was differ-ent back then, at least for a small window of time. The Spirit of God moved heavily upon people. God used most anyone willing to share the gospel. Nowadays, the average Christian will witness once or twice a year; back then Christians witnessed with boldness because lost people were so open. Prayer warriors had prayed open the floodgates of heaven. For that brief few years we saw miracle after miracle. It was so commonplace to see hundreds of people weeping, asking God for mercy, that we took it for granted. Oh, that people would pray!

Anyway, back to love. That evening Michael preached a simple message. All present were in their twenties (including us). At the end of the message we sang. Many wrapped their arms around their bodies and rocked back and forth, almost as if they were in pain. Some wept. Michael called for prayer and they all went on their knees. I softly talked to one girl after another, answering their questions and praying with them. Several people prayed out loud, asking God to save them. After a time, only soft murmurs were heard. I was still on my knees with my hands laid on the chair in front of me when I felt someone slip in beside me, and then a large hand grasp mine. I opened my eyes, startled. It was Michael. He stared into my eyes, then dropped his head in prayer. I confess, at that moment I ceased praying. Michael was well known for not touching ladies (even old ladies that wanted to shake his hand after a church service). Now he held my hand while he prayed!

He never spoke on that long hour trip home. We even stopped and had something to eat, and yet he remained embarrassingly silent. I was so rattled I talked non-stop.

When we pulled into the church parking lot I moved to get out and he reached out and grabbed my hand again, yet still he remained totally silent. It was late. I was exhausted. I had been up for almost 24 hours. My emotions were spent. I wasn't even keyed up, I was so tired. I sat now silent and unmoving, then my tired tongue softly spoke my thoughts. I reminded him about the young boy he had baptized the previous Sunday evening. I talked about how the boy kept jumping up in the water so he could see his parents. Then I said the unthinkable: "You know, someday I would love to give you a son."

To my memory I had never ever thought such a thing, but what's said is said. Michael reacted like a rocket. Out of the car he shot and into the dark; around the building he ran. I just laughed. I was too tired to really be concerned. He came tearing back around by the time I climbed out of his car and had gathered all my gear. I was almost to my VW when he came around the house again. This time he came streaking across the lighted parking lot like a long-legged spider. I had put all my stuff in my car and turned around to watch him. He came running straight to me, then grabbed me around my waist and threw me in the air while shouting, "Let's get married." And we did, just eight days later on a Sunday evening. As you can imagine, it was a simple wedding. I made my wedding dress with white satin in the style of a peasant dress. There was no time for flowers or any extra finery or even invitations. The church building was full to overflowing as everyone came out to see the famous preacher marry the hillbilly girl. I guess they needed to see for themselves that it was really true.

It's a doozy of a fairytale. I have been his wildcat, barefooted princess for 40 years. How good can it get? Real, real good.

You might think, "This can't happen to me! It's too…different." Every love story is unique, full of wonder and romance. Yours will be, too. My goal is not to package romance, but to let you see that God's ways are bigger and better than our greatest dreams and hopes.

Now let's figure out how to get you a man worth getting.

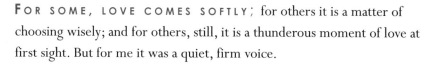

FOR SOME, LOVE COMES SOFTLY; for others it is a matter of choosing wisely; and for others, still, it is a thunderous moment of love at first sight. But for me it was a quiet, firm voice.

So why did God tell me ahead of time who would be my husband?

One thing I know: Michael was God's man, a preacher that needed a faithful prayer warrior. He was in the thick of winning thousands of soldiers to the Lord, men who were soon heading off to a deadly war. He was tall, dark and awesomely handsome as well as half-famous. Hot females chasing after him would be a constant threat to his ministry, and they did chase him—by the herds. This could have been an extreme temptation to his flesh.

Think about this: Several girls all thought it was God's will for Michael to be their husband. How was it that these fine Christian girls all truly believed he was the one for them, and, yet, were wrong?

What if all these girls were RIGHT? Maybe they were being moved by God's warriors to pray for this one man? It is possible that any of these girls could have made a fine help meet for Michael. God was looking for a help meet that would pray, not for herself to have a wonderful prince, but for a help meet to start HELPING this warrior of God to do the job God had for him to do.

There was a spiritual battle going on that was far more important than our moment in time of sweet love. God needed a warrior that would preach the gospel to thousands and thousands of lost souls.

Michael needed a help meet to pray for him a long time before he needed a wife. I prayed. My mama reminded me to pray. We are commanded to pray for laborers.

Do you sit waiting for God to give, yet you never ask for the laborer's strength, honor, and boldness? What young warrior NEEDS your faithful prayers?

What specific thing are we told to pray for?

Our duty is to pray for those who are busy giving the gospel to those who have never heard. We can and do make a difference in eternity when we pray. If that were not true then it would be pointless to pray.

"Pray ye therefore the Lord of the harvest, that he will send forth labourers into his harvest" (Matthew 9:38).

"Therefore said he unto them, The harvest truly is great, but the labourers are few: pray ye therefore the Lord of the harvest, that he would send forth labourers into his harvest" (Luke 10:2).

II Thessalonians 3:1-2 says, **"Finally, brethren, pray for us, that the word of the Lord may have free course, and be glorified, even as it is with you."**

Why does God want us to pray?

He tells us to pray that the word they are preaching will have free course. The devils that would otherwise hinder them with sickness, strife, or worldliness will not be able to slow down the gospel message!

Verse two goes on to tell us how to pray for these preachers, **"And that we may be delivered from unreasonable and wicked men: for all men have not faith."**

Called to Pray

God uses the prayers of his saints as much as the message of the preacher.

"Verily I say unto you, Whatsoever ye shall bind on earth shall be bound in heaven: and whatsoever ye shall loose on earth shall be loosed in heaven" (Matthew 18:18).

In summary:

One of the most important commands God gives us in his word is to pray for laborers for the fields, men and women who will go forth to give the gospel. Yet who obeys his command to pray for laborers?

- ♥ We have a command to pray.
- ♥ We have a responsibility to pray.
- ♥ Do you pray for laborers to give the gospel?

God Designed His Will to Come Through PRAYER

Do you pray for those who bear responsibility for your well-being? Your father will need wisdom to know how to deal with the young man who comes to ask for your hand in marriage.

Your pastor might know a young man who would be a good mate for you. Why would your pastor think to bring this young man to your father's attention? Have you prayed for your pastor to have wisdom and peace? Do you seek God's blessing on your pastor?

Maybe one of the men of the church has a young man who works for him that would be a great husband for you. Do you pray for the men of the church to grow in Christ? Does your future beloved languish because you do not pray for him and those over him?

If you want a Thread to weave through your life and marriage, if you want a godly prince to hold you in his arms, loving you with all his heart, then know this: it starts with prayer! Begin today praying for your coming prince to be the warrior God wants and needs.

Will YOUR prayer make a difference in eternity? Will it change events? Will it enact God's plans? What is happening in the heavenlies? What could be different if you learned to be a faithful prayer warrior? Here is the story of a man who found out just how God answers prayer.

Battles in the Heavens

There is a book in the Bible named after the young man, Daniel, whose story it tells. It is about a boy who was taken to be a slave in a foreign nation. He and three other young men excelled as talented, educated, disciplined young slaves who could handle affairs of state. Daniel often found himself in trying circumstances caused by his uncompromising faithfulness to the will of God. Many men were jealous of his rise to power and sought ways to accuse him, yet he remained faithful and steadfast to God. You may remember some children's stories about Daniel. Once he was put in a lion's den, but was untouched by the deadly animals.

In the book of Daniel, chapter 10, there is a story of Daniel asking God for supernatural understanding concerning end times. For twenty-one tense days Daniel prayed and fasted, yet his prayers were not answered. Finally, Daniel discovered why it took so long for God to respond.

The Bible describes a Star-Wars event of good and bad angels fighting. It even tells that the evil spirit forces that hindered Daniel's prayers were assigned oversight of Persia—the nation in which Daniel lived and prayed. The Prince of Persia and his spirit minions were able to prevent the warrior of God from delivering God's answer to Daniel. A heavenly battle raged for 21 days—the forces of darkness resisting the forces of light. Finally God sent the warrior angel Michael and his host to break through enemy lines and deliver the answer to Daniel.

When the warrior arrived with the answer, Daniel was sitting by the river. Daniel took one look at the out-of-this-world being and fainted flat on his face. The warrior of God grabbed Daniel and told him to stand up so he could give him the information he had requested. The angel indicated he couldn't stay long because he had to get back to the battle and assist his comrades in the heavenly war. How strange is that?

So how does God answer prayer? He uses our PRAYERS (requests) to send God's forces to bring the answer. Sometimes that means a major fight between God's forces and the spirits of darkness. Did you ever think what your prayers might be unleashing? What if Daniel had been irritated with the men who bothered him over the years and had allowed himself to pray for their destruction? Would Daniel be praying amiss? God warns us not to pray amiss. The reasons are sobering.

It is interesting to note the Bible tells us several times that Daniel was dearly loved by those who live in heaven. The Bible mentions several whom God loved, but Daniel was loved by those in heaven—the righteous angels who are God's ministers sent forth to minister for those who are heirs of salvation.

Why, of all people, do the residents of heaven love Daniel? I think it is because Daniel prayed, made many requests, releasing these angels to subdue the forces of darkness—something they loved to do on God's behalf. When you read the book of Daniel you will notice that, of all men in the Bible, Daniel most faithfully prayed and sought God concerning every issue.

Unseen Beings

When we pray for wisdom concerning a matter, most of us just assume God will somehow whisper into our little pea brains and suddenly we will know truth. It is not that simple. There is a whole world around us of unseen beings shaping our daily lives—many strange and wonderful things in the immediate heavenlies that we do not know or see. Yet they are more real than we are.

God does not force himself or his blessings upon us. He trusts us to see the need and make a request. In other words, we direct affairs with our prayers. God may want to help, but he does not do so until we ask. "You receive not because you ask not." Just as a military commander in the field must anticipate the need and request armaments or additional troops, so God set up a chain of command that leaves us in charge of the battle. He says, WATCH, PRAY, ASK…and it will be given you. The angels wait for orders. God waits for us to ask. Just think of all the times heaven waited on you and you never asked. Disappointed angels. They hate to see us defeated when they were so ready to help. Daniel prayed and kept on praying until the answer came through. What if he had stopped after one week? **"Ask, and it shall be given you; seek, and ye shall find; knock, and it shall be opened unto you"** (Matthew 7:7).

Help Meet's Prayer

Remember my love story? I believe that sometime in his youth Michael asked God for someone to faithfully pray for him. His prayer released a group of angels. It is possible the angels went to several girls to provoke them to pray. Maybe the other girls prayed amiss, not for the warrior, but for themselves to get a wonderful husband. One angel thought if he found a girl young enough she would not be sidetracked to always be thinking of marrying. He fought a heavenly war to get my attention to pray. Forty-six years ago Satan sent a serious storm, yet God's forces prodded the church leaders to go ahead with the meeting. The young man of God stood to speak, and an angel focused on me, a 13 year-old girl. The angel reflected back to my newly saved parents who truly believed in prayer. The angel whispered into my young, believing ear, "He's the one." As I left that day, the angel made sure a brochure of the day's event was in my hand. When I got home he pulled it loose from my purse so I would see it and be reminded to tell my mom about the unusual thing that had occurred. My mom soberly taped the paper on the wall. The young preacher's prayer would be answered. My mom would pray, I would pray, and thus God's warriors would be fighting beside this busy, young preacher for the next seven years and beyond. Thousands upon thousands of men would come to know the Lord through the young preacher's ministry. People would marvel that God had raised up such a talented, faithful man. God could have raised up thousands of such men had someone been faithful to pray for each one.

Your Treasure Chest

This is your first tool to add to your Treasure Chest. It is the beginning of the Thread you will weave into your life.

♥ Pray for your future beloved. Pray that he will be strong. Pray that he will walk faithfully.

♥ Establish lifelong habits: When you wake up at night, PRAY. When you look into the mirror, say a silent PRAYER. When you stop at a red light, remember to PRAY.

♥ Make a list of people you are committing to pray for.

Discovering God's Will

MORAL TO THE STORY: God often leads us down his path through the counsel of those who are wiser.

A CAUTION: Stubbornness can wreck your life. High-mindedness can leave you a high and dry old maid.

How will I know whom God wants me to marry?

This is one of the most asked questions of all time. Finding and marrying that one person God made for you is the most important decision in your life. Since it is so critical to the success of the remainder of our life, surely God has a formula for us to follow, a step-by-step plan that leaves no room for error.

Not so. (See Man's Comment on page 35).

God's ways are not our ways. The way of the heart—the way of romance—is a way of mystery and surprise, full of passion and illogical attraction. Everyone's love story is an amazingly different journey…Here is Lydia's story.

CHAPTER 2

COURTSHIP TO *whom?*

story two

M Y NAME IS LYDIA. BY THE time I turned 23 years old I was beginning to wonder if I would ever marry. But I am not one for sitting around worrying. That summer I signed up to help at several youth camps. Between camps I came home for a short break, never suspecting my life was soon to be changed forever.

That first evening I noticed my dad seemed in a hurry to rush my younger siblings off to bed, but when he stopped in my room for a talk I knew something was up. As he sat on the end of my bed he quietly said, "Lydia, a young man has asked for permission to court you."

My first reaction was excitement; then a dream-like disembodiment washed over me. I was going into what you might call a serious case of shock. I mean, I had hoped and waited for this moment, some wonderful fellow to love me and ask for my hand in marriage, but now it was happening and all I could feel was a strange disconnect. As if from a distance my dad asked if I could guess who it might be. I tried to guess and could have continued guessing all night, but I would never have guessed it to be Billy Hill. I had met him off and on over the years in different groups, but never really had a conversation with him. The last time I saw him was early summer and he never said a word to me. Really, he never talked to any of the girls. He seemed aloof and stiff, and I was a little scared of him. Besides, I had always assumed I would at least know the guy I would marry. Now, my mind hesitantly considered the idea of this stranger being my husband…as in MY husband. It took an hour of my dad's gentle persuasion before I finally agreed to give it a chance by just getting to know the guy…then we would see. No promises.

We emailed a few days—mostly him answering my questions about who he was and why he had picked me and what did he want to do with his life (See "Billy's Story" later this chapter).

Nervous? Are you kidding? I was a MESS. I mean, can you imagine it happening to you? A total stranger wants to marry you…how would you feel? Exactly!

Patience is an act of the will, or at least acting patient is, so I made up my mind that I would not initiate any form of contact. If he emailed me, then I would email him in return. I was scheduled to go to another camp in a few days, and for my sanity's sake I didn't want to leave it all hanging. I really wanted just to meet Billy before I left, but I decided that unless he mentioned us meeting I would not say a word. It was really hard waiting and wondering, but I had spent 23 years practicing patience for this moment in my life; now was not the time to goof up. I did let him know I would be going back to camp in a few days. Thankfully he was a "go-get-(h)er," so I didn't have to wait. That evening he arranged for our families to spend the next day together, which happened to be the Fourth of July.

My dad was totally wonderful. He did everything he could think of to make the meeting less strained, but I was still a ball of nerves. So there we were, the prospective husband and wife, meeting face-to-face. We stood like wooden statues awkwardly shaking hands. I struggled to no avail to overcome my sudden shyness. Then Billy asked to see the barn. That was familiar territory, so I began to relax as I showed him my animals and talked about the good times I had raising them. We swapped stories, but we were both distracted with wanting to get on to pertinent issues. Finally I couldn't wait any longer so I asked him point-blank what he thought courtship was. Then he said it, bold as day: "I want to get to know you with the intention of marriage."

The day ended and I knew that, at least, I could stand him.

Progress.

My mom and dad reassured me that I didn't have to rush, but I knew I couldn't sit around and agonize forever. I had to know. How can a girl know if she will fall in love and be wonderfully, happily wed to a total stranger? I called Billy and told him that I was going to spend the next day in fasting and prayer and asked that he not call or email me so I would not be distracted.

I prayed and talked with my dad, then went to visit an older woman who had wisely mentored me many times. After talking and praying with her, I went home to talk with my mom. I weighed each person's advice. I knew they dearly loved me and wished for my happiness. Their advice was cautiously given, leaving me room to make my own decision. **"Where no counsel is, the people fall: but in the multitude of counselors there is safety"** (Proverbs 11:14). **"Without counsel purposes are disappointed: but in the multitude of counselors they are established"** (Proverbs 15:22). By the end of the day I had peace. I sat down and wrote out my carefully thought through reply. I called Billy and read my letter over the phone. I told him, "I don't love you, hardly even know you, but I feel God is in this, so I am willing to learn how to love you if you will teach me."

The morning after I said yes to courtship I went for a jog. As I ran, I was crying and asking God to let me please fall in love with this man before we got married.

One month later we were engaged. I know it seems fast, but I had full confidence and assurance from God that this was his will for me. I found safety and rest in knowing that my parents liked and admired him. I could immediately honor him because I knew he walked honest and upright before

God. It was deeply moving to see in a good man's eyes profound thanksgiving, joy, and love for me. I felt precious to him because he had chosen me above all others. It was easy to open my heart toward Billy. And yes, God answered my prayer. I fell totally and completely in love with this wonderful man. Three months later, we married.

The rewards of trusting God have been greater than we could have imagined. I am thrilled for the opportunity to tell our love story. I hope it happens for you.

Billy's Story

Q. What attracted you to Lydia?

A. When I first met Lydia I wasn't what you would call really attracted, nor was I ready for marriage. Both Lydia and I happened to be working in a family center. Our initial meeting was relaxed. She knew my brother, so she stopped to talk to him about ministering to the youth. She was bright and interested in what she was doing. I shared her interest in ministry. I saw that she had a drive for life. Her face constantly reflected joy and active interest in life and ministry. This is very appealing in a female.

I agree with this. Guys look for girls with a cheerful countenance, responsiveness, and who find a quiet joy in whatever they're doing or saying.

I unconsciously filed the info away for a coming day.

At a later time I took note that she had a really high regard for her dad.

From what I've observed this quality exists in most Christian girls. It is an attractive quality. If they have a good father they should appreciate him.

I liked that. I also knew she was happy to live at home, yet she was very active in serving in many different ministries, and was taking part in productive activities.

Yes, it is good for a young, unmarried girl who is out of school to be involved in ministry. She should be investing her time in worthy activities (long-term rewards) and not spending too much time just hanging out with friends (short-term rewards).

This was important to me because I knew I wanted a wife that would be satisfied with being a stay-at-home wife, yet I also wanted a woman that had a lot of drive to get things done. Even though I still hadn't yet thought of her as a possible wife, this knowledge was what eventually produced a stirring of interest.

Also, I noted she wasn't a flirt. <u>I always disregarded any girl I ever saw flirting or hanging onto a guy's arm.</u> **(Grabbers…beware!)**

I agree; flirting cheapens a girl.

Q. How did you come to believe Lydia was God's will for you?

A. I had come to the point in my life where I was ready for marriage. I had spent the year getting certifications and furthering my education, and <u>I knew I was ready to take on the responsibility of a wife.</u> My an-

Important for a man to know he's ready for this responsibility.

tennas were up. Over the years I had been attracted to different girls, but for one reason or another they moved off my radar.

Lydia and I were both working at the same camp that year. I watched her, noted her ready smile. In a way she reminded me of my mom. Unexpectedly I caught myself perking up every time I heard her name called over the loudspeaker. I decided that before I found myself getting too attracted I needed a reality check on my feelings. Was God leading me this direction? I didn't really know this girl at all; was this for real?

One afternoon I was asked to drive one of the three buses for the girls' ministry. It was a perfect time for me to <u>put a fleece before God</u> in order that I could have some physical evidence that God was directing my path toward Lydia. I asked God to confirm to me His direction by putting Lydia on my bus. Soon a stream of girls began filing on the bus, and then their leader stepped in. I actually breathed

As an entertaining and enlightening study read the account of Gideon and the fleeces (Judges 6) to understand a Biblical view of the term. You may be surprised to find that "putting a fleece" before God is not a good thing, that it is a blatant sign of doubt. Just count how many times Gideon contradicts and doubts the messages given to him.

a sigh of relief…Lydia wasn't among the group. Then the head leader came out and directed everyone off my bus. Now my bus sat empty. I sat spellbound, watching the door, waiting. The door swung open and there was Lydia's smiling face. She led her group of young girls onto the bus.

Q. Were you ever apprehensive about the whole courtship approach of choosing someone you hardly knew?

A. Yeah, when Lydia came out and got on the bus, I felt total panic. It was such an in-your-face positive fleece. Now I had to take action in a matter that seemed vague and unreal. Finding a wife was uncharted territory. It was daunting.

Q. So how did you proceed?

A. I searched the internet to find anything she might have written to anyone. I found her blog and read all her posts. If I had read <u>flirty nonsense, or noted anything that lacked chastity in her manner, or seen pictures that alerted me to anything off color, I would have dismissed her.</u>

I emailed my sister, who was a friend to Lydia, and asked some questions: Was Lydia a hard worker? Did she have a good head on her shoulders? Was she flexible? Also, I needed to make sure she wasn't legalistic. I asked about her stand on music, dress, and movies, which are things that I knew would affect my future children.

I spent some time thinking about all that I had read that she had written and what my sister said about her. It was all good. She was the kind of woman I had always wanted. Plus, I was highly attracted

The nature of someone's speech tells a lot about them and where their life is headed. There are distinct differences in the speech of a person who directs their life (proactive/wise) and someone who lets their life direct them (reactive/foolish). The reactive individual talks of wishes and hopes whereas a proactive individual talks of plans with definitive action. The reactive individual talks of people, things, gossip and "tabloid" news whereas a proactive individual talks about concepts, opportunities and meaningful current events. The fool's speech consists of vain babbling, flattering, and slander whereas the wise speak of righteousness, praise and wisdom. The book of James equates the tongue to the helm and rudder of a great ship or a horse's bit. The way it directs, the rest follows (James 3:1-12). You cannot direct your life with words of nonsense and back-biting and expect a life of blessing and meaningfulness. What subjects fill *your* conversations?

to her. I went home for the weekend and talked to my dad. My dad offered to call her dad, and so it went.

"My son [and daughter], forget not my law; but let thine heart keep my commandments: for length of days, and long life, and peace, shall they add to thee. Let not mercy and truth forsake thee: bind them about thy neck; write them upon the table of thine heart: so shalt thou find favor and good understanding in the sight of God and man. Trust in the Lord with all thine heart; and lean not unto thine own understanding. In all thy ways acknowledge him, and he shall direct thy paths" (Proverbs 3:1-6).

God really blessed me with a jewel.

Let's look at how Lydia approached knowing God's will:

- ♥ She was busy walking with God and praying for wisdom all through her youth.
- ♥ She didn't chase Billy down.
- ♥ She didn't say NO when her dad surprised her with an offer from someone that she barely knew.
- ♥ She sought out her parents and another older counselor for support and prayer.
- ♥ She prayed and fasted, asking God for wisdom and direction.
- ♥ She was open to considering Billy because he had proved himself righteous.

What did Billy do that helped him understand God's direction regarding a mate?

- ♥ He spent his youth considering what he wanted in a woman.
- ♥ He waited until he knew he was in a place in his life when he could support and care for a wife before he started seriously looking.

- 💜 He kept his eyes open, noting the chaste girls which might one day be possibilities, setting aside those who showed themselves not the kind of girl he wanted for the mother of his children.

- 💜 He followed his natural stirrings and interests to consider Lydia.

- 💜 He sought God to give him a clear answer.

- 💜 Once he had what he believed was an affirmative from God, Billy still used the mind God gave him to search out information that had a bearing on the suitability of Lydia as wife and mother of his children.

- 💜 When he had all the information before him concerning Lydia, Billy sought his father's counsel.

- 💜 When everything was set, he pursued his chosen woman with diligence until he won her love.

 Not every story is like this, though. It's great that they're happily married, but not every relationship needs to move this fast.

God Works Through Man and Woman, though Man has Final Say

You will remember from "The Kid's Love Story" that several girls approached Michael telling him they believed God had told them he was to be their husband. He was not impressed or moved. He knew God would have to speak to him first and foremost concerning this important decision. He would start his marriage by being the spiritual leader God intended man to be. Although I felt God had spoken to me, I never said a word. But I made myself available to work, serve, and minister. Yet for seven years he never noticed.

How does a girl find direction regarding whom God would have her marry?

- 💜 She honors God in her youth.

- 💜 She is open to counsel. She seeks knowledge and understanding from others. She knows that stubbornness is foolishness.

- 💜 She shows herself hard working and willing to be a good wife.

- 💜 She prays for those in authority over her so that they will be watching for any young man who might be a good match.

♥ She waits with patience and joy.

♥ She watches for an opportunity to serve.

♥ When a man of honor asks for her, and those who have watched over her feel he is a good man, then she genuinely seeks the Lord for his direction.

Courage and Loyalty

Two books of the Bible are named after the women the books are about—Esther and Ruth. Both women had marriages that were either arranged or planned by others.

Esther was a young Jewish orphan who lived with her uncle and had the misfortune of being exceedingly beautiful. One day government officials came and took her away from her home. She was taken to the castle and was told she was being considered, along with countless other girls, as a possible wife to the heathen king. He had discarded his first wife because she had not obeyed him. After a night with Ester, the king chose her to be his queen. Can you imagine how traumatic this must have been for this young virgin?

But her ordeal was just getting started. Through political intrigue, laws were changed that threatened the lives of all Jews. No one knew that Esther was a Jew. She could have stayed silent and been safe, but Esther knew that God had put her in this place for a reason. She had to find a way to break the bond of a strong, evil, political leader. It took courage, wisdom, and a great

Search the Word and you will discover it never says God will tell you whom you are to marry, nor that He'll confirm your decision. He's outlined the character qualities of a godly man and promises wisdom to those who ask, but it is your life and your choice. Yes, many times God worked and directed very specifically in men's lives even concerning marriage, but recognize that He did so to further His own goals and will, not for the individual's sakes. He orchestrated various marriages in the Old Testament because He needed a specific lineage through the nation of Israel to Jesus--not because of the people themselves.

If you want to know what "God's Will" is, read the Bible, because the Bible is the written record of God's will to man. Therefore, if the person you are interested in fulfills the qualities God sets for a godly man, then the choice is in accordance with God's will (barring no other entangling issues).

God esteems a man who uses prudence and foresight and plans ahead. Read James 4:13-15 and note it is not wrong to have plans, only to have them and not give place for the intervention of God. He has his own specific plans, and sometimes they cross our lives. When they do, be prepared to yield yours.

deal of shrewdness. In the end she won the king's favor and saved the Israelite people. Because one young girl was wise and sober minded, and because she was willing to lay down her life, a whole nation was spared.

Think about her life. Her marriage was arranged. She had no choice. Her husband was a divorced heathen. Yet she never woke up at night and thought to herself, "God, why did you put me here?" Her story is one of courage.

The other book is about a woman named Ruth. She was a young widow caring for her old mother-in-law. Ruth was given an opportunity to leave the old woman, but chose to stay and help her. This would have greatly limited her chances of marrying again and having children. Every day Ruth worked in the fields of Naomi's relatives in order to feed them both. A wealthy man named Boaz took note of this hardworking girl who labored in his fields, gathering the leftovers after his workers had already harvested the grains. Boaz was impressed by both her hard work and her faithfulness to her mother-in-law, yet the older Boaz still never considered Ruth for his wife. It was the old woman who took matters into her own hands, forcing Boaz to notice the young Ruth. When you read the story you will notice that Ruth trusted and obeyed Naomi concerning Boaz. The couple's firstborn son is in the line of Christ. Ruth's is a story of loyalty and faithfulness. Faithfulness is highly valued in Scripture.

It is interesting to me that, of all the women who ever lived, Ruth and Esther have books in the Bible bearing their names and telling their stories of courage and loyalty. Think about that: courage and loyalty. Nine times in Scripture this phrase appears: **"Be strong and of good courage."**

Read the stories of these two young girls, Ruth and Esther. These stories were written for you. Come to know these girls. Think about their hardships, their pain, fear, worries, and victories. Put yourself into their shoes and ask yourself how you would respond to situations they went through.

Your Treasure Chest

Our romantic notions often take precedence over God's will.

♥ Are you willing to seek wise counsel?

_____

_____

_____

_____

_____

♥ Will you be open when it is given?

_____

_____

_____

_____

_____

♥ Make a written commitment now.

_____

_____

_____

_____

_____

_____

_____

_____

Prophet-Natured Man

MORAL TO THE STORY: Be flexible for your man.
A CAUTION: Your most important job as a Prophet's wife
is keeping a chaste and commonsense attitude and
conversation (not bad-mouthing folks).
Without it your marriage will be miserable.

What sort of man attracts you? Forceful, Gentle, Artistic,
Thoughtful, Athletic, Brainy?

Did you know that God created men to express different
aspects of his image?

Which expression would best suit you?

CHAPTER 3

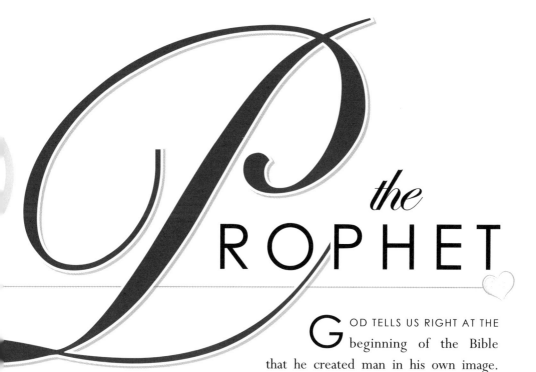

$\mathscr{P}$the ROPHET

GOD TELLS US RIGHT AT THE beginning of the Bible that he created man in his own image. **"And God said, Let us make man in our image, after our likeness"** (Genesis 1:26). What is God's image? What is God's likeness? The word OUR is plural. Why does God refer to himself as more than one?

Strange as it may seem, answering these questions will help you understand men; and, most importantly, gaining knowledge in this area will better prepare you to be a good wife. Let's start with a simple question:

What does the word *likeness* mean?

When you look in the mirror what looks back at you is your likeness. It is amazing to think that God created man in his likeness.

What does the word *image* convey?

When the Bible uses the word image, it is usually referring to graven figures that people used for worship. Image refers to the shape of something. God made man in his image…his likeness, like HIM.

Why does God refer to himself as OUR?

God is Three Persons

When you think of God do you think of God the Father? Or does Jesus come to your mind, or maybe the Holy Spirit? The Bible relates that the one God is manifested in three persons. It is impossible for us to understand, but God has introduced himself to us as Father, Son, and the Holy Spirit.

Now back to God's image.

God created man in his own image. Which image? Well, all three persons, of course. God's relationship to us and his ministry to us is different with each person of the godhead.

Your husband-to-be will fall into one of these three categories: He will be like God the Father, a King, or what I have dubbed a Command Man. He will be healing and kind like Jesus, a Priest, or what I have called a Steady Man. He will be in the image of the Holy Spirit, a Prophet type, or a man of ideas. I call this type of man a Visionary.

When you can identify a man (your dad or brother) as expressing one of these three traits, it will help you to understand men in general. I have never known a man that is a balance of all three. Sometimes a man is mostly one with a little of another, but never balanced. What I am saying is that it is not realistic to expect any man to be perfectly balanced. We must appreciate them as they are.

So what about us ladies? Do we also come in three varied expressions of God's image? Ah…that is an entirely different subject to be discussed later in this book…and you will be surprised. For now, we are discussing the male. It should help us understand the men in the several wonderful love stories you are about to read.

There's no sense in reinventing the wheel, so the next few pages will be a modified version of information found in my previous book, *Created To Be His Help Meet*.

Who Will Your Man Be?

Prophet

GOD IS A PROPHET AS SEEN IN HIS PERSON, THE HOLY SPIRIT. He made some men in the image of that part of his nature. As a man moves into his late twenties and early thirties his image will become much more pronounced. Some of you will marry men who will be shakers, changers, and dreamers. One word that describes them is Visionary. They see what can be or should be and seek to change things.

The Prophet or Visionary is "the voice crying in the wilderness," striving to change the way things are done, or change how humanity is behaving or thinking. Prophet-type men are street preachers, political activists, organizers and instigators of any front-line social issue. They love confrontation, and hate the status quo. "Why leave it the way it is when you can change it?" They are the men who keep the rest of the world from getting stagnant or dull. They are consumed with a need to communicate with words, music, writing, art, or actions. The Prophet always has a "cause."

Good-hearted prophets can be a lot of fun. They are never Mr. Dull. They can love with a passion and be aggressively loyal to their friends and family. They can take the lead in calling the world to repentance and showing them a path of righteousness.

However, if they are not balanced, these Prophet/Visionary types may get fanatically focused on one or two weird issues and, in the process, upset the entire family. You will hear them going on and on about issues like whether or not we should celebrate Christmas. Should we accept a license from the state? Should a Christian opt out of the Social Security system? Why go to a doctor? No birth control! They may be extreme in their separation from "the world." The issues they focus on may be serious and worthy of one's commitment, but, in varying degrees, these men can have tunnel vision, tenaciously focusing on single issues. They can drive some women crazy.

The Prophet type will make a great boyfriend because he will focus totally on his sweetie. He will be very romantic, giving you flowers and gifts. If you catch the heart of a Prophet you will be his consuming passion, his greatest challenge, his dream come true. A few weeks after marriage, though, his focus will turn to other challenges. As his new bride you will feel abandoned. It is important for all girls to understand this great truth regardless what type you marry: You need a life, a vibrant life, before your man comes on the scene. A clingy useless wife that lacks drive, goals, ambitions, or dreams is just that—useless. Right now, do you have a life with purpose? If so, then when your new Prophet/Visionary husband suddenly becomes focused on some strange, new, driving project, your life will continue to go on smoothly and happily. Don't be offended when he focuses on something other than you. It is his nature. He cannot do otherwise. Of course, as a wife you will still need to be ready to "ooh and aah" when he comes back to share his new vision with you. When he does turn his attention back to you all the other wives will be jealous, for you will have the most romantic man around.

If you marry one of these wild-headed fellows, expect to be rich or poor, rarely middle class. He may invest everything in a chance and lose it all, or make a fortune. He will not do well working 8:00 to 5:00 in the same place for thirty years, and then retiring to live the good life. If he works a regular job, he may either not show up half the time or he will work like a maniac 80 hours a week and love every minute. He may purchase an alligator farm in Florida or a ski resort in Colorado, or he may buy an old house trailer for $150 with hopes of fixing it up and selling it for $10,000, only to find out that it is so deteriorated that it can't be moved. He will then have his wife and all the kids help him tear the top off and carry the scraps to the dump, saving the appliances in the already crowded garage, so he can make a farm trailer out of the axles. Now that he has a farm trailer and no animals, expect him to get a deal on three old, sick cows, and…he may never be rich in money, but he will be rich in experience.

A girl who lives a static life of waiting to be married is not attractive. Think what it conveys: "I'll just sit here idly while waiting for someone to come and give me a purpose, and a house and money and food and make me happy and love me." It's very needy. A man wants a companion, not a sympathy case.

He will easily pick up and relocate without any idea of what he is going to do for a living at the new location. In his zeal for the truth, he may end up splitting the church. He may be fanatical in his demand for doctrinal purity and proper dress and conduct. Like a prophet, he will call people to task for their inconsistencies.

I am sure it was men of this caliber who conquered the Wild West. They would have been the mountain men and the explorers, going over the next mountain in search of knowledge and adventure. They would not be the farmers who settled in one spot.

The upside of the Prophet/Visionary is his creativity and tenaciousness in the face of difficulty.

The downside of the Prophet types is that if they are not wise, they can be real fools who push their agendas, forcing others to go their way.

Good intentions don't always keep Prophet types from causing great harm. If they are not wise they can stir up pudding and end up with toxic waste. Often the difference between a productive Prophet and a destructive Prophet is a good, supportive, stable woman. An unwise wife with negative words can turn a Prophet into an antichrist, an inventor into a destroyer. Every…I say *every* Prophet needs a good, wise, prudent, stable wife who has a positive outlook on life.

Come to think of it, my husband is a little like a Prophet. I remember, on more than one occasion, helping him tear down someone's old barn in order to drag the junk home to fill up our old barn. This is a new idea you need to keep in mind. Most men are a mixture of types, but predominately one.

In you are fortunate enough to catch the attention of a Prophet/Visionary guy, you will never be bored. In fact, you should be just a little bit reckless and blind in one eye if you are going to enjoy the ride. If you end up with one of these guys, you need to learn two very important things: learn how to be flexible, and learn how to always be loyal to your man. You will be amazed at how much happier you will be and how much fun life can be if you learn to just go with the flow—his flow. Life will become an adventure. And once you get it into your head that your husband does not have to be "right" for you to follow him, you will FINALLY be able to say "bye-bye" to your overwrought parents, even when they are screaming that you are married to a crazy man. People looking on will marvel that you are able to love and appreciate your husband, but you will know better, because you will see his greatness.

Greatness is a state of soul, not certain accomplishments. Thomas Edison was great after his 999th failure to make a light bulb, though not recognized as such. The Wright brothers were great when they neglected their lucrative occupation of fixing bicycles and "wasted time" trying to make one of them fly. If the light bulb had never worked and the plane had never flown, and no one remembered their names today, they would have been the same men, and their lives would have been just as full and their days just as challenging. Did Edison's wife think him great when he used his last dime on another failed idea? If she didn't, just think what she missed.

The Prophet man needs his woman's support, and he will appreciate it when it is freely given. Without her, he feels alone. This guy will be a little hard to live with at first. Big, wild fights are the usual beginnings if a nice, normal girl marries one of "the weird ones."

That Crazy Boy

Having the blessing and guidance of parents is priceless for many reasons. You are embarking on a new life—start it right. Once married, the Scripture teaches: **"Therefore shall a man leave his father and his mother, and shall cleave unto his wife: and they shall be one flesh"** (Genesis 2:24). When you marry, your father will *give you away* in marriage. You will belong to another. If you marry a Prophet-type man, this verse of Scripture will take on much greater significance. Here's why. If your mother has a gentle spirit, she will have a very difficult time understanding your "crazy" husband. Her gentle heart has always been "never to offend anyone" regardless of his or her error, but if your husband has a heart of a prophet he will be standing on truth "no matter whose toes I tromp!"

Poor, kind Mama…it will take her a while (probably after the third child) to come to appreciate this MAN who reigns as the leader of you and your home.

God, in his great wisdom, knew how dismayed the sweet-hearted mama would be; hence he gave instructions to Adam when Eve and, by extension, to all couples thereafter, as we find repeated in the books of Matthew, Mark, and Ephesians. The need for observing this precept is revealed in Mark 10: 4-8. **"And they said, Moses suffered to write a bill of divorcement, and to put her away. And Jesus answered and said unto them, For the hardness of your heart he wrote you this precept. But from the beginning of the creation God made them male and female. For this cause shall a man leave his father and mother, and cleave to his wife; And they twain shall be one flesh: so then they are no more twain, but one flesh."**

In our ministry we receive thousands of letters seeking help for hurting marriages. Many issues could instantly be solved if both the man and his new bride obeyed this simple rule of *leaving and cleaving*. There are good reasons why the term mother-in-law evokes negative thoughts in the minds of many. Once you marry, your honor and allegiance belongs to your man. Of course, you will probably forget what is written here...so I have an idea to help you keep this important bit of information ready for your coming day.

The Scroll

Take a sheet of pretty paper and write a commitment: "I, _____, make a commitment this day, _____, to honor, reverence and obey my Prophet/Visionary husband for the man he is. I will appreciate his dreams; I will not listen to anyone bad mouthing him, and I will remember that I am his help meet to stand with him on all that he wants to accomplish," etc.

Roll your document and tie it with a ribbon, then store it away in your Treasure Chest. If you do marry one of these rascally Prophet types...this rolled-up, written commitment might save your husband a whole lot of irritation. From time to time, as you go through your things, you will see this scroll and it will stay fresh on your mind.

God needs these Prophets to be able to function with clear and ready minds. Stand by his side, confident that he is the man he is supposed to be, and you will allow him to do just that.

In Summary

If you marry a Visionary Man, learn to enjoy the trip, for if he ever makes a better light bulb, he will want you to be the one who turns it on for the first time in public. It will be your face he looks into to see the marvel of what a great thing he has done. You are his most important fan. When you know your man really needs you, you can be happy with just about anything.

♥ Prophet/Visionary Man will not notice what he eats, so don't be offended when he doesn't seem to appreciate your fine cooking. What he does appreciate is your interest in his present project—not your opinion or even your input—just the light in your eyes as you listen to him tell his newest wild idea.

♥ Prophet/Visionary Man will talk and talk and talk to his honey if she approves of him. He will be subjective, thinking about feelings, moods, and spiritual insights. One of his greatest needs will be for his wife to think objectively (proven truth) and use common sense, which will help keep his feet from flying too far from solid ground. He spends his life looking through a telescope or microscope, and he will be stunned that what he sees (or thinks he sees) that others do not seem to notice or care about. Every small issue will become mind-consuming, and he will need his wife to casually talk about the big picture and the possible end results of relationships, finances, or health if he continues to totally focus on his present interest. His sweetheart needs to stay in a positive state of mind, yet not jump into his make-believe world, trying to be too much of a cheerleader on dead-end issues. Let him burn out on things that are not wise, but don't throw water on his fire. Let him find his own balance through bumping into hard realities.

♥ Prophet/Visionary Man is an initiator and provoker. He is a point man, a trailblazer, and a voice to get things done. He will start the party and keep it going until the Kingly Command Man gets there to lead.

♥ Prophet/Visionary Man's focus is so intense that matters can easily be blown out of proportion. A wife must guard against negative conversation about people. An idle conversation by her can bring about the end of a life-long friendship. This is true with all men, but especially so with a Prophet. By beginning before you marry, you can learn not to be instrumental to Satan's arsenal in sending fiery darts to your husband.

♥ A Prophet-natured man, with his tunnel vision, might spend money unwisely, leaving his wife feeling insecure. To stay happy with this man, you must remember that your treasure is not of this world. Treasure your husband and children and don't mourn the loss of monetary things.

Start now by searching your heart to discover your motive in what you say about people. What is your intent when you speak? Do you criticize in order to build up yourself and make others think that you alone are perfect? If you mention people and make them look a little bad and yourself a little "taken for granted," your future husband may get the idea that friends and family are treating you unfairly, and he may become withdrawn and suspicious. You could unwittingly render your husband unteachable. If you want your husband to grow into a confident, outgoing man of God, then he needs to have a clear conscience toward his friends and family. God says a woman's conversation can win her lost husband. In the same vein, a woman's idle, negative conversation can cripple a strong man and cause him to become an angry, confrontational, divisive man.

"Likewise, ye wives, be in subjection to your own husbands; that, if any obey not the word, they also may without the word be won by the conversation of the wives; While they behold your chaste conversation coupled with fear" (1 Peter 3:1-2).

> *"For he that will love life, and see good days, let him refrain his tongue from evil, and his lips that they speak no guile..."* (1 Peter 3:10).

♥ Prophet/Visionary Man needs a lady who does not take offense easily. She needs to be tough. He needs his lady to be full of life and joy. His lady will need to learn to tuck in that quivering lip, square those shoulders, and put on that smile.

♥ Prophet/Visionary Men can be leaders, but because they have tunnel vision the leadership will have a more narrow focus.

Your Treasure Chest

"Through wisdom is an house builded; and by understanding it is established: and by knowledge shall the chambers be filled with all precious and pleasant riches" (Proverbs 24:3-4).

♥ What can you do to prepare yourself to be a good wife of a Prophet?

♥ Will you start today praying for this wild man?

♥ Find all the statements that list what you need to become to be a good help meet for a Prophet-type.

Priest-Natured Man

MORAL TO THE STORY: The wife of a Priest-type needs to be as active helping others as her husband is. This will bring him honor.

A CAUTION: A Priest's desire is to please. Your impatience or unthankfulness can destroy his vision for serving others, as well as destroy your health.

CHAPTER 4

the PRIEST

BIBLE STUDENTS RECOGNIZE that in the Godhead Jesus is the Priest. His ministry on earth was mostly priestly, and in a lesser degree, prophet. But one day he will come back as prophet to judge, and then reign on earth as king, thus fulfilling all three roles and manifesting the complete image of God. Every man on earth manifests one of these three images in predominance over the other two.

You may marry a man that is priestly in nature. He will be the most steady and easygoing of the three types, not given to extremes. The steady nature of the Priest type is reflected in his tendency not to make snap decisions or spend his last dime on a new idea; nor does he try to tell other people what to do. He avoids controversy. He doesn't invent the light bulb like the Prophet, but he will be the one to build the factory and manage the assembly line that produces the light bulb and the airplane. He would never lead a revolution against the government or the church. He will quietly ignore hypocrisy in others. As a general rule, he will be faithful till the day he dies in the same bed he has slept in for the last 40 or 50 years. <u>This man is content with the wife of his youth.</u>

I recently saw a very adventurous young lady get engaged to a Priest. A few years ago, no one on earth would have anticipated this match. But knowing his faithful attitude, it's not surprising she would find a lot of security in that.

Joys and Tribulations

If you marry one of these steady, Priest-natured men, your new husband will never put undue pressure on you to perform miracles. He will not expect you to be his servant like a King type would. You will not have to spend your days putting out emotional fires like you would if you married a Prophet type. You will rarely feel hurried, pushed, pressured, or forced. The women married to the Prophet look at you in wonder that your husband seems so balanced and stable. The wife of the Kingly Man marvels at the free time you will have. If your dad happened to be a Priestly, Steady Man, then chances are you will appreciate your husband's down-to-earth, practical life for the wonderful treasure it is.

The down side to the Priestly natured man is the irritation his very steadiness produces in an impatient, romantic woman needing a little reckless adventure to spice up her life.

This type of man is steady and cautious, and for a spoiled young girl it is hard to see his worth and readily honor him. He almost seems old when he is still young. He seems to just let people use him. His strength is being a people person. Everyone will like him, enjoy his easy manner, and feel comfortable around him; they will not feel judged or ignored by him. He will like helping others, having his home open to casual get-togethers and visiting around. A good wife will make herself conform to his gifts. She will use her time to make her home a pleasant place to gather. She will learn to cook for groups and become a gracious hostess. Her strength and ministry will be hospitality. This will bring him honor. All of this sounds simple, but for most couples it's not.

The steady Priest man is not a shaker and mover. Even if he's not content with the status quo, he is the last one to speak up. His even nature keeps him from the flamboyant emotional displays that you might see in the Prophet types. His lack of fervent religious expression will provoke his wife into judging him as unspiritual. Wives are blinded by the church's standard of "the spiritual man" and become critical of their new husbands.

The steady Priest natured man is content to take a long time in making critical decisions. He tends to be more cautious than the Prophet type. An impatient young wife often finds it difficult to quietly wait for him to make up his mind. In her agitation she leaks criticism, which tears at his confidence and makes him even more cautious and noncommittal. He just wants peace, to be left alone to do his daily routine and enjoy the company of people who are not all fired up, passionate, or critical.

Are you controlling?

What can you do now to change your attitude so that you are not guilty of trying to revamp what God designed?

Know Your Man

Girl, you hope to be God's gift to some young man, but know that you come unassembled, just as he does. You will not bring to marriage all the skills necessary to make it into a fairytale come true. You must be humble enough to bend and merge into the new identity. When you come to understand men as God created them to be, you will not waste your marriage trying to change your new husband into what you think he should be.

The key is to know your man. In what image has God created him? You, as his help meet, will need to learn to conform to your man. God's Word

That's a very good point about fairytales. Notice how fairytales are never about marriage; they're always about whirlwind romantic courtships. They cover a few years, and then conclude with an "ever after" that, in reality, lasts ten times longer than the fairytale did. Fairytales are very poor indeed at equipping a girl for a marriage that will comprise most of her years.

says, in Hebrews 13:8, **"Jesus Christ the same yesterday, and today, and forever."**

Of the three types, the Priest will most want to please his wife. **"Counsel in the heart of man is like deep water; but a man** [a wife also] **of understanding will draw it out"** (Proverbs 20:5).

If you get such a man, you will need to learn how to stand still and listen. Seek to always have a gentle spirit. Look up "shamefacedness" in the Bible, and learn what it means. This study will mold you into what you need to become. Start now praying for your husband-to-be to have wisdom.

This is going to sound different, but many of these "nice" men prefer their wives to show some initiative. A Kingly man tells you what to do and how to serve him, and a Prophet wants you to do what he is doing. But if you marry a Priestly Man, he will want you to walk beside him, yet grow in your own right before God and man.

I agree with this. The danger here is that the woman could try to take over the dominant role and try to lead, which doesn't work.

Priestly men like their wives to be involved in business. He will be proud of your accomplishments. He will want you to use your natural skills, abilities, and drives. Your achievements will be an honor to him, but if you are lazy or slothful it will greatly discourage him. Study the Word of God concerning idleness so that you will not fall victim to becoming a lazy bum.

All men dislike for their wives to waste time or money. Silly behavior weighs heavily on a young husband, robbing him of his pride and pleasure in his new wife. A Priestly Man really values a resourceful, hardworking woman who shows dignity and honor. It is very important to the Priestly Man that his wife be self-sufficient in all the tasks of daily living. If you marry a Priest you will be urged to explore your own creative genius.

Men can be a little weird about money. For many men there is a direct link between their productivity and their self-worth. Money, with its numerical value, is a concrete measure of productivity. This is why, when a girlfriend or wife flippantly spends her guy's hard-earned money, it can be hard on the fellow. He'll feel cheated and belittled that you hold such small regard for the result of his effort and time. Whenever you buy something, it shows the man that you equate that item to that much of his life (which is his time), and he may mentally calculate the exact number of hours he had to work to cover the superfluous item.

Start today learning how to <u>pay bills, make appointments, and entertain guests</u> with a competence that will bring satisfaction to your husband-to-be. Your hobbies should be creative and useful so that you learn things that will help you teach your children. If you are busy and productive now, so you will be when you are married. Your skills and achievements will be your husband's résumé. When those on the outside take note of your wisdom and competence, it will reflect well upon your husband. At the end of the day, your Priestly husband will enjoy weighing what he has accomplished with what you have accomplished and will rejoice in the value of having a worthy partner in the grace of life.

> Yes, very useful.

- ♥ Your Priestly Mr. Steady will not expect you to cook, clean and serve him, but he <u>might enjoy being in the kitchen cooking with you.</u> If he does, and if you are a perfectionist, unhappy with his contribution, then you will be stealing something precious from your marriage. A fine chef can be hired! He married you to be his help meet.

> Agreed. I like to help out alongside other people. I want to be involved somehow in the work or preparation so that I know I am being productive. I get joy out of this.

- ♥ He will be in a state of quiet contemplation much of the time. He will want to share his deepest feelings and thoughts with you, so be still until he figures out how. He will enjoy the company of others and be most comfortable spending time in small talk with anyone who drops in. Of the three types, he is the one who will be most liked by everyone.

- ♥ Your Priest will always be in demand. People everywhere need him to fix a car, build a house, set up their computer, figure out what's wrong with their phone, heal them of cancer, and the list goes on and on. You begin to wonder if you will ever have him all to yourself. The answer is, no. He belongs to people. When you need that special time alone, take a vacation, and leave the cell phone at home.

- ♥ Your kind husband-to-be will be wonderful with those who are hurt, sick, or dying. He loves to comfort and seems to know what a person needs in times of great sorrow. His still, quiet presence brings peace. To the Kingly Command Man, this is nothing short of a miracle.

I think I have a healthy envy of the Priestly Man. Just about any priestly man would be a good catch in my book.

♥ This type of man does not focus on the eternal picture, nor is he looking through a microscope at the details, but he does respect both views as important. His vision is as a man seeing life just as it is. He can shift his sights to the sky and know there is more up there than he can see, and he wonders about it; or he can stare into a muddy pond and appreciate that there is a whole world in there that he knows nothing about. In most of life, he is a bridge between the other two types of men. He is a very necessary expression of God's image.

♥ A Priestly man will not waste money nor take reckless chances. If you marry this type man he will never make you feel insecure, although, he might be tight fisted when you want to spend money.

Wisdom is the Principal Thing

As a single girl you must be wondering, how can I know what type my husband is and how should I respond to him? How can I know if I am just being an enabler, someone that tries to be so helpful they cause another to remain weak, thus keeping them from taking on their rightful responsibility, or if I am encouraging him into greatness?

"Wisdom is the principal thing; therefore get wisdom; and with all thy getting get understanding" (Proverbs 4:7). Then God says in Psalms 111:10, **"The fear of the LORD is the beginning of wisdom: a good understanding have all they that do his commandments: his praise endureth for ever"** .

Being a really good help meet requires, first, a heart to do God's will, and second, a basic understanding of God's requirements as revealed in his Word, and, thirdly, wisdom. Without wisdom you will falter in confusion and doubt. When you have children you will be frustrated in not knowing how to respond to difficult issues. Wisdom opens the door of discovery;

wisdom whispers peace, because your soul can rest with knowing truth. Wisdom will be your friend when all else fails. **"Say unto wisdom, Thou art my sister; and call understanding thy kinswoman"** (Proverbs 7:4).

Anyone can have wisdom, but few ever attain it. It is a gift promised by God for all who ask. Imagine that! In James 1:5 God promises us, **"If any of you lack wisdom, let him ask of God, that giveth to all men liberally, and upbraideth not; and it shall be given him."**

Just asking for wisdom brings it to you. We have studied prayer. Put it into practice now! Ask God to bring you wisdom, then expect the angels of heaven to soon begin delivery. Don't stop there. Ask God to give your future husband wisdom, and keep on asking every day of your life. God answers prayer. He has a storehouse full of unused wisdom that no one has asked for; such a waste of heaven's priceless resources.

"For wisdom is better than rubies; and all the things that may be desired are not to be compared to it" (Proverbs 8:11).

This is a Thread day! It is the moment in your life when you can begin building on God's divine gift of wisdom to aid you in your pursuit of wifehood and motherhood. **"For the LORD giveth wisdom: out of his mouth cometh knowledge and understanding"** (Proverbs 2:6).

Your Treasure Chest

If you marry a Steady Priestly man you need to be very busy preparing yourself for your new place in his life.

♥ What are some of the things you need to be studying?

_____

_____

_____

♥ Write in your notebook a list of things you are committing to learn in order to be a better help meet to a Priest.

King-Natured Man

MORAL TO THE STORY: The wife to a King must learn to serve him with honor.

A CAUTION: Don't be offended at his lack of serving or helping you in the mundane things of life.

God the Father is dominant, sovereign and in command. He is the King of Kings. He created a few men who are like him in this aspect; they are kingly men. In my book *Created To Be His Help Meet* I called them Command Men, because that is their most dominant feature. Though men in general are dominant compared to women, the King type is enbued with an extra dose and, seemingly, a deficit in gentleness and patience. They are often chosen by other men to be military commanders, politicians, preachers, and heads of corporations.

CHAPTER 5

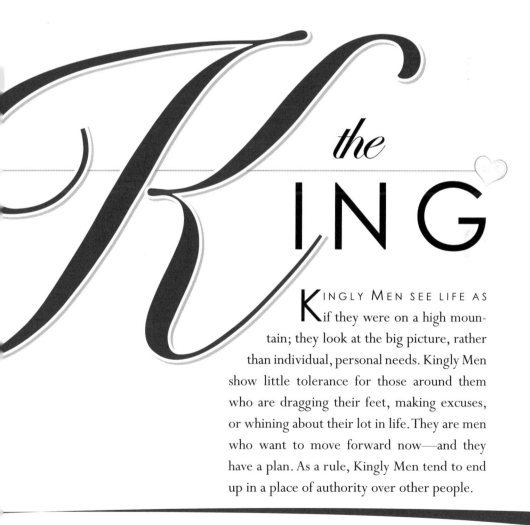

the KING

KINGLY MEN SEE LIFE AS if they were on a high mountain; they look at the big picture, rather than individual, personal needs. Kingly Men show little tolerance for those around them who are dragging their feet, making excuses, or whining about their lot in life. They are men who want to move forward now—and they have a plan. As a rule, Kingly Men tend to end up in a place of authority over other people.

If you should marry a King, you must be prepared to give him honor and reverence on a daily basis if you want him to be a benevolent, honest, strong, and fulfilled man of God. Every king wants a queen. He will best fulfill his potential to become an effective leader when he has the confidence and admiration of the queen at his side.

In the chapter later in this book called "Fleas" you will study the word reverence in detail. If you happen to marry a Kingly man, this study will cause your coming marriage to be glorious instead of heart-wrenching. Being a Queen comes with pleasures and honors, but it also carries extreme demands. It is a life of service, first to your King and then to those who are under your man's care.

What to Expect If You Marry a King

These types are known for expecting their wives to wait on them hand and foot. A Kingly Man does not want his wife involved in any project that prevents her from serving him. If you are blessed to win the favor of a strong, forceful, bossy man, then it is very important for you to learn how to serve with joy.

Kingly Men are not as intimate or vulnerable as other men in sharing their personal feelings with their wives. They seem to be sufficient unto themselves. It can leave the sensitive woman feeling shut out. A woman married to a Kingly Man has to earn her place in his heart by proving that she will stand by her man, faithful, loyal, and obedient. When she has won his confidence, he will treasure her to the extreme.

A King-natured man has a tendency to gather around him those who will assist him in establishing his kingdom and will dismiss anyone who stands in his way. If a wife supports her King, he will honor her with glory, but if she becomes his opposition, he will go on without her. She can be left feeling awfully alone, for the kingly man may not stop so she can cry on his shoulder; he may go forward and leave her crying alone.

She is on call every minute of her day. Her man wants to know where she is, what she is doing, and why she is doing it. He corrects her without thought. For better or for worse, it is his nature to control.

If you marry a Kingly Man, you will wear a heavier yoke than most women, but it can be a very rewarding yoke. You will always know exactly what is required of you. For a wise woman this can bring a calm sense of safety and rest.

The Kingly Man feels it his duty and responsibility to lead people, and so he does, whether they want him to lead or not. Amazingly, this is what the public is most comfortable with. Very few people have enough confidence to strike out on their own. The feeling of being blamed for mistakes holds many men back. The Kingly Man is willing to take the chance, and it is for that purpose God created these men. Their road is not easy, for James said, **"My brethren, be not many masters, knowing that we shall receive the greater condemnation"** (James 3:1). If you marry this type, he will need you to stand by him. He will grow much faster as a man and a leader if you march forward as a couple united in mind and heart. If you pray for him, support him, encourage him, and act as his faithful right-hand man, he will be more capable to serve a greater number in wisdom and humility. YOU could be a blessing or a curse to many people by how you relate to your Command Man.

A good King sees the bigger picture and strives to help the greatest number, even if it costs him his life and the lives of those he loves. If he is an honest man, he will take financial loss in order to help lead those who need him, but in the end he will usually come out on top. If he is not an honest man, he will be selfish and use the resources of others to further his own interests. A good wife can and does make the difference in how a leader is able to lead.

A King wants a Queen, which is why a man in command wants a faithful wife to share his fame and glory. Without a woman's admiration, his victories are muted. If a wife learns early to enjoy the benefits of taking the second seat, and if she does not take offense to his headstrong aggressiveness, she will be the one sitting at his right side being adored, because this kind of man will totally adore his woman and exalt her. She will be his closest and sometimes his only confidante. Over the years, the Kingly Man can become more yielding and gentle. His wife will discover secret portals to his heart.

And not all kingly men lack gentleness. I've been praised for being gentle, so there's hope for us young monarchs.

A King who has "gone bad" is likely to be abusive, selfish, and overbearing. It is important to remember that much of how a Kingly Man reacts depends on his wife's reverence toward him. When a Kingly Man (lost or saved) is treated with honor and reverence, a good help meet will find that her man will be wonderfully protective and supportive. In most marriages, the strife is not because the man is cruel or evil; it is because he expects obedience, honor, and reverence, and is not getting it. Thus, he reacts badly.

- ❤ Kings usually like fine meals served on time and in good order. If you are an especially good cook, your gifts will be greatly appreciated. A Kingly Man is not one to help out in the kitchen.

- ❤ Kings like to talk about their plans, ideas, and unfinished projects. They will be very objective, very unemotional, and not enjoy small talk. Their vision is like a man looking from a high mountain, focused on the distant goal. The King's wife needs to help him remember individuals' needs.

- ❤ A Kingly Man will be most uncomfortable and at a loss when dealing with the sick, helpless, and dying. Where there is no hope, there will be no need for a King. If you marry a King, don't be offended if he shirks being with the sick or weak.

- ❤ A born leader is a man who can, when necessary, adapt principles or rules to the circumstances for the greater good of the greatest number of people.

- ❤ A Kingly man will not confer with his wife concerning the way he spends money. If his wife "feels" it is her right to help decide how the money will be spent, she will engage in a war she will never win. Even though she is not part of the decision making, a Kingly wife will feel secure in her husband's ability to "take care of her", due to his commanding confidence.

Mama Says He's a Dud

If your father is a gentle, kind man, and if your mother has always been... how shall we say it...a little dominant, then what I am about to teach you might save your future marriage. When you marry, or even while you are in courtship, your forceful mother will not appreciate or understand your dominant King betrothed. She might say he lacks humility, which indicates his lack of spirituality. If it is clearly apparent to all that he does indeed love and honor God, then she will simply say he is arrogant and selfish. As a Kingly type, he may be a little overbearing. It goes with the territory. He will expect service, and will assume you will jump with all joy just to do his bidding. It is his nature.

If you are unwise, you will be swayed by your mother's scorn. Don't let it happen to you! If you are wise, you will recognize that your mother measures all men by your father's Priestly nature. To her a good man is gentle, kind, and considerate. Through her eyes you will see only the negative side of your husband's type, and it will cause you to become critical of him, too. Be patient with her. She is honoring your dad by measuring all men according to him, but your King man will walk a different path.

Right now, if you know that your thoughtful soft-spoken daddy is a Priestly type and your mama has always sort of ruled the roost, then you will need to make a document much like you did in the chapter on the Prophet-type man. This one will need to be more personal than the first one you wrote concerning the Prophet man because it will be read by you (who are probably a gentle heart) and by your forceful mom.

Take a pretty piece of paper and write a letter to yourself, to be read sometime in the future when you are finding it difficult to submit to your dominant man. Explain to yourself this potential problem and how you will respond to it when it arises. Make some real commitments. Date the document. Then roll it into a scroll and tie it with a ribbon. Put this document in your Treasure Chest. Someday—sooner than you think—you will be married. There will come a time when you are discouraged with your demanding husband and you will say something negative about him to your mom. She will take the opportunity to tell you what has "been on her heart." At that moment you will recall the Ribbon document. Taking it out and reading it will change your heart. Showing it to your mother will, hopefully, change her heart as well.

These documents are separate from the book's Treasure Chest, in that they will be a written testament to you for your future marriage. You might forget what you write on the pages of this book, but when you prepare Ribbon documents for your Treasure Chest, you will not easily forget it. Just the act of preparation will cause its content to be written on the pages of your heart.

Keep in mind that your mother is not the enemy. She is Mom. She is the one who cared for you when you were sickly; she is the one who believed in you when you were down. She is the one who would have given her very life for you if you were in need, but, because she is Mom, she will be the first to speak out when she thinks you might be hurting. Treasure her for the wonderful friend that she is, but remember, once you are married your allegiance changes. Right at the beginning of the Bible, God tells us, **"and thy desire shall be to thy husband, and he shall rule over thee"** (Genesis 3:16). One day you will be Mom to a grown daughter, and in that day you will understand the protective instinct your mother has for you. Until then, be wise, be loving, be patient with your mother, and stand by your man.

This is another Thread moment; only this time we used another ribbon.

Your Treasure Chest

♥ If you marry a King you will need to keep in mind that he is not trying to lord over you...he is just in the image of a supreme leader.

♥ Write your commitment to your King.

_____

_____

_____

_____

_____

_____

_____

_____

_____

_____

_____

_____

_____

_____

_____

_____

_____

_____

_____

_____

_____

_____

_____

_____

_____

_____

Dreamers, Servants & Go-to Gals

Moral to the Story: Learn and live well.

A Caution: Stubbornness shuts the door on understanding.

God has two sets of blueprints for the human race: one for male and one for female. The inside is as different as is the outside. God created us different and expects a difference in the way we function and relate in life and in marriage. This sounds absurdly obvious, but the practical implications are controversial.

The BIG Question: What type of man best suits me?

CHAPTER 6

THREE *types of* WOMEN

WHEN GOD SAW HOW LONESOME poor old Adam was, he said, "It is not good that the man should be alone; I will make a help meet for him." All females agree with God that it is not good for those wonderful, eligible men to be alone! Some men are slower to come to see their need for us tender sweeties than others, but most all men finally come to a place where they are genuinely lonely and want a mate.

After observing all the animals in pairs and naming them (e.g., "Mr. and Mrs. Giraffe"),

Adam came to understand the need he felt. Only then did God wake him up to his new bride. The Bible records how the first couple found each other. It was a marriage made in a garden. **"And the LORD God caused a deep sleep to fall upon Adam, and he slept: and he took one of his ribs, and closed up the flesh instead thereof; And the rib, which the LORD God had taken from man, made he a woman, and brought her unto the man. And Adam said, This is now bone of my bones, and flesh of my flesh: she shall be called Woman, because she was taken out of Man"** (Genesis 2:23).

From this passage we can see that woman was made from the man's body…in man's image. A woman reflects the man from which she was derived. She was made from him and for him. Eve (and by extension, every woman) was created to fulfill a need in the man. He needed a helper who could meet his needs. So—a help meet, that is, a helper suited (meet) to his needs. Her body, soul, mind, and emotions were created to be a blessing and help to Adam.

The reason a good portion of your thoughts are wrapped up in thinking about certain men and the hopes of marriage is because you were hard-wired with the overwhelming need to be a wife and mother. It is a God-given need that only a man can fulfill. I can't think of one thing I would rather have than a man to really love me. It is supreme. A lovely person is easy to love. That is our goal. God wants to make you become a lovely help meet. To be a good one takes effort…lots of effort.

Question?

That introduces another question: "Well, if women are created in the image of man, and man comes in three types, are women created in different types?"

We are…sorta. Since we are females, I like to call us a more feminine version of Prophet, Priest and King. I'll call us girls Dreamers, Servants and Go-to Gals. To keep all this clear here is a chart:

	⚓	👑
Prophet-type	Priest-type	Kingly-type
Visionary Man	Steady Man	Command Man
Dreamer Gal	Servant Girl	Go-to Gals

I'm a Dreamer, similar to the Prophet type. A female's type is not as predominant as a man's. Remember, man was created in God's image and we in man's image, so we are one step removed from the original, which, thankfully, tempers our extremes. Are you a Dreamer? Do you like to create, sew, design, paint, or write? The little three-year-old girls that love to dress up like ballerinas or princesses are the Dreamers. If you are a Dreamer, then you need to keep your head out of the clouds while dancing your way into your vision of the future. Don't get involved in projects that take you away from your responsibility to honor your husband. Spend your youth honing down your gifts and developing skills. Someday, if you honor your man, your gifts will greatly benefit your marriage. Girls that are Dreamers have a tendency to become Antsy Girls when things don't seem to be happening as fast as we think they should.

An example of a Prophet in Scripture would be Elijah. Remember he is the man who called down fire from heaven. Most, though not all, Old Testament prophets are Prophets in nature. It is not as easy to identify the female version of the Prophet/Visionary/Dreamer, no doubt due in part to the fact that there are fewer women featured in the Bible. There are several obviously negative examples of the Prophet-natured woman. The most prominent is Delilah. Her story is found in Judges 16. She was the object of Samson's tender feelings, as well as his uncontrolled lust. The story of Delilah is that of a wicked woman trying to discover the secret of Samson's strength. When he repeatedly refused to reveal his secret, she put on her acting charm. She wept, brokenhearted, blaming him for not trusting her with the secrets of his heart and therefore not loving her. It worked. He was deceived into telling her that his secret lay in a covenant he had with God, the sign of which was his long hair. At the first opportunity she sheared his head, leaving him powerless. He paid with his eye-sight and then his life. Sorry to all you Dreamers for the negative example. I can think of some really cool ladies who are Dreamers, which includes me, of course.

The Servant

My daughter who wrote the Teacher's Guide for this book is a Servant, similar to the Priest type. From the time she was a small child, she "mothered" her little sister. She always enjoyed caring for the elderly. She was a wonderful young daughter, helping me do anything around the house. She is a peacemaker, kind, and considerate. Because she was known for being such a sweetheart, she had 27 different offers for marriage. My other girls had no such track record…not even close. Men are not intimidated by a female with a kind Servant's heart. It is so feminine, very different from males. This type definitely has its perks.

It is important for a Servant not to become a pitiful, little-brown-bird-person. Maintain your individuality and develop your gifts. Always keep in mind that it is good to be an Encourager, but not good to be an Enabler. An Encourager helps people better themselves. An Enabler does things for people that they should be doing for themselves, healing their self-inflicted wounds and sympathizing with their poor vices to the point that they are enabled to continue their negative behavior without facing the consequences or assuming responsibility to change. This simple concept could be key in your life.

Hidden Flower/Servant Types

Girls that are of the Servant type tend to become Hidden Flowers if they don't stay focused on serving the greatest number. Keep looking for a vision. Get a purpose in life that is bigger than you, homeschooling and even family. Prayer will be an important part of your ministry.

An example of a Priestly/Servant type man found in Scripture is, of course, Jesus. The Apostle John must have been a Priestly type also. A female example would be Ruth who faithfully served her mother-in-law.

The Go-to Gal

My son's wife, Zephyr, is a Go-to Gal, similar to the King type. That is not to say she is overtly bossy; she knows her place as a wife. But she is strong, capable, and gives a sense of taking care of the greater number of people. Go-to Gals ooze with confidence, have strong opinions, and do well organizing people. These types often have a queenly presence. Beware: Girls that are that dominant can easily become Grabbers.

An example of a Kingly man in Scripture is King Solomon. David was in fact a king, but in personal nature he manifested himself as a Priestly type. A female example of a Go-to Gal is Deborah. Her story is found in Judges 4. She was a judge in Israel and such a strong personality that the armies would not go to battle without her being with them.

Examples

When I think of Queenly/Go-to Gal, two different ladies come to mind. One is a pastor's wife. He is regal and so is she. When she walks into a room, she glides with her head held high. The King Male/Queen Female combination is often bad, but because she has purposed in her heart to serve and honor her husband, their marriage is powerful. She brings it strength and honor. Her resolve allows him to grow as a minister without having to take time to pamper her as his weaker vessel. Together they do well in raising a family in a challenging ministry. In the back of this book, her husband will tell an awesome story about his strong, capable wife.

The second Go-to lady that comes to mind is a dear older friend of mine who is married to a Prophet type. She has served him, understood him when all others shook their head in bewilderment, and been a help to him in all that he has undertaken, no matter how dead-end the project appeared to be. As he gets older his Prophet-like traits are dimming, but his love for her shines like a beacon for all the world to see.

My Gifts

A man has a natural need to protect, defend, and cherish, therefore he is drawn toward a weaker vessel. A woman's need to be cared for causes her to be drawn to a man who makes her feel secure. These natural needs help us find life mates that best fit our abilities and drives. But power struggles still arise especially when a girl has not been taught what God says concerning honoring her husband.

Some of you who have strong gifts might ask, "Well, what about my God-given gifts and drives? Are women just supposed to lay down their abilities and let the man do his thing, even when she may be more gifted and capable than he is?" Yes! That is exactly the way it is, and no, not at all. The key is to recognize your natural type, not so you can take the lead, but so you can understand how it might weaken or aid your service to your first-in-command—your husband (Ephesians 5:22-24).

WHY?

Why did God put the man in charge? Why can't the stronger of the two personalities be the leader, or the smarter of the two make the decisions?

God knew we would complain, so he gave us a careful, logical answer. Now for you girls who live by your feelings (like me), I know it is painful, but try to think logically for just a moment. The answer lies in the very nature of a man and the nature of a woman. Understanding and appreciating these Biblical realities is the foundation of all that makes a cherished help meet.

Man's Nature: God did not create man with knowledge of good and evil. He was created to develop into a higher plane of wisdom and character. God knew that this growth process would be challenged by the devil and by man's own innate propensity to advance himself. There was danger in creating a man with autonomy, as evidenced by the perpetual failures of the male gender. But God in his wisdom created the male with an innate caution and natural skepticism rooted in his cold logic and unemotional responses. Granted, that which guards him against believing a lie can be twisted to become the basis of rejecting the truth, as history demonstrates. The devil is the master of deceit. He is the father of lies (John 8:44). His trickery is how he wins converts. No one would ever follow Satan's lies unless he was tricked into believing it was the truth. So God created man with extreme resistance, reluctance, stubbornness, and a skeptical mind.

Female's Nature: God created the female to express in excess a narrower band of the image of God. She is the softer, kinder, believing side. God designed the woman to be sensitive and vulnerable for the sake of the little ones whom she must nurture. The soul of a mother must be quick to feel, to hurt, to love, to have compassion, to take in the broken, and to believe the best. Vulnerability is both a woman's greatest natural asset and the point of her greatest weakness. Our very nature makes us susceptible to being tricked. We were created to be protected by our men while we nurture the family and maintain a connection with the emotional side of God.

Male and female together complete the image of our Creator, but we are vastly different. We each carry a strength and a weakness. Our roles were designed around these strengths and weaknesses. Neither can perform the role of the other well.

The Helper

The Hebrew word *Ayzer*, from which the English words help meet come, means one who helps. Woman was created to be a helper who was suited to meet the man's needs, to fill in between the lines. The female is a softer image, one step removed from the original. I am his curves. I am his sweetness, thoughtfulness, compassion, sensitivity and so on. I was created to help him be successful, to bear his children and train them according to his will. God did not create a help meet for the woman, for the responsibility is not hers. He is the one responsible and in authority. He needs a suitable helper. I Corinthians 11:8-9 says, **"For the man is not of the woman; but the woman of the man. Neither was the man created for the woman; but the woman for the man."** This passage should alter our way of thinking about marriage somewhat. Maybe we should be asking, "Would I be a good helper for that man? Would I be capable of supplying all his needs, filling the emptiness in his heart, and serving him in a way to make him successful in all he chooses to try?" And then we would change the way we pray. "Lord, help me learn to be the kind of woman a good man will need to help him in all things."

The Woman Was Deceived

Satan could have tempted this lonely man at any time, but the Deceiver waited for the creation of the needed weaker vessel. **"For Adam was first formed, then Eve. And Adam was not deceived, but the woman being deceived was in the transgression"** (I Timothy 2:13-14). Satan knew that the man could not be easily deceived, but the woman could.

The very first command God ever gave to a woman was, **"Thy desire shall be to thy husband, and he shall rule over thee"** (Gen. 3:16). God goes on to tell us, **"But I would have you know, that the head of every** man is Christ; and the head of the woman is the man; and the head of Christ is God" (I Cor. 11:3).

"For the husband is the head of the wife, even as Christ is the head of the church: and he is the saviour of the body" (Eph. 5:23).

God gave man the kind of nature that would be suitable to hold the superior office in the chain of command. A wife's position under her husband is where God put her for her own spiritual, emotional, and physical safety. It is the only position where a wife will find real fulfillment as a woman.

God is not impressed by our gifts, our types or our strengths. He is impressed by our willingness to abide by and appreciate his program by conforming to the needs of our man. God calls married women help meets. He NEVER called a man to be a help meet to his wife. This is not a two-way street. God commanded us wives to submit to, obey, and even reverence our husbands. He also tells us why we are assigned the role of helper.

"For a man indeed ought not to cover his head, forasmuch as he is the image and glory of God: but the woman is the glory of the man. For the man is not of the woman; but the woman of the man. Neither was the man created for the woman; but the woman for the man" (I Cor. 11:7-9).

"But I would have you know, that the head of every man is Christ; and the head of the woman is the man; and the head of Christ is God" (I Cor. 11:3).

"This is a great mystery: but I speak concerning Christ and the church…and the wife see that she reverence her husband" (Eph. 5:32-33).

Created For the Man

Now that we know what God says, we can more clearly see our role as help meets. It all comes back to one important truth. We were created for our man. It is our job to fit into his life, being whatever he needs. We need to think about how we can best use our gifts, talents, and our type in this honored place of second in command.

Think about this: I am married to a King type, yet I am writing this book, which means I am using my Dreamer drives. Serving my husband is first, but when a man knows that his wife is serving him first and foremost, her gifts will then become an extension of his gifts. **I complete my husband; I don't compete with him.** The Scripture says we become one flesh; we are heirs together. If we seek God in fulfilling our roles and walking together as one, we create a complete picture of the person God wants us to be. We are stronger, smarter, more resourceful, more talented, and more able to help if we work as a team. Amos 3:3 says, **"Can two walk together, except they be agreed?"**

Creating Balance

God created the genders different so that together we can bring balance as a couple in the struggles of life. I know a married couple composed of two Priestly personalities. I doubt they have ever had a fuss. They are the nicest people you will ever want to meet, but their oldest son is a Kingly type, and he is a real pain toward his brothers and sisters and people in general. He needs at least ONE parent to be dominant in order to keep him in his place. I feel sorry for the boy, having to grow up finding his own way as a King. I have only very rarely seen two Priestly types marry.

As a rule, opposites attract. A person finds someone of the opposite type interesting because of the mystery, because the other possesses traits they envy and find attractive for their very lack of those traits. Look around and you will notice that Priestly men seem to be drawn to Go-to women and Dreamers. Kingly men usually marry gentle Servants. Prophets often marry Servant-type girls. Of course, a positive female influence in a boy's life can change his perspective in what he values in a wife. The same thing goes for negative influence. <u>If a boy's mother is a Dreamer that has allowed her unstable emotions to rule the family in a destructive way, he will unconsciously avoid girls who have any of the same drives.</u>

I'm mainly attracted to Dreamers that some friends don't consider beautiful at all. Go-to Gals seem to be diva types that are often physically beautiful, which has caught some of my friends' attention. Nothing's wrong with outward beauty, but it isn't an overly important trait to me. If emotionally attracted to a girl, she can appear to me the most beautiful person in the world, inwardly and outwardly, even though others might think she has average or less physical beauty.

This is why I think <u>the young man needs to FIND the woman</u> that attracts him and not have it initially set up by parents or other authority figures. A man knows what kind of woman commands his interest.

Yes. However, I think in most western cultures (or at least, American culture) the parents will not go forward with an "arrangement" if the man expresses an obvious dislike for the girl.

It is a good thing that opposites are drawn to each other, because when a couple of different personality types work together as one, they will come closer to a balance of God's image than a man would alone. For example, my husband is a King type. I am a Dreamer, but as his wife I first function as a Servant. Notice the triangle of all three types. I know that we as a couple lack some Priestly attributes, but together we come closer to being a balance of all three types than my husband would if he walked alone. As a wife I can help to bring balance. I can finish out the image, complete the picture.

So the question is not, "What am I?" A better question to ask is: What type of man would I best complement with my gifts? This subject is explored more in the Teacher's Guide in the back of the book. Shalom, my middle daughter, discusses different couple combinations and the pitfalls and joys of each.

Now let's summarize the Prophet, Priest, and King types so they will be easy to spot.

How to Spot a Prophet

It is fun to observe men and guess if they are Prophet, Priest, or King. Here is a simple guide: Percentage-wise, there are a lot of Priests, a few Prophets and fewer Kings. Most men are a mixture of two types, though one is typically dominant, which helps bring a better balance to their personalities. Prophets will have a little King or Priest to tone them down. If they are pure Prophet/Visionary types, they are easy to identify.

Most young boys have been caused to conform to what their parents deem acceptable, and many Prophet/Visionary boys are taught to control their proclivity to tunnel vision. Even when very young, Prophet traits will be obvious in a child. A boy Prophet will be easily fixated on ideas, mechanical workings, or troubling social or spiritual issues he feels need to be addressed. These young men are usually sensitive souls. The Prophet can be a perfectionist, which means he will judge others and himself, sometimes harshly. He, compared to the other types, will likely be more prone to frustration and depression. This kind of male will focus on pursuing excellence in areas such as music, art, or even computer science, but they are more likely to launch out into frontier research and find something different from the status quo. They will be prone to talk in extreme depth about one subject until they dissect every part and discover something no one else has never thought about.

The man who designed the layout for *Created To Be His Help Meet* is a Prophet. I can see him smiling as he reads this, and his response is, "Oh, *really?*" He is an artist. His stare can get locked on something, or worse, on someone, and he looks as if he is lost to the world, and in a way he is. But he needs a help meet who will smile when she sees the glaze drawing over his eyes, because she knows behind that vacant look is a masterpiece being constructed or an idea about to be hatched. He will need a cheerful soul for a wife, one not given to offense or negative chatter. A Servant-type female willing to serve and enjoy his talents would greatly please him. However if he married a Go-to female, and if she really knew her place to serve him, then she could put him on the map! His art could be known to the world due to her strong drive and abilities. It depends not so much on the woman's type, as it does on her heart to serve her man.

One of my daughters is married to a total Prophet. He has such tight tunnel vision that when he is working on a project he forgets to eat and sleep. My daughter (his wife) is also a Dreamer. They own and run Bulk-HerbStore.com. Thankfully, she has been taught to be his wife first and creative second. Together they are a lightning rod for ideas. If she did not follow God's plan for a woman, then neither their business nor their marriage could withstand such boiling, sometimes disjointed energy. Since she does, they are indeed a dynamic duo. 💜

In the end it is not so much what type you are as whether or not you are willing to place his talents and ambitions first and then utilize your gifts to assist him. Believe it or not, though this approach may look like you are sub-

Though there is insight in understanding people's types, in the end salvation and character are the most important qualities.

jugating your personality and burying your gifts, in the end, if you achieve a balanced marriage and make your man successful you will discover the greatest, most fulfilling expressions of your own talents.

How to Spot a Priest

A Priestly/Steady type is a laid-back "good ol' boy." He is not hyper, not explosive, not brash, and as a rule he likes to hold a regular job. Farmers are often Priestly. He is every mother's choice as a perfect husband for her young daughter.

You will spot him because he likes to do things for people. Everyone calls him when there is a need, because he is nice to have around.

I agree. In fact, I resemble these remarks to a tee. I also like to think people call me when there is a need because I can help them with meeting that need, and not because I am "Nice to have around."

He usually makes a good daddy and provider. Any girl that has been in difficult relationships thinks this type of man is heaven-sent. All divorcees are looking for this type of man because they are fed up with wild-eyed Prophets and commanding Kings. The Priest is the salt of the earth. I am sure you can think of several older men who fit this description, and you like them. There are many Priestly types because…we need them.

Usually it is the girl who has a strong streak of Go-to or Dreamer that notices the Priestly man who is getting things done. The Priest reacts positively to her admiration. That is why kind, soft-spoken, easy-going men often seem to be attracted to the strangest types of females—dominant, bossy, opinionated, or maybe even flashy girls. I have met the most accommodating Priestly men who are married to the most assertive women, yet the men seem to really enjoy their wives. Often I have seen a shimmer in the man's eyes as he met his wife's eyes after she said or did something a little over the mark. The only way to define the shimmer was amusement.

Unfortunately, most young girls have stars in their eyes, so romantic that they first swoon over the King type because he is the one standing up front

Hilarious and true. The boldness of some women amuses me. Brashness however is a different thing—very unattractive.

commanding. Then their attentions are captivated by the two or three Prophets because they are the ones shouting that everyone needs to stop wasting time and get on with the project. The Priest is noticed when he is quietly doing something…because that is who he is. If a girl is blessed by having an opportunity to work on the project with the Priestly man, she will come to appreciate what a good, steady man he is. He is the kind of man "you need to get to know" to really find out that he is indeed fascinating.

All men seem to bloom after they marry (if their wives are of one spirit with them) into a stronger, better version of what they were as single men.

> I know that happened to me big time. Ask anyone who knew me before I was married.

A Priest might take on some characteristics of a Kingly type. A Prophet might tone down and become more Priestly. A Kingly type will take on a few Priestly traits. It is common to hear young girls say of a newly married young man, "He seems so different now that he is married. I never even noticed him before. He is really a strong man. He must be dressing differently." I just smile. Clothes don't change a man, but a good woman serving him will bring out the MAN in him.

Females are not necessarily attracted to good looks, whereas most men put good looks as the number one qualification for any female they are considering.

Females are attracted to different types. So when sisters or mothers or friends start gasping at your choice in a man, you need to understand it has nothing to do with your man; it has to do with his type versus their type.

I know most of you are wondering what kind of man is best for your type. The problem of being a young woman and picking out a type that you would rather marry is this: You are probably fickle and don't know what suits you best. No offense intended, just an honest observation of young girls. But do keep in mind: Opposites typically attract.

> This is true, but don't underestimate one thing: Vivaciousness and joy will do a hundredfold more to make a girl look attractive than the best makeup and hairstylists money can buy.

> Amen to that, brother. Check out these two verses: Proverbs 17:22 **"A merry heart doeth good like a medicine…"** and Proverbs 15:13 **"A merry heart maketh a cheerful countenance…"** So, a cheerful countenance doeth good like medicine (my own paraphrase).

How to Spot a King

We have a boy in our church that is a King type. He is so cute. Since he was just a little guy he has ushered his brothers and sisters, one sister older than he, up to the front and directed them in singing specials. They all look to him in honor and reverence as he directs their paths. He smiles as if they are his pride and joy. All the siblings will do better because he is there appreciating his team. King types are usually firstborn sons.

My oldest son, but second born child is a King. He even walks like he owns the world—shoulders back, pushing forward with long forceful strides. He oozes of leadership and command.

They are easy to spot even in their youth. Look around at the young boys in your church. Do you see a King in the making? Isn't it engaging to see his leadership and confidence? Sometimes these boys will have real conflict with their mother and father because they will unconsciously expect their parents to bow to their leadership. If a boy's mother is a strong woman, he could hold her in contempt for not being submissive. If a boy's father is strong, there could be a "battle of the bulls." Parents need extra grace raising Kingly sons through their teenage years. It is worth the effort.

Start praying for the young Kingly boys you know to have the wisdom and kindness they will need to navigate their young years. Also remember to pray for their parents.

Strong Kingly types are not as common. It seems as if there is only one in every group. Not all King types have gifts in teaching, preaching, or directing a large company, but they do have a natural tendency to lead. This type is always being judged because they are the men who take charge. James 3:1 says, **"My brethren, be not many masters, knowing that we shall receive the greater condemnation."**

Leaders get the blame if things don't go as well as expected. It is human nature. The wife of the King must understand this. She should more than understand; she has to have the wisdom to see it, dismiss the clamor of others, and at the same time remember that her man, like everyone else, has soft tender spots that need her gentle healing hand. Regardless of her type, the King's wife will need much wisdom.

Your Treasure Chest

♥ Could you serve a King?

♥ Seek God for the wisdom you will need to help him be all that God would have him be.

♥ Write these verses in your notebook and on the pages of your heart.

"Likewise, ye wives, be in subjection to your own husbands; that, if any obey not the word, they also may without the word be won by the conversation of the wives; While they [lost husband] behold your chaste conversation coupled with fear. Whose adorning let it not be that outward adorning of plaiting the hair, and of wearing of gold, or of putting on of apparel; But let it be the hidden man of the heart, in that which is not corruptible, even the ornament of a meek and quiet spirit, which is in the sight of God of great price. After this manner in the old time the holy women also, who trusted in God, adorned themselves, being in subjection unto their own husbands: Even as Sara obeyed Abraham, calling him lord: whose daughters ye are, as long as ye do well, and are not afraid with any amazement" (I Peter 3:1-8).

♥ Explain what "let it be the hidden man of the heart" means.

Learn And Live Well

MORAL TO THE STORY: Knowledge can save your life.

A CAUTION: Shrugging off learning can be devastating.

Married life is not all romance and passion—maybe five percent. The rest of your time is devoted to the routine of living.
There will be unexpected trials and burdens that will catch you
and your sweetie totally by surprise. Whether your family, not
to mention your passion, survives life's curveballs depends on
knowledge…yours.

CHAPTER 7

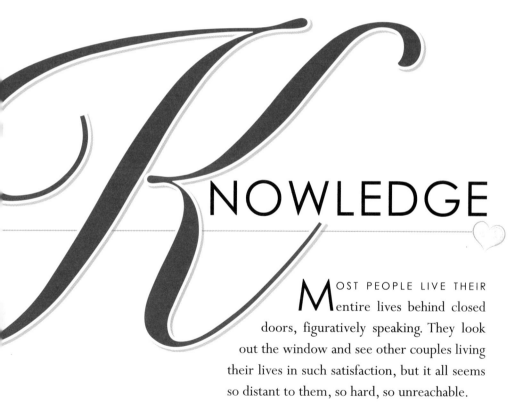

KNOWLEDGE

MOST PEOPLE LIVE THEIR entire lives behind closed doors, figuratively speaking. They look out the window and see other couples living their lives in such satisfaction, but it all seems so distant to them, so hard, so unreachable.

A man comes into marriage believing that his wife will be the fulfillment of all his longings, all his dreams, and all his expectations. After only a few short weeks he looks into her eyes and finds only dissatisfaction. A wife blames her husband for being a loser sitting in front of the TV or spending his life on some other useless time waster. The husband is frustrated that something is not the way it should be. He sees the disappointment in his wife's eyes and it leaves him powerless to go forward, so he drops into the nearest chair to lose himself in mindless pursuits. And so he stands behind the locked door thinking his youthful dreams were just wishful thinking, not really possible. He loses hope. Without his vision, she has no vision, or she pursues her own vision apart from him. Half of the Christian couples settle into a life of ho-hums. The other half will part ways and try it again, and then again, and maybe again, with different spouses. Failures keep pairing up, hoping to find a workable combination. **"Where there is no vision, the people perish"** (Proverbs 29:18).

For most people it is a simple lack of knowledge that keeps them chained to the floor, daydreaming their lives away one day at a time. Living behind closed doors means always living in expectation, waiting, waiting, never doing anything better with their life. Do you daydream your life away even now? It is a sign of things to come.

Actually, if I had to point to one moment in my life when I saw clearly the need to take hold of everything I could to learn and grow in wisdom, it would be the night the Death Angel came to visit me. It was then that I finally rushed through the door of being actively involved in pursuing truth and have never returned. I'll tell you that story, but first you need to understand a few simple truths.

Proverbs 24:3-5 says, **"Through wisdom is a house builded; and by understanding it is established: And by knowledge shall the chambers be filled with all precious and pleasant riches. A wise man is strong; yea, a man of knowledge increaseth strength."**

Life is not that complicated. There are only a few simple principles that God set into place that make the whole process not just run smoothly, but really fly.

Proverbs 24:14 says, **"So shall the knowledge of wisdom be unto thy soul: when thou hast found it, then there shall be a reward, and thy expectation shall not be cut off."**

Where It Starts

<u>Many girls waste their youth by being entertained with movies or novels, shopping, playing the social game, yakking on the phone, texting, etc., or just lying around waiting for one of these things to happen.</u> When someone hands them a book like this, they grimace and say, "I'm not much of a reader…it's just so hard; it's boring," or "I'm just so busy, I don't have time to read books like that; besides, I've already read one like that before." And so their life stays limited for lack of knowledge, understanding, and wisdom. This chapter is a wake-up call.

"The heart of the wise is in the house of the mourning; but the heart of fools is in the house of mirth." (Ecc. 7:4) The house of mourning is a place of death, sorrow and ending. It makes the heart reflect and consider its own mortality and the heart of the wise is there, considering issues of life and death, purpose and vanity. Their pursuit is of wisdom and redeeming the time the Lord has given them. There is value in such thoughts but not those of the house of mirth and feasting. A fool's heart is full with thoughts of entertainment and pleasures, of laughter and merriment. Their pursuit is of fun and abundance. They never consider the future; for them all there is is today. What value do those things bring the heart? How do they redeem the time?

Fellowship, mirth, laughter and amusement are a spice of life but who would serve a meal of just ground cinnamon or table salt? What an ill-balanced diet it would be. Spices themselves give no substance and nourishment, but exist to enhance and contrast the flavor of the main dish.

Where does your heart dwell? The subjects you think about will tell you. To which do your actions and past bear witness?

The next story is my testimony about how I finally woke up to the extremes of life, and how I finally grabbed hold of hungering for truth and wisdom. It took a big, bad angel to get my complete attention.

THE DEATH ANGEL

Most people that hear this story think it was just my imagination playing tricks on me. It happened more than thirty-five years ago. I was just a young wife when the Death Angel visited, but I am convinced today, as I was then, that this truly happened just as I relate it.

I lived in a small community of mostly young military couples. All of the young families were expecting, or had a baby or two already. The girl directly across the street was nineteen years old and was married to a soldier of the same age who was in training to go to Vietnam. Her baby was born a few days before mine. One cold morning she came over to tell me the military authorities had called her, reminding her that the Health Department had issued a requirement that babies two-and-a-half months old should start on their vaccinations. This was a new mandate, starting the baby shots earlier than ever before. Somewhere I had read that there were problems with these vaccinations, especially for such young babies, but who was I to question the Department of Health? Besides, the shots were free and we could afford that! My best friend, Carla, who lived next door, also had a two-month-old son, but when I invited her to ride along, she wasn't interested in getting her baby a shot. Mrs. Soldier Girl and I took our babies and stood in the cold in a line outside a small trailer that served as the local Health Department, waiting for our babies to get their shots. We chatted and visited with not a care in the world except to stay warm. I think back to that day and ask myself, how were we to know what was to come? Then I wondered, why didn't we take the time to ask questions, demand information, or seek out advice? I know the answer. We were young; we believed that everyone else knew better than we did. Until that moment neither of us had ever been put in a position to know just how terribly a thing can go wrong due to a lack of knowledge.

Mrs. Soldier Girl called that evening to ask if my baby had a big red hot spot where the shot was administered. He did. Both of the babies had high fevers. I knew it was going to be a long night. As I rocked my son, trying to soothe him, I began to wonder why Carla had resisted getting her son a shot, and I sincerely wished I had listened to her when she tried to explain to me what she had read concerning the shots. Finally, the medicine I gave my son caused him to sleep. It was cold in our old farm house, so I nestled my baby boy up to my body and fell asleep. He cried off and on all night.

I awoke sometime in the predawn hours, the blackest part of the night. Other than my newborn's soft groans and my husband's light snores, the night was deathly quiet, like when there is a heavy snow that blankets the sound. I couldn't say why, but I lay tense and fearful, waiting...for what, I knew not. I was afraid. I moved ever so gently to lay my hand on my son's head. It was burning hot. I moved my head to his tiny chest and heard a strange rasping sound. Profound terror gripped me, causing my whole body to sweat. Then, as if I could see the shadowy figure, I knew that the Death Angel stood there at the end of the bed. My body was rigid, my mouth dry; I tried to control my breathing, but could manage only great gasps. I reasoned with myself that I was just an emotional female, and that nothing was really there. Yet conviction held ground in my mind and soul…I knew what I knew, and I knew that the Death Angel had come to our house.

I gave up trying to convince myself that it wasn't real, and I began to pray as I have never prayed before. I pulled my baby up tight to my chest, defying the figure at the foot of the bed that dared to enter this room. Time passed as I begged God's mercy. I began to pray aloud, getting louder and more insistent as my panic grew. Finally I jerked the covers off Mike and shouted, "Wake up now and pray. The Death Angel is in this room! Pray for our son!" My startled husband sat up, confused and alarmed. Then he grabbed the covers away from me, mumbling that I had lost my mind. I jerked his covers off and smacked him on the back as I screeched, "Get up and pray for your son!" By this time he was awake and truly concerned for my sanity. He tried to comfort me, but I cared nothing for comfort; I only wanted to hear him pray, asking God for mercy and commanding the Death Angel to leave the room. I told my husband what to pray. He reminded me that I could pray just like he could pray, so why did I wake him up? But he was my spiritual head and I knew that now was the time for the top command to pray. Thoroughly chilled, he grabbed the covers to lie back down but this time his normally obedient wife shouted, "You will never sleep again until you pray for our son!"

He turned over and tried to see me through the darkness, trying to perceive what had provoked such a passion. What I was doing was so out of character that he was genuinely mystified and somewhat intrigued. He wondered if maybe I was right, that the Death Angel was indeed standing there in the room. I am not a "spiritually sensitive" type—ready to lead him into all truth. He has always been the spiritual leader of our home, by anyone's standard. I could sense that he had made a decision. He reached over me and laid his hand on our son's head. He prayed. As he prayed, I sensed the Death Angel leave the room. For the first time in several minutes, the constriction in my chest released; I could breathe again. Our baby fell into an exhausted slumber. We lay there wide awake, man and wife in the dark, staring at the ceiling, whispering about what had just happened. He believed me. We watched the early morning light slowly begin to lighten our bedroom.

Suddenly red and yellow lights darted across our ceiling. I sat up and pushed the curtain open, peering across the street. The cold thin window pane frosted over and I rubbed it clean to see better. Then I saw the ambulance. It was parked across the street at Mrs. Soldier Girl's house. I still remember the feeling of profound relief that enveloped me. I still remember the shame that followed. *My son was spared…but her son was taken?* I watched as a police car arrived. *Why police?*

We quickly dressed. Mike rushed over to see what was wrong, and was told the following story:

All night the baby had cried. The young parents only had a couple of nights left together before the soldier was shipped out to war. When they awoke in the morning the baby was no longer breathing. At first the poor stricken couple was charged with neglect because the authorities assumed the baby died of cold. Later it was determined that it was the common three-month "Crib Death" that had taken the child. No one dared blame the vaccination that our babies had been given the day before.

Did I learn anything? That night changed my life. Never again did I stand in line like a dumb sheep waiting to receive what "professionals" said I needed. I learned that "professionals" were people who were just following orders from people whose only goal is to make a buck. It is true they might have gone to school a few extra years and learned a different vocabulary; but they were not my baby's mom, and they couldn't make wise decisions for him. Time has strengthened my resolve. The older and more "professional" I get, the less I respect "professionalism" as the voice of knowledge, understanding, and wisdom.

Now, no matter what the issue, before I submitted, I would LEARN everything I could possibly know for the sake of my children's health and my family's well-being. The door was open. I started to learn…really learn.

Everyone has opinions and agendas. If you have a reasonable basis on which your concerns, beliefs, hopes, or opinions are founded, then stick to them while remaining teachable.

You alone live with the consequences of decisions made concerning your life—you bear the responsibility. As an adult, do not be quick to delegate your life decisions to others.

How easily do you accept the "expert" advice of others, knowing that most travel the broad way that leads to destruction (Mat. 7:13) and are governed by their heart, which is **"deceitful above all things, and desperately wicked"** (Jer. 17:9)?

You need to learn about:

FROGS

Did you know that down in the Amazon there is a tree frog that has horribly toxic poison on its back? This poison does not appear anywhere else in nature except in the gut of schizophrenics (people with multiple personalities). Isn't that weird? What does the gut have to do with the brain? This poison is not in the gut of healthy people. Is it found in any other diseased individuals?

Thanks to a mom and dad who were desperate to find help for their autistic son, we now know that the same toxin is in the gut of autistic kids. Where did their bodies get it? Did it develop there from something they ate? How does the gut relate to a brain disorder called autism? Right now you are unmarried and autism is not an issue with you, but what about two years from now? What are your chances of having an autistic child in two years? Higher than you think! Once an unknown disease, autism is now destroying the lives of one in every 100 children. Each year a greater percentage of healthy two-year-olds suddenly develop strange digestive disorders and bizarre behavioral problems. When the disturbed parents have their child tested they are informed he has autism. Why? What is causing these children to get sick? What can you do to avoid the chances of your child developing autism?

Jerked Around

What do frogs and autism have to do with preparing to be a help meet? You might think I am jumping around in my book. Couldn't I have had my editor make the material a little more uniform?! I want you to understand that LIFE will jerk you around. Get prepared! You spent so much time waiting to be the beautiful bride in a long, flowing, white dress, and then in a space of a few weeks you feel like you accidently boarded a high-speed train. You go from the long, lazy days of being single to suddenly being on-call 24/7. When you're tired, when you have a headache, when you feel icky, when you don't want to get up and cook, well, you have to anyway, because now you're married. Within a few weeks of becoming a glorious, married princess you will find yourself kneeling in front of the potty barfing your guts out because you have a little one on the way. Doesn't sound very princess-like, does it? I know these things because I am the older lady. Been there, done that, seen it ten thousand times. Your time's coming.

Shock Training

I married a preacher. Actually, he was the pastor of a church at the time we married. It could happen to you. Learn now. Just two short weeks before we married, I was just a crazy 20-year-old who was peacefully enjoying the easy life that most 20-year-old girls enjoy. I had no idea I was about to be married. (You can read the rest of my story in *Created to be His Help Meet*.) Now that I was a pastor's wife, I was expected to know all, do all, and be all. I was suddenly responsible for keeping a large house clean, doing all the laundry, washing every dish, cooking every meal, entertaining large groups of people at the drop of a hat, and stretching money so thin that the grocer couldn't see color. Besides that, as a pastor's wife I was expected to know how to counsel women, teach Bible classes, and generally be a wise, discerning woman of God. In the midst of all this responsibility I had to learn to live with and serve a messy, demanding husband!

I came into marriage missing a few spokes in my wheel. Don't let it happen to you.

You spend your time pining away for your one true love and suddenly... voila! You're married and it's a lot more than you bargained for. Now is the hour you should be preparing to be a help meet.

Preparing to Be a Mama

Most every young girl thinks it will be months and months...maybe years before a baby comes. Surprise! Pregnancy is not as easy to control as most girls think. Now is the time to learn how to have healthy babies and what to do if your child has health issues.

In a garden, strong healthy plants get that way by being planted in strong, healthy, balanced soil. Your body is the soil for your coming children. Good health starts before conception. The more you know now, the more you will be prepared to handle what life might send. It is time to start reading on health issues for your future pregnancies. There is a list of good reading in the back of this book.

Help Meet Food Preparation 101

Every girl should know how to prepare different kinds of meats. You should know how to buy and prepare fresh vegetables. It is really important to know how to use dried beans. Using dried beans as a base, you can feed a lot of people healthy and tasty food with just a little money. Another important piece of information is how and where to purchase healthier food at a better price than the corner grocery store. "My mother doesn't know all this stuff, and she's done all right!" I hear you saying. Yeah, well, it depends on who you marry whether you can do all right with ten percent knowledge. My mom knew a lot, but she was never married to a pastor, and that adds a whole new list of responsibilities. If you marry a doctor, or a lawyer, or a farmer, then you'll have another list of responsibilities.

Thinking about marrying a farmer brings up another list of things to learn. You should have already learned how to make butter, cheese, yogurt, and kefir. Most of you think you'll never have the opportunity to obtain raw milk, so you will not need to know how to make yogurt. But what if you marry a farmer? Would you know even the basics on how to grow a garden? Learn how by offering to help someone with their garden. Read gardening books.

Don't take for granted that life will continue its status quo, for life will surprise you. It is your responsibility to be ready. Knowledge is worth more than anything when bad times hit. Almost all families have bad times of some kind. A little information can guide you through bad times with far less pain, so it is part of preparing to be a help meet. Start reading cookbooks. My favorite is *Nourishing Traditions* by Sally Fallon.

Birth Control

I wish I could avoid this subject, but it will be the single most discussed subject once you are married. This is a smidgen of how your future conversation will go:

He says, "We need to use something."

She replies, "We decided before we married that we wouldn't do anything."

He demands, "Well, we've got to do something! Three babies in two years —and you're completely bedridden for the first five months of pregnancy!"

She moans, "What? What do you want to use?"

He throws up his hands. "I don't know, but something! You're the woman; what do you suggest?"

She looks baffled, "I don't know…how should I know what to do?"

He responds, "Well, go figure it out!"

If you are like most girls, the issue of birth control has never crossed your mind. Some girls, and guys, come to marriage with a principled conviction against doing anything to limit or control the frequency of conception. Others are adamant against using any mechanical or chemical means of birth control, but are willing to practice abstinence or a rhythm (timing) method to prevent unwanted pregnancies. Certainly no Christian will want to use any method that causes the destruction of the fetus after conception.

My object here is for you to learn about your body, come to understand the entire process, and learn what God says on the matter. If you don't give it any thought now, then chances are you will be pregnant and puking within three weeks of marriage. Your first child will be a girl. Now, how can I know that? Because, if you are like most girls, you will plan your wedding for the week after your period ends. That is when most women are fertile. During the first three days of fertility the woman's slight discharge is beneficial to female sperm. The fourth day, the woman's slight discharge is advantageous to male sperm. Did you even know that there are male and female sperm?

How do I know all this stuff? I study. Knowing things helps.

Birth control is a subject that you need to study. When Eve sinned, God placed a curse on her, **"Unto the woman he said, I will greatly multiply thy sorrow and thy conception; in sorrow thou shalt bring forth children; and thy desire shall be to thy husband, and he shall rule over thee"** (Genesis 3:16).

Man's curse of hard physical labor is found in Genesis 3:17-19, **"…cursed is the ground for thy sake…thorns also and thistles shall it bring forth to thee…in the sweat of thy face shalt thou eat bread."**

The curse on the woman, and every sister of Eve, is multiplied ovulation—having babies more often. According to this passage, it seems that the woman probably didn't have a cycle every month like she does now. A woman's cycle might have come only every six months or even once a year like some mammals. At any rate, the curse of the multiplied conceptions would have meant the cycles came more often, which would translate into closer pregnancies. This is hard on a woman's body; it is part of the curse.

As a single girl, you need to decide before marriage if you are willing to cheerfully and confidently go along with your husband's wishes, knowing he may change his mind. He might begin marriage believing in birth control and then change his mind. Never go into a marriage thinking you will change his mind. That attitude is controlling.

This is one point on which you must agree beforehand or there will be contention in the marriage. Once you are married if you stand against your husband…you will be standing against God. Know your mind; make sure you both agree before the wedding is planned. Get familiar with different natural forms of birth control as well as the timing of your own body in the event your husband wants to space the children.

Don't let some nurse at Planned Parenthood tell you that IUD's are not abortive, or that "the pill" is not a problem. Trained professionals are trained to lie.

It is your body. For you to have a strong healthy body and strong healthy babies, you need to learn.

Good, godly information is available at: www.familyplanning.net

Practice Makes Perfect
(homework ideas for practicing)

Hospitality
Homework Time: Go out and earn some money. Take that small sum and plan to have four families over to eat. Not families that make you feel comfortable, but families that need someone to be their friend. Do all the preparation before and cleanup after.

I think these are good, practical ideas.

Stretch the Dollar

Homework Time: Go out and earn some money. Find a family who is struggling financially. Tell the mother you are doing a *Preparing to Be a Help Meet* project and want to see how much you can buy for her kids on a limited and fixed budget. Get their clothing sizes and any preferences they may have. Tell her it is her lucky day, because as a learning project it is important that you cover all expenses. Look around until you find a good secondhand store or look for garage sales. Start shopping. Learn to stretch the dollar. Learn to please every kid. Learn to make wise decisions quickly. Make sure you buy something for the mama.

Responsibility

Homework Time: Tell your parents you want to learn what it is like to have the entire responsibility of caring for a family for one week. Let them help you choose a family. Volunteer your services in accordance with when it will be convenient for the chosen family. Most overworked moms will jump at the opportunity. Go ready to clean, cook, wash clothes, keep kids, homeschool, car-pool, and even keep Grandpa. Be a servant and let them grade your services. Don't be offended when they say you were edgy or too slow! If you are offended at their grade, you will spend your first years of marriage offended. Part of the class is to learn _not to be offended_ when judged and found wanting.

 Use it as a motivation to improve yourself.

Homeschool

Homeschooling for your future children starts today! Many years ago I read a book on how to introduce an infant to great music and instill in them a natural musical talent. When my first baby was born I had already purchased old records and a record player from the Goodwill store. In her first hours she faintly heard strains from some of the best violinists in the world. Did it work? It did.

By the time my second child was born I had read how to introduce a newborn to math. That works as well. The time to read up on subjects like that is now.

I often wonder what could have been for my children if I had learned all that information before I married. Good homeschooling does not come just from textbooks; it also comes from research and life.

Homework time:

Start today going up and down the library aisles and plan to introduce yourself to a new subject each week. Or, if you are computer-oriented, spend your time studying vital subjects rather than idly "surfing." I was a young mother when I decided to stop wasting my time with entertainment and start trying to learn. My first subject was mushrooms. It was fascinating. The mushroom subject opened up the subject of different kinds of fungi. This past year, as we harvested our corn, I noticed a few plump purple kernels. I quickly put the strange corn in a pile for burning. It reminded me of the barley fungus blight I had studied so many years before. This blight that hit Europe several centuries ago didn't destroy the grain; it just caused a few of the grains to take on a strange fat-looking shape. It was the common folk who finally realized it was their diseased grain that was destroying the brains of the people, making them go totally crazy.

Over the years I have covered the strangest subjects, some of which have come in handy at the oddest times. Almost forty years ago I started studying herbs; now two of my children are herbalists. Later I studied space, air movements, and flight. One of my sons is a pilot. My study became their school.

Why do I tell you all this weird stuff? I want you to know that walking through the door of knowledge will make you a stronger, healthier, smarter and more resourceful person. It will make you a more capable wife, a wiser mother and an interesting person. It could save your life or that of your child.

The human brain is not made to hold everything, but a good library, online or otherwise, can make it possible for you to be an expert on many subjects. Following is a list of books (and DVDs) to purchase, use, and add to your Treasure Chest.

HEALTH AND HERBOLOGY

Nutritional Herbology by Mark Pederson

ABC Herbal by Steven H. Horne

The Whole Soy Story by Kaayla Daniel

The Herbal Drugstore by Linda White MS and Steven Foster

Nourishing Traditions: The Cookbook that Challenges Politically Correct Nutrition and the Diet Dictocrats by Sally Fallon

Organic Body Care Recipes by Stephanie Tourles

Seeds of Deception (genetically altered seeds) by Jeffrey M. Smith

UNDERSTANDING MEN

For Young Women Only: What You Need to Know About How Guys Think by Shaunti Feldhahn and Lisa A. Rice

The Truth About Guys by Chad Eastham

Understand Your Man: Secrets of the Male Temperament by Tim LaHaye

GIRLHOOD / WOMANHOOD

Passion and Purity: Learning to Bring Your Love Life Under Christ's Control by Elisabeth Elliot

Let Me Be A Woman by Elisabeth Elliot

Before You Meet Prince Charming by Sara Mally

A Chance to Die: The Life and Legacy of Amy Carmichael by Elisabeth Elliot

Authentic Beauty: The Shaping of a Set-Apart Young Woman by Leslie Ludy

The Ministry of Motherhood by Sally Clarkson

RELATIONSHIP

Created To Be His Help Meet by Debi Pearl

When God Writes Your Love Story: The Ultimate Guide to Guy / Girl Relationships by Eric Ludy and Leslie Ludy

The Five Love Languages for Singles by Gary Chapman

I Kissed Dating Goodbye by Joshua Harris

When Dreams Come True: A Love Story Only God Could Write by Eric
  Ludy and Leslie Ludy

FINANCES

Total Money Makeover by Dave Ramsey

CHILD TRAINING

To Train Up A Child by Michael and Debi Pearl

Hints on Child Training by H. Clay Trumball

Standing on the Promises by Douglas Wilson

FAMILY LIVING

Homesteading for Beginners Volumes I-II by Erin Harrison

Your Treasure Chest

"Through wisdom is an house builded; and by understanding
it is established: and by knowledge shall the chambers be filled
with all precious and pleasant riches" (Proverbs 24:3-4).

♥ Write a summary of what you learned in this chapter.

In Pursuit of Happily Ever After...

MORAL TO THE STORY: As a single girl, actively pursue an aggressive life of ministry, learning, and serving.

A CAUTION: A caution drawn from this story is: Be patient and wait on the Lord (and your man).

"There is difference also between a wife and a virgin. The unmarried woman careth for the things of the Lord, that she may be holy both in body and in spirit: but she that is married careth for the things of the world, how she may please her husband" (1 Corinthians 7:34).

In this love story you will meet a Princess named Ellie. Ellie was active, aggressive, serving, ministering, and patient. As you read her story, give attention to the time in her life when she gained the real purpose in her life. Note the scripture that guided her. This is Ellie's story.

CHAPTER 8

the ITALIAN PRINCE

story three

MY NAME IS ELLIE. IT WAS AROUND my nineteenth birthday, and I was wondering if there were any good guys out there. I thought the best person to ask was my protective older brother. So while we were on the phone I nonchalantly threw out the question, "Adam, have you met any good guys who would be good for me?" Now, thus far, my brother had given the hostile stare to every potential suitor that had looked my way, approving of none; but I hoped that in all of his recent travels he had met someone of whom he approved.

Without hesitating he answered, "Yeah, I've met one."

"Good," I said. I didn't ask him any more about the mystery man. I wasn't looking for him to set me up; I was just wondering if there were any good guys out there.

I had already had my experience with a charmer three years earlier. I was fifteen years old and my family started going to a new church in Denver. There was a handsome older boy there whom I noticed right off because the very first Sunday he looked right into my eyes. It was clearly a special look, and I was excited to get his attention. We soon became friends. We spent time talking, playing group games, and laughing together, and by the end of the year I was deeply infatuated with him.

Our relationship took an inevitable turn. There came an awkward moment when his mother approached me and said, "I'm looking for a good wife for my son."

I was shocked. Did she know I had secretly thought about marrying him?

Probably. Parents have very sharp eyes and usually observe more than they let on.

I was confused and unsure of what to do, so I sought God. Do you know that there are turning moments in a person's life, pivotal points that decide their future? God waits for you to decide which way you want to go. I am so glad that at that moment I wanted only what God had for me.

It was the truth I read in I Corinthians 7:34 that turned my heart away from her son.

"There is a difference also between a wife and a virgin. The unmarried woman careth for the things of the Lord, that she may be holy both in body and in spirit".

My life headed in a completely new direction. I laid aside the boy crush

Read the book of Daniel. There were many pivotal moments (life and death in his case) in his life, but it didn't start that way. His first "test" was shortly after being taking into captivity and being given the king's meat and delicacies to eat. It was a dietary decision: eat the fine food provided by King Nebuchadnezzar or adhere to his people's dietary laws and abstain. It was a small matter that he was faithful in. Years of faithfulness in increasing larger issues lead to pivotal decisions. As Jesus told in the parable of the talents, he who is faithful over a few things will be put in charge over many things.

If it feels God is not moving or advancing your life or spiritual walk, ask yourself, "Have I been faithful with the truth and things I have been given? Have I sown what seeds I have?" Prove to God, yourself, and everyone else that you have flourished with what you have.

thing and threw myself into pursuing a life of knowing and serving God. When I was sixteen, I worked part-time as a nanny. I took extracurricular art, music, and speech classes. I received certification from the Institute of Floristry to do floral design. I started teaching English to immigrants in the inner city of Denver, and I went from being a Sunday School teacher to becoming the Sunday School superintendent with my older brother. <u>My brother and I also took our first cross-country trip together before I turned seventeen.</u>

> Cross-country trips may be some of the best times for discussing life goals and perspectives with family members.

I eventually went on to start my own business. I named it Ellie Designs and I started doing floral arranging for weddings and other events. I also did interior decorating, gardening, landscaping, and housecleaning. When I wasn't working, I was busy doing ministry, taking courses, and spending time with like-minded friends.

One day, three or four months after asking my brother if he knew of any good guys, the phone rang. It was a guy asking for my older brother. I told him that my brother was out of town, and I politely asked if I could take a message. He told me his name and said he was moving to our area to attend Bible College. Later that day my brother called, we talked for a little while, and then I remembered the guy who called. I said, "Somebody called for you."

"Who was it?" he asked.

"I think he said his name was Anthony Taylor."

My brother didn't say anything for a few seconds, and then he asked somewhat sharply, "What did he want?"

"He said he is moving here to go to Bible College."

Again my brother didn't say anything for a few seconds and then he said very seriously, "Oh no, Watch out!"

I was startled by his reaction and I asked him, "What? What are you talking about?"

To which he responded, "Oh, nothing; never mind."

I didn't have to wait long before I met the mystery man. My brother was back in town when Anthony first came to our church, and he sat with our family for the morning service. I couldn't wait for the preacher to finish his message so my brother could introduce me to the guy with the warning "watch out." As soon as the service ended I stood up and turned towards my brother with expectation, but he quickly turned away and escorted his friend out of the pew without an introduction. I was so disappointed!

A few minutes later I walked into the lobby and there was Anthony, leaning up against the wall. He was well-dressed, and my first thought was that he looked like a super-handsome Italian prince. He didn't look my way, and he was soon gone. About ten minutes later I heard the church's back doorbell ring. I walked down the steps to answer the door and I saw Anthony standing outside. I opened the door and he began to walk past me without even saying, "Thank you," so I stuck out my hand and said, "Hi, my name is Ellie." He gave me a quick handshake and then, without even glancing at me, walked on by.

We slowly became friends over the next two years. He was very discreet with girls, so it was hard to get to know him well, but his passion for ministry and the things of God were evident. I wanted to know him better, so I began to set up soccer, ping-pong matches, and volleyball games. It took many months before he started coming over a couple of times a week to events that I was putting together. Of course, I cooked fantastic meals and treats, and I made sure that I looked cute for the get-togethers.

I was able to observe him in many circumstances. One time we were playing a game and someone got very angry at him. I was impressed with the way he patiently calmed the angry man down. I also noticed that instead of hanging out with the cool kids, he was often seen with inner city children, immigrants, and street people. I remember seeing him many times sitting in the park talking with strangers about Jesus, and once in a while I attended one of the weekly Bible studies he was leading with various people he had met.

Over a couple of years, our friendship grew stronger. Then he gave me an essay he had written for college and asked me if I would edit it. I read the essay over and over again. It was life-changing! In the essay he explained that a person could not be saved by the act of praying a prayer, stopping their sin, or making Jesus the Lord of their life; a person could only be made righteous by faith in Christ alone. I began pointing others to Jesus instead of things they had to do in order to get to Jesus.

Instead of leading me further away from God and toward himself, Anthony was leading me closer to God. He treated me in such a way that if I married someone else, my future husband could have thanked him. I respected him more than any man I had ever met outside of my immediate family, yet I still had not allowed myself to dream romantically about him. <u>This is probably because I never sensed that he was thinking romantically about me.</u>

Worthwhile guys are always thinking about her honor and avoiding the mere appearance of evil in their relationships with girls. I haven't always done that, but I'm learning like all the rest of the guys.

Now, over two-and-a-half years had passed since I first laid eyes on my Italian prince and still we were just friends. I had real yearnings, but I was committed to keeping my eyes on serving God as a single woman until God made my romance happen. About that time, I decided to go on a four-month mission trip. The whole four months I never wrote or phoned him, and he didn't contact me. I stayed focused. Toward the end of my trip, I was on a train thinking about going home and seeing Anthony again. As I watched the beautiful Asian countryside pass by, I realized that I did not want to spend the rest of my life without the godly man that I had come to greatly honor. I had delighted myself in the Lord. I knew he would give me the desires of my heart. He so promised in Psalms 37:4. I remained full of peace and delight.

Within six weeks of my return, my dream finally came true. He came to visit and asked me to take a walk with him on the beach. We walked to the waterside and stood there for a few minutes. I asked him, "Well, what do you want to do?" He said, "I think we should pray." Then he dropped to his knee. "But before we pray, I want to give you something." He pulled out a ring and pressed it into my hand, and then asked me to marry him. For the first time, I looked deeply into his eyes. He had never told me he loved me, but he had loved me. He had never tried to kiss me or even hold my hand, but he had treated me like a treasure. I said, "Yes!"

He took my hands and we prayed together, dedicating our lives to God. Then he said, "I have a gift for you," and started digging in the sand right where we were kneeling. He dug up a box and opened it, revealing two dozen red roses. As he handed me the roses, he finally told me the three glorious words every girl longs to hear: "I love you."

It wasn't until after we were engaged that my older brother told me that Anthony was the one good guy he thought would be good for me.

My handsome Italian prince and I have now been married for almost seven years, and for better or worse, for richer or poorer, through it all, we have rejoiced in one accord. I have traveled around the world with him and watched him preach the Good News to thousands. We just returned from living in Africa for the summer with our three kids and another baby on the way. Just today, we talked with a friend whose eyes filled with tears as he thanked my husband for preaching the gospel to him last year.

My love story gets better every day.

How did Ellie prepare to be a help meet? Here is what she says you should be doing:

- ♥ Get seriously busy making something of your life for Christ's sake, serving him in ministry to others. Make sure your life has purpose.

- ♥ And when it comes to Prince Charming, don't be a flirt and don't get frustrated at his slow approach. Don't try to push him to commit before he is ready. Be prepared to wait.

From the Italian Prince
My first impression of Ellie was that she was joyful, pure, confident, and full of productive activity. The more I got to know her, the more I realized my first impression was exactly right.

I will never forget the first time I met her. I was locked outside at the back of the church building, and she came to open the door for me. I recognized her as the sister of my friend Adam, and for some reason my heart started racing when I saw her. In that moment when she opened the door I became so nervous that I just started walking past her without even telling her thank you. Then she put her hand out in front of me and introduced herself. I quickly shook her hand like a wooden soldier. As I walked away from her, I wondered why I had been so flustered. For months I was on edge whenever I was around her. ♥

A female friend of mine said that all the guys she ever felt worthwhile (it was a really short list and one I wasn't on) were incredibly slow moving when it came to relationships.

For those of you who don't know me, you would probably think that I was just a shy guy, but that is not the case at all. I was able to become casual friends with other girls, but Ellie was different. She was much more attractive to me than other girls, and <u>she made me nervous.</u>

Girls I like make me "nervous", too. I often stumble all over myself when I try to talk to them.

Two years after I first met her I finally decided that, if she would have me, I would marry her, but still I did not speak. I carefully hid my feelings from her. It was another year of quietly watching her and getting to know her, plus preparing my life to include caring for her as my wife, before I knelt down to ask her to marry me.

Even though Ellie must have sensed my high regard for her, she didn't push or try to take the reins of our relationship. She waited. Again she proved her worth. For two and a half years we were friends, and then she left on a four-month mission trip. <u>When she returned it was as though I saw the sun for the first time after hibernating in a cave for the winter.</u>

Absence of a loved one can make the heart grow fonder.

Three weeks after she returned I finished Bible School. Within the hour of graduating I was sitting with her dad asking for his blessing to marry his daughter. He was shocked! He knew I had never said anything romantic to Ellie. Not once had I told her how gorgeous she was, how much I enjoyed being around her or how I longed to just hold her hand. I had waited until I knew it was the right girl and the right time. Her dad asked me when I wanted to get married and I said, "Soon." I had waited so long for this wonderful girl…I asked her dad not to tell Ellie a word. I wanted the privilege and the honor of asking her myself. He totally agreed.

Two long weeks later I took Ellie to a secluded beach and asked her to be my bride, my princess, my help meet. She said yes! ♥

We now have a daughter, and my dream for my daughter is that she would grow up to be just like her mother - joyful, pure, confident, diligent, and content.

Here are some things we need to consider after reading Ellie's story.

- ♥ She was busy with school, ministry, service and even setting up socials.

- ♥ Ellie was patient. <u>For years she had her eye on her "Italian Prince" but never pushed herself or demanded that he make up his mind and declare his interest!</u> Her busy life helped her stay focused on serving God. If she wasn't busy and fulfilled, she might have been trying to get the hesitating Prince to rescue her from a life of boredom.

- ♥ Ellie had purpose. Her life was doing something that gave her fulfillment.

- ♥ Patience is not sitting around waiting. Ellie regularly organized and hosted social activities in hopes of gaining his attention. It worked.

 Be proactive but not forward.

Your Treasure Chest

God's estimation of a Virtuous Woman?

♥ She is a hard-working, creative, frugal, cheerful, kind and pleasant lady.

♥ What things are you already involved in?

_____

_____

_____

_____

_____

_____

_____

_____

_____

_____

_____

♥ What are you going to begin doing that will develop you into the kind of treasure Ellie became?

_____

_____

_____

_____

_____

_____

_____

_____

_____

_____

Grabbers, Hidden Flowers, and Princesses

MORAL TO THE STORY: The kind of female you are will determine the kind of male you attract.

A CAUTION: If you want a husband that is not a pervert, then act like a princess so as to attract a good, wholesome prince.

The next few stories are disasters. All these girls got too antsy. What does antsy mean? You'll see.

CHAPTER 9

FINDING *balance*

WE HAVE READ THREE BEAUTIFUL LOVE stories: The Kid, Courtship with Whom? and The Italian Prince. We learned about the three kinds of men and three kinds of gals. Now it is time for some ragging.

Don't be discouraged, for sometimes we have to explore the negative to get positive results. Remember, your goal is to grow and change so as to attain a glorious marriage. If you feel a little beat up, well…charge on and grow. Life is a series of tests. Discard and forsake those shabby things you have put in your life and start building that which will be a glory to God.

Many young girls have come to me bemoaning, "How do you let a guy know you think he is really fine without being a come-on?"

Others girls have said to me sanctimoniously, almost bitterly, "I am so embarrassed at the way that girl hangs on to guys. She sure doesn't act like a chaste virgin." Their critical observations are warranted, but sometimes it drives them to the other extreme—to become a Hidden Flower. Their reserved attitude often comes across as snooty and puts good men off.

I've actually had this happen to me because I'm reserved, don't hug girls, etc.

No man wants to get involved with a girl who thinks she is super-spiritual, holy, and wise. This chapter will help you find balance.

In order to help teach balance, I have divided girls into three kinds: Grabbers, Hidden Flowers, and Princesses. This is not a biblical categorization like the three types we discussed earlier, but it is a very representative description of today's girls. I think the categories will help you gain a picture of what you want to become and what you need to avoid.

Grabbers

Grabbers are girls who go out hunting guys, latching onto the arms of any possibility. The problem is that the good guys will look down on girls who come on to them. Some girls are such renowned Grabbers that they hang

Advice from Zack* to his teenage sister:

My sister asked me how she can get a good guy to be interested in her. I tell her that sometimes girls come across as, "I'm so cool" or "I'm too spiritual to have the time of day for you."

I really don't get into girls who have that "better than you" look. I know that the girls say they don't mean to come across that way, but that is what the guys are seeing.

I told my sister she needs to always make guys feel that they are liked and appreciated. Look at them and smile with an accepting look, not flirty, but a pleasant interest in them and in their interests. Never put on airs of being a defensive, chaste virgin.

*Zack is cool, 18 years old, talented, and has his eye on the girls.

In Response to Zack's comment:

"I don't mean to come across that way" is really a useless argument and a cop-out. Especially when the whole point is to get other people to notice you. You are what other people see you to be. It can really come across as just another way for an "uppity girl" to absolve herself of responsibility to change.

on any arm that doesn't already have a swinger on it. No one really knows if they have a special boy friend; they are just "boy crazy". There are plenty of guys who will welcome the attention and the good time, but they won't value what is cheaply given.

The good guys looking on will disregard Miss Hanger-On as a possible mother of their future children even if they welcome her attention and flirt back. If her actions are not wifely and motherly now, why expect her to be different in the future? **"The heart of her husband doeth safely trust in her, so that he shall have no need of spoil"** (Proverbs 31:11). This girl is destroying her marriage before it happens.

Some guys, even good ones, like getting their male ego tickled, but when you are married to a guy that you managed to snag this way, you'll be left wondering if he still likes come-on females after he is married.

> Yes, he does. You can state that emphatically. If he married a girl that got his attention by constant flirting and flaunting her body, various girls will continue to get his attention that way after he's married. The biggest problem with being a "Grabber" is that it practically guarantees you're going to marry the wrong kind of guy—and that will probably become an even more acute problem 25 years later when you don't have a 20-year-old body anymore and lots of other girls out there do.

That's a real problem. As a young wife, you will be in a constant state of jealousy, so shun being a Grabber.

Even if a Grabber doesn't literally hang onto a man's arm, a man will recognize the Grabber's intent of grabbing at the relationship. An example of this would be the girls who approached my husband Michael, telling him they knew God had told them he was to be their husband. That is a spiritual Grabber. In the Teacher's Guide we will discuss patience in order to avoid becoming a Grabber.

> I know if any girl had come to me and asserted God told her I was to marry her, I can promise you I wouldn't. I'd be seeking the fastest route away from the crazy and/or grabby girl. On a fundamental level, I don't think any man wants to be married to a self-proclaimed prophetess.

Hidden Flowers

Hidden Flowers are treasures concealed from public view, either behind closed doors or disguised as icicles. They might as well be wearing a sign that says, "Find me if you can, that is, if you are worthy of such a glorious gal as I." These girls live at home, seldom minister to others outside their families, usually don't help out in events, steer clear from getting involved in projects outside their small circle, don't work outside the home, wouldn't consider a mission trip unless it was very scheduled and chaperoned, and, of course, seldom meet any cool dudes.

I've heard guys ask, "How can you get to know a girl enough to consider her if she is so protected that you can never find out anything about her or talk to her?" The answer is to be found, not in recreational dating, but in arranging social activities, dinners with other families, get-togethers, etc. These events allow young people to interact, talk, and see how others respond in various situations, in a "safe" environment.

It is not their spirituality that makes these Hidden Flowers as "useless as they seem." A few have adopted their cloistered life style as a matter of principle. They think they are doing what God would have them do. Others just live in a very protective environment and are guarded by parents. Some are shy and uncomfortable in public, due to lack of experience. Some are afraid of the world. They, or their parents, fear the world will gobble up the girls. Many believe that somehow God is going to just find the perfect man and send him an email telling him to go to her house and ask for her hand in marriage. For whatever reason these flowers remain a secret to the many guys out there looking for a quality girl.

Nuns don't get married unless they leave the convent. See "The Sound of Music."

They are good girls that would make great wives, but they have a misguided idea of how a righteous girl should spend her time. If they remain homebound too long, they might wake up to find that they have become Hidden Old Maids. Many quality young men complain that they cannot find a virtuous woman. When most young men get of age to marry, they will choose the

If you want to be found, be findable.

best they can find among their acquaintances. They don't knock on doors.

I know several productive, charming, happy women who never married because they stayed Hidden Flowers too long. If they had it to do again… well, they would tell you to read this book and do what it suggests. Chances are, if you are reading this, you want to become a Princess who marries a real Prince…so read on.

Both Grabbers and Hidden Flowers are on opposite ends of the spectrum. Both loose out. One never marries; the other marries a jerk. There is a balance. The Princess wins the Prince.

 ## Princesses

A Princess will not be a come-on, neither will she stay hidden. She will be busy, productive, and her life will have purpose, and her purpose will not be just to get married!

When a man is looking for a help meet, he will notice girls who are busy helping. A girl who is enthusiastically involved in projects and activities exudes an energy that makes her attractive. A young man of energy and vision who plans on conquering a little portion of the world and making a difference is going to find a partner who is already engaged in the same. He is not going to want to marry a liability, a high maintenance wall hanging. When he sees you aggressively helping at church, in camps, at home, friends, etc, he will take notice.

So become busy workers. When you work with children, your motherly skills will be noted. Offer to cook for church meetings. Smart girls will take charge of the clean-up routine, demonstrating a true servant's heart and a go-to personality. People will talk about good food and who prepared it. Everybody appreciates hard work and a good attitude.

Men not only listen, they watch. All men appreciate women that are joyful, cheerful, and entertaining. A too-sober girl, a girl that has a slightly cautious air tinged with just a touch of critical attitude, will be passed over. All men are repelled by self-righteous women. It is a common

Good guys tend to be busy and don't have time to stick around and get to know what a "sweet" girl someone is behind their shyness or composed reservation. Make a good first impression, make an effort to show on the outside what's inside. It doesn't matter the kind of person you think you are; it matters what you do. People are known by their doings (Pro. 20:11).

fault that seems to overcome even the sweetest girls once they are married. If your countenance as a single girl suggests even a hint of thinking yourself "wiser" and more "spiritual," you will most likely stay a single girl. So if you feel your mind drifting into self-promoting piousness, relax, kick yourself, and put on a smile. You can read more about this subject in my book *Created To Be His Help Meet*, in the chapter on Jezebel.

Generally, men like their girls to be informed and ready to give an opinion when asked. Don't be a dingbat spending all your time on clothes and hair. That is shallow and temporal. Some men like their ladies well dressed and looking sharp, but that wears old in a few years. And if that is all there is to you, you might just end up being somebody's show doll: "Don't say anything, Stupid, just look pretty." Listen to Bible teachers; ask significant questions. Keep up with current events. Learn about health issues, herbs, and natural healing. <u>Be open to read and learn a wide variety of subjects.</u>

For me, a girl who is a good conversationalist is way more attractive than a "knockout" who could star in a movie but who couldn't keep up an interesting tête-á-tête.

Sorry to mention this, but I have to tell it like it is. Most men want a girl that takes care of her body, keeping it toned, strong, and healthy. It is a sign of what she will be in her future. After all, men are visual beings. They like to look and enjoy. Don't let yourself become a fat lassie.

Learn what men like. Ask your brothers how most young men like girls to wear their hair. You will hear, "<u>Guys like girls with long hair.</u>" If you're smart you will listen to what you are told. You will also be told that guys don't really like piles of make-up or strong perfume. Again, if you are wise and not stubborn, you will listen and comply.

Don't be moody. Guys do not like complaining or touchy-feely, you-hurt-my-feelings type of girls. Most young men know someone's mother

Not super-long, though; keep it manageable. Don't try to set any world records! Remember to strike a balance; don't go to any extremes. From time to time girls tend to want to cut their hair just a little bit shorter to see what it's like. Once you marry, the guy will probably want you to keep it the same length. Girls like change but guys typically don't. On a related note, **"But if a woman have long hair, it is a glory to her: for [her] hair is given her for a covering"** (1 Cor. 11:15).

who makes the whole family miserable by her moodiness. All young men hope they escape that plague. Guys talk. They will alert other young men to any female they see sulking.

Antsy Leads to Grabbing

In the story, The Kid's Love Story, you read how I had to wait seven years until Michael noticed me. Then in the story of the Italian Prince you saw Ellie had to wait for a long time without a clue before her Italian Prince let her know she was his chosen sweetie. Waiting, wondering, hoping and too much thinking can make a girl Antsy. Antsy is not good. It can turn a good girl into a Grabber.

The Antsy babe is not lustful; she just admires the guy and is thinking about marriage. She might be a little demanding…pushy…or, well, you decide. A King or a Prophet man will not tolerate a pushy female. You will clearly see this in action in the stories in the next chapters.

Don't complain. Ever. Try not complaining about anything for a week and you'll realize what an ugly crutch it is. When evaluating a girl as a potential, I listen to her conversations and imagine the nature of them multiplied out 50 years. I shudder at the thought of enduring that much complaining, gossiping, whining, or sheer shallowness. Or will I find her conversations stimulating, encouraging, uplifting, and educational?

Your Treasure Chest

♥ Give an honest appraisal of yourself:
   I tend to be a...?

_____

_____

♥ What areas can I change to be more like a princess?

_____

_____

Learning Patience

MORAL TO THE STORY: Patience is crucial. Even when a little pressure is kind, polite, and thoughtful, it is still taking control.

A CAUTION: Desperation leads to becoming a Grabber.

Some of the following negative stories are depressing, but necessary for your admonition. Don't lose heart, for, as painful as it may be, there is nothing more influential than seeing the pain someone else experienced having traveled a road that diverges from yours. I hope these stories open your eyes so you can see pitfalls to avoid and so you can find the bridge to a good life.

CHAPTER 10

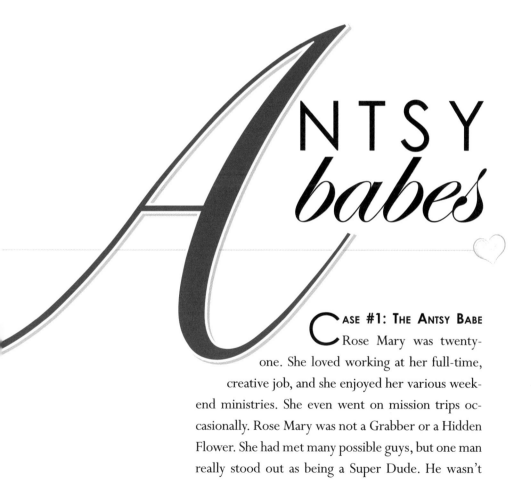

ANTSY babes

CASE #1: THE ANTSY BABE
Rose Mary was twenty-one. She loved working at her full-time, creative job, and she enjoyed her various weekend ministries. She even went on mission trips occasionally. Rose Mary was not a Grabber or a Hidden Flower. She had met many possible guys, but one man really stood out as being a Super Dude. He wasn't

tall, dark or handsome but he was cool, smart and in control. On occasion he came into town and dropped in on her family. Rose Mary loved it when he visited because she and Super Dude really hit it off. They talked for hours about everything from politics to Bible doctrine. But Mr. Super Dude never seemed to progress from being a friend to a Possibility or, even better, a Probability.

Then Mr. Super Dude wrote her on Facebook. Okay, progress. After much writing, visiting, more writing, and another visit, Mr. Super Dude still said not a word of anything personal. How good of a friend does a man need to be before he progresses?

Rose Mary was frustrated. Had she invested her energies in a shadow? Why did he make a point of writing her, visiting her family, but never gave any indication of interest? They were both old enough, so…duuuuh. She got antsy…then she began to stew, fume, talk with friends trying to decipher if he might be interested. She finally got angry. What she wasn't was patient. *He is* not *going to keep me hanging on*, she fumed. Rose Mary developed a serious case of female pride. So she wrote Mr. Super Dude and told him in a very nice way that a man should either be serious or not become good friends with a girl.

Now Rose Mary no longer has a friend, a Probability, and certainly not a Possibility. Was Super Dude biding his time until he had all his ducks in a row like the Italian Prince who waited until he finished college and was financially stable? We will never know—neither will Rose Mary.

If Super Dude was considering her, then she surely scared him off with her demand. I would guess he is a King. Kings react forcefully and finally when rebuked or challenged. But then, no man (Prophet, Priest or King) likes a woman to force his hand prematurely. Sometimes though, a man will need a

I'm not sure she should have been sitting around waiting for him. And certainly cutting off their friendship was a bad idea. This raises some questions: Can a girl and a guy not just be friends? Can't they even become good friends and not have further expectations? If there is nothing inappropriate or indiscreet going on, isn't it okay? I'll say right here I don't have the answers to these questions, but I know that for me it is hard to see any girl as "just another friend." There is always going to be the question in the back of my mind, "Could this be the girl?" At a certain level of involvement, however, I believe that it is wise for girls and guys who are "just friends" to discuss their views of each other and their intentions. This keeps everything above-board, open, honest, and realistic.

wake-up announcement. <u>What is a proper wake-up announcement?</u> We will visit that idea and tell the story of a girl who softly "woke up" her man, and won him.

<u>Notify</u>, but do not <u>inform</u>. Seek his notice but do not demand his intentions

If a girl were wise she would know that to demand is to take the lead. **If you lead your husband into the relationship you will lead him thereafter.**

Proverbs 8:11, **"For wisdom is better than rubies: and all the things that may be desired are not compared to it."**

A demand is…well, a demand. When a girl responds to a man's informal interest with informal hope, not demand, a man interprets it as humility. This is a very important lesson to learn. You may think the difference is only semantics. Not so. For a man, it often makes the difference in whether he drops a girl or continues in the developing relationship until he marries her. Remember, a King or Prophet-type man will respond to humility in a female with gentleness and interest.

Stop right now and ask God to give you understanding as you continue to read. You must come to appreciate this concept. Learning it will help you in every facet of your life.

"When pride cometh, then cometh shame: but with the lowly is wisdom" (Proverbs 11:2).

Interview with Ellie

(By Beth, Princess-in-waiting)

This next section is an interview with Ellie, the bride of the Italian Prince. Ellie tells us a story of one of her friends who did not demand a man to make a decision, yet she did boldly state her interest in him.

Interview:

Q: How did you know that the Italian Prince was the one rather than the other guy you liked when you were younger?

   A: I had grown very close in my friendship with the Prince before the four-month trip to Asia, and I knew spending time away from him would help me see our relationship from a new perspective. I knew we couldn't get much closer in our friendship without having things turn romantic, yet I also knew we could walk away from our friendship with no regrets. As I thought about the possibility of not having a friendship with him, I realized <u>I didn't want to spend the rest of my life without him.</u> So I knew when I returned from the trip that if he would have me, I would have him, too! I never had confidence to move forward with the other guy. Besides, at the earlier experience, I was too young to feel comfortable about marriage. When I was younger I was not a good judge of character. By the time I met my Italian Prince, I had matured and knew what I was looking for in a guy. I spent a lot of time watching him and figuring out what kind of person he was before I ever gave my heart to him.

Funny how most people only discover this in the negative sense--i.e. you rarely ever hear anyone say, "I realized I wanted to spend the rest of my life with this person." A short absence often brings feelings to light.

Q: How did you find the patience to wait for him to make a move?

A: I wanted to be married, but romance and the desire for marriage did not consume me. A girl who becomes desperate places herself in a dangerous situation. She is more likely to settle for a guy who, in a non-desperate state, she wouldn't even consider an option. When I was single and wanted to be married, I often reminded myself of the verse, **"For I have learned, in whatsoever state I am in, therewith to be content"** (Philippians 4:11). <u>I knew if I wasn't content with what I had (singleness), I wouldn't be content with what I wanted (marriage).</u> After being married for seven years now, I can definitely say that was a lesson worth learning!

Very wise.

Q: You said in your letter that you weren't into the Italian Prince all girly like. Is that correct? I know that you were busy with your life, but still?

A: I was young and I had goals and things I wanted to experience and accomplish before I got married. Paul wrote the verses in 1 Corinthians 7 for every single Christian girl. It says that a virgin cares for the things of the Lord that she may be holy both in body and in spirit. I saw my single years as a window of opportunity to give God my energies, my desires, my strengths. I treasure those years and thank God for the fruit that resulted from the ministry He brought into my life.

Q: Your story inspires me. There is this guy that I've liked for over a year and he hasn't made a move or anything. I don't even know if he's interested in me.

A: I have a friend who wanted to marry a guy who was clueless as to her interest. One day he told her that he couldn't find any good girls to marry, and she responded, "How about me?" They were soon married, and he says that the first time he thought of marrying her was when she asked that question. I think there could be a place for dropping hints or even stating your interest. Without knowing your situation, it's hard to say what I would do, but I have seen examples of young women letting the guy know where her interests lie, or having a brother/father/close friend let the guy know. Of course, if you do this it may end the casual friendship you have…or it could get the ball rolling!

Beth's Parting Remark

Thanks for the interview…and the idea of letting him know that you've got the answer if he's got the question!

Popping the Question

As a general rule, popping the question is a big no-no. Remember the antsy Rose Mary basically did the same thing as Ellie's humble friend. The difference was: Rose Mary was steamed. A guy can tell the difference. Ellie's friend came across with a smile and a big hope. A man would feel honored, not pressured.

Remember, I'm the kid who knew from the time I was thirteen who would be my honey, yet he said not a word for over seven years. I popped the question…you can read our whole story in *Created To Be His Help Meet*.

You will remember the joke I played on Michael, pretending to be engaged to the military guy? It was Michael's wake up call to see me as a potential bride.

Humble Response

Can you see that Ellie's friend was humble with her question?

She was hoping but not demanding that he "declare himself or else." When a woman demands that a man state his intentions, he will feel trapped. But when she expresses her interest in a way that doesn't draw a line in the matrimonial sand, he will feel honored.

A good man will not want to hurt a girl. If you lead him to think that a continuing casual friendship is leading you to a place of pain in the event he doesn't carry it through, out of regard for you he will discontinue the relationship immediately.

In a stand up demand, the girl is demanding the guy surrender the secrets of his heart immediately.

Ellie's friend humbled herself by letting it be known she would be honored if he would consider her, but she asked for nothing. There is a big difference in the way a man and a woman think.

This verse shines significant light on the contrasting results of these two girls stepping forward in the relationship, **"When pride cometh, then cometh shame: but with the lowly is wisdom"** (Proverbs 11:2).

Now back to Antsy Babes:

Case #2: An Old Antsy Babe

A mature, older woman had been single for a number of years. She decided to try an online matchmaking site to find a match. She was offered a match and talked online with a very nice older gentleman with whom she enjoyed corresponding. They were cautious, only writing once a week and then keeping their correspondence strictly non-personal. He began to call occasionally. Oh, it was bliss hearing his voice. The friendship seemed

Guys hate that. Most of the time the secrets of a guy's heart are a secret even to him right up to the moment he makes a firm decision. Trying to force the issue before he's ready makes him feel vulnerable and defensive.

to be progressing just fine, but weeks passed into months and still Old Joe showed no signs of taking the friendship up a level. Then he missed a few weeks of calling and didn't write for a while. The sweet, gentle Miss Oldie fretted, "Why doesn't Old Joe write or call? Has something happened?" She impatiently waited a few more weeks before she wrote, asking if everything was all right. "I hope you are not ill or anything? I was concerned." Old Joe wrote that everything was just dandy; he had just been down a little. So Miss Oldie felt better about waiting for another couple weeks. Then she got very antsy. Whoa—hold your horses, Miss Oldie! Nothing has been promised; there is no understanding. He owes you nothing. Don't demand he state his intentions.

After another week, Miss Oldie had had enough. She thought, "I would rather know that he is not interested, so I can get on with my (EMPTY) life. So she wrote Old Joe a very polite, dignified letter. It was easy for the old guy to read between the lines. He had been married before and knew when a woman was telling him what to do and when to do it. He grinned and waited another month before responding. He wrote a polite, kind, thanks, but no thanks reply.

The moral of the story is:
Patience is critical. Even when a push is kind, polite, and thoughtful, it still exerts pressure that the man instantly perceives as asserting control. One last story will show you there is more than one way to scare off a man.

Case #3: Antsy gone Grabber
Women have numerous ways of taking control. Many men are either weaklings or so sexed up they simply don't care if the girl is mowing them down, but most good men will not put up with a girl who tries to leapfrog his schedule. I want to tell you the story of an Antsy Babe turned Grabber—literally. Remember, desperation can turn even a fine girl into a Grabber.

April was twenty-two years old and ready to get married. She had her wedding all planned: dress, bridesmaids, food, flowers, the works. When Jacob came to her church, she pounced. He was just what she had always hoped for. Her eyes shot daggers at the other girls who eye-balled him, saying, "Don't you even think about him…he's mine."

That evening, as Jacob walked back to the parking lot in the company of the rest of the church group, he was surprised to feel a soft arm wrap around his. He jerked his head around to see who had been so bold. He was shocked speechless when she squeezed in beside him in the car, then laid her hand across his thigh. His healthy hormones raced into overdrive, forcing him to struggle to choke down the impulse to do some heavy smooching right in front of the fam—yikes!

Alone in the bright lights of his private room, he reassessed the situation. It felt oh so good. It didn't really matter which of the many pretty girls it was that draped her arm across his leg and pressed her soft breast against his arm…it was the female part that felt so good. He tried to place the face that went with the body…oh, yeah; now I remember. She is sweet, but I don't really know her.

Of course, now it would be difficult for him to get to know her, because his flesh had been stirred to the point his mind and soul would not function on a pure level. Not that she was a bad girl, he knew that…she just had no clue as to the workings of manhood.

He felt both drawn to her and repulsed by the guilt she caused in him. He liked what the flesh was feeling. It was heady that such a cute girl obviously thought he was the DUDE, but he hated the feeling of losing control of his life. He knew if she continued her fleshy pursuit, he might give in, wanting to marry her for the wrong reasons, and that would mean that for the rest of his life he would have a marriage built on the flesh alone.

Jacob did what a man has to do: **"Flee also youthful lusts: but follow righteousness, faith, charity, peace, with them that call on the Lord out of a pure heart"** (II Timothy 2:22).

He quit a good paying job and left town. The girl waited for his email or texts, and watched Facebook. Nothing. I suspect he was a Prophet, since they are more likely to do the unexpected. A Priestly man would have stayed in town, but just tried to stay hidden until the chase was over. A King might have given her the evil eye or a rebuke. This Prophet just ran. Very biblical.

Lessons Learned

Would Jacob have gone for April if she had not turned Antsy and become a Grabber? It's possible. Now let's think of a way she could have gently told him she was interested without becoming a Grabber. What if she had been smart enough to just briefly catch eyes with him…just once (very important to be just once) so as not to appear to be a Grabber or take control? Then if she happened to blush, well, he would clearly have gotten the message that she thought he was a hunk. It might have awakened his interest in her; then, again it might not have. A girl has to hope but not demand.

The key is that he could have decided whether he was interested and/or if he was ready for such a move. Good men carry the load of responsibility. They need to feel as if they have stability to offer their bride. Remember how the Italian Prince waited until one hour after he graduated from college before he spoke for Ellie. He was wise enough to know that once he spoke he would be so distracted with the thoughts of her becoming his lover that he would not be able to focus on the task at hand, which was finishing what he had already started (school). Once he was free from that responsibility, he was eager to marry as quickly as possible.

It is possible that a man who shared a "look" with you three years ago has been nurturing thoughts of having you as his bride. This might be a Priestly young man patiently working to save money so he will have something solid when he marries.

Patience is so important.

Yep, that's me.

Why Do I Paint Such a Mean Picture of Grabbers?

People wonder why so many marriages are hitting the rocks. You don't have to be a Christian counselor to figure that one out. Most marriages start with guys either looking for or giving in to a Grabber. When a girl is safely married, having captured her man on the lure of flesh, she will not feel cherished as a person. Maybe it's because she's not.

Marriages forged in the heat of lust will burn out fast. It takes a lot of

Whirlwind romances often have violent ends. I think there is a quote to this effect by the apothecary in William Shakespeare's play, *Romeo and Juliet*.

work and a lot of giving and healing to save these marriages. You don't want to go there.

I don't think you need another case.

> *"For the lips of a strange woman drop as an honeycomb, and her mouth is smoother than oil: But her end is bitter as wormwood, sharp as a two-edged sword. Her feet go down to death; her steps take hold on hell"* (Proverbs 5:3-5).

Learning Patience

Patience is a virtue that produces lasting results. Ask Ellie and her Italian Prince. She waited over two years for him to even give her a hint, yet he said that he carefully concealed his love from her.

How do you get patience if it is not natural to your nature? That is what we need to learn.

Case #1: Praying for Patience

I know a young lady who seriously lacked patience. She was also quite stubborn, a trait she was rather proud of until she began to notice that stubbornness and lack of patience seemed to walk hand-in-hand. Contrary to the notions of some girls with strong personalities, stubbornness is not a virtue in a female, for it is a masculine trait. Anyway, this girl observed that several of her friends had lost one of their Possibilities due to lack of patience, so she planned to master the art of patience so as not to suffer the same disappointment. For weeks she diligently prayed for patience. She had learned that God promised wisdom for just asking, so she just assumed that God would reward her with patience just for asking. She claimed the verse, **"Ask, and it shall be given you; seek, and ye shall find; knock, and it shall be opened unto you: for every one that asketh receiveth; and he that seeketh findeth; and to him that knocketh it shall be opened"** Matt. 7:9.

Soon her life went from humdrum to chaos. Her parents pushed her; younger siblings tortured her; overtime at work strained her, and a wonderful, handsome Possibility taunted her with hope unrealized. Finally one day she came into work looking worse for wear. Her hillbilly co-worker eyed her woebegone expression and said, "What's up your craw?"

This fine, upstanding girl broke down, "I can't figure out what's happening to me. Everything in my life seems to be pulling at me all at once. I can't seem to please my parents; my younger siblings are acting crazy; we are swamped here at work; and now I hear that this wonderful guy that has been hanging around our house has been hanging around Barbie's house too. I can't understand it. I have been asking God to give me patience, and instead I get more trials than I can bear."

Her wise co-workers stood for a few seconds before they burst into laughter. "Well," says the preacher who works in her department, "How do you think God is going to work patience into you? God clearly says in Romans 5:3-5, **'And not only so, but we glory in tribulations also: knowing that tribulation worketh patience; And patience, experience; and experience, hope; And hope maketh not ashamed; because the love of God is shed abroad in our hearts by the Holy Ghost which is given unto us.'** Be careful what you pray for, girl...he answers prayer."

Your Treasure Chest

Learning patience will bless all the days of your life, it will bless your husband, your children, your friends, and even your church. Weave the Thread of patience well.

♥ Write down areas of your life where you can begin practicing patience.

_____

_____

_____

_____

_____

_____

_____

_____

_____

_____

_____

_____

_____

_____

_____

_____

♥ So far we have learned:

- ♥ The importance of prayer.

- ♥ To seek counsel and to be open to consider a man we might otherwise pass over.

- ♥ With Ellie we learned to have a purpose in life, staying busy and motivated serving the Lord.

- ♥ Hopefully, we will not fall prey to becoming Antsy, thus becoming Grabbers, nor will we remain Hidden Flowers.

- ♥ Our goal is to become real Princesses.

♥ That brings us to the real possibility of becoming a Make-Believe Princess. I implore you to take what I write seriously so your life will not end up just Pie In the Sky.

Foolish Illusions

MORAL TO THE STORY: Maintaining a chaste conversation, both spoken and written, will reward you with gladness.

A CAUTION: Every deed, every word, everything will be revealed in detail some day. **"…and be sure your sins will find you out"** (Numbers 32:23).

When you're in love, your priorities change. Previous plans and goals don't seem quite as important anymore. That "special someone" is suddenly the most important thing in your life. A dangerous fact is that when you "think" you're in love, the same thing happens…it just doesn't last.

CHAPTER 11

PIE *in the* SKY

story four

MY NAME IS TARA. I AM nineteen and have never been your average girl when it comes to guys. Yes, they make good buddies, but I could never understand the girls who spent all their time giggling about their latest crushes. I made up my mind from a young age not to waste my time or emotion on a guy I couldn't picture myself marrying. Looking back, I can see I had too much spare time. If I had been busy, I would not have had time to text, text, text.

Here is how it happened.

Matt was the most sensitive guy I had ever met. He wasn't the kind of man I had pictured myself with, but we seemed to fit together so well. Because I grew up with an insensitive and very emotionally unflappable father, I never thought of sensitivity as a positive character trait for a man to have. But when you become the object of all that emotion and thoughtfulness it is very appealing. Matt always knew how I was feeling and seemed to relate. He was romantic and read poetry. He made me feel like I was the most special and wonderful girl on earth. In a way, it made me feel guilty, because I didn't know how to do the same for him. Like my father, I am rather insensitive, and very realistic. But I tried. Even though I knew I wasn't being myself, I tried to be emotional and as dependent on him as he was on me. It just felt so good.

Girls just love attention of this sort. It becomes intoxicating, like alcohol, and bends their perception of reality, like a drug.

We had briefly met through mutual friends. We seemed to hit it off. A few months later we started writing, and over the span of about four months he became one of my best friends.

That's the first red flag—internet "love" is just pie in the sky. It looks great, but it is not a real pie.

Because I am a very self-reliant and guarded individual, I found it amazing how much I opened up to him and trusted him on the internet. The transition from close friends to something more may have been slowly building throughout those four months, but neither of us realized it until he helped me get through some very difficult issues. He was extremely honest with me and very sympathetic. I gave him my cell number and we began talking and texting all the time. Looking back, I see that we didn't have a chance of remaining "just friends".

When a guy and girl spend all their time communicating and confiding in each other, they are going to run into trouble eventually.

I set myself up without knowing it. I didn't see it coming, and while I was still trying to figure out my own feelings, he had already moved on to considering himself in love with me. **Knowing that the man I cared for was in love with me was a wonderful feeling, and I felt pressured to return the sentiment.** I convinced myself that I loved him, despite the fact that deep inside I knew I was forcing it. I thought love would be amazingly clear, but it seemed so elusive. I pushed the doubtful thoughts from my mind; we were both so shocked and surprised by this development that instead of taking things slow to evaluate whether it was real or not, we plunged ahead, discussing whether or not my family would like him and what kind of weddings we'd always dreamed of.

We also discussed his past and some of the issues he had struggled with for years, and once again I persuaded myself not to let it bother me, for I was his healer. Our relationship was good for him.

Red Flag number 2: You don't have brains when you're in love and you can't "fix" your guy!

I convinced myself it wasn't that big of a deal, that we could work through it. I was foolish and blind.

My parents were absolutely shocked when I told them about Matt. It was the last thing they would have expected from me. But because I had never shown much interest in a guy before, they took me seriously and said he could come meet the family. They made sure to emphasize that he was coming to be approved, not to visit me.

They had no clue as to how serious we had become through texting and talking on the phone. After talking to my dad on the phone a few times, Matt bought his ticket and finally arrived. It had been eight months since we met—the only time I had ever seen him. Things were awkward at first, and I started wondering what I'd gotten myself into. <u>I pushed all my doubts and fears aside and pretended to be just as much in love as he was.</u> But slowly, over two or three days, little pieces of his character that I didn't recognize

> The more you desire something the less qualified you are to make a good decision about it. The very desire that drives the decision clouds you from being able to judge the decision well. As attraction can become all-consuming, it is doubly important to be mindful of the counsel of wise family and elders.

online began to show and it scared me. When someone writes, they project the person they think (or maybe wish) they are, not the person they really are. It became obvious that he wasn't the man I foolishly convinced myself I loved. But still, I told myself it was too late, I can't back out now. After all we had been through and all our plans, I couldn't just end everything. He was so sensitive. I could not hurt him.

I made up my mind to go through with it, to stop thinking about things so much and make it work. The same day I made that decision, a close friend approached me and said she had to talk with me. She hesitantly told me things she, herself, had noticed in Matt, things I had convinced myself were okay or "normal". While she talked, I set my feelings aside and tried to see truth, because I truly wanted God's will in my life.

Hearing these concerns from someone I loved and trusted was a reality check for me. It hit me that I didn't really love Matt, and that I didn't actually want to spend the rest of my life with him. I could see that all we had was a result of modern technology and runaway emotions. It wasn't real tried and true love. Through her gentle counsel I came to realize that I didn't want to have to deal with his past problems for the rest of my life, nor did I want my children to start life with a daddy that came with baggage.

It wasn't easy to admit how wrong I had been, but I was relieved to know I was walking in truth. I went straight to my parents and told them everything. They told me I was doing the right thing. So that night I ended the relationship. Matt took it very hard and tried his best to change my mind. But I knew I was doing the right thing, and the freedom I felt was remarkable.

Life was hard the following weeks, but I deserved it. I had fooled myself into thinking you can know someone from chatting on the internet. I learned that is just not true, and I am thankful I escaped my folly. All of the pain I went through could have been so easily avoided if I hadn't continued to play my little mind games and convinced myself of lies. I learned the hard way, but I will always remember one thing: lying to yourself doesn't change the

"A prudent man foreseeth the evil, and hideth himself: but the simple pass on, and are punished" (Proverbs 22:3).

truth. <u>I feel wiser now, so maybe something good came out of my disaster</u>
<u>after all, although I know a part of me will never be the same.</u>

~ *Tara*

Chaste conversation: **"While they behold your chaste conversation**
coupled with fear" (I Peter 3:2).

Holy Fear: **"The fear of the LORD is the beginning of wisdom: and**
the knowledge of the holy is understanding" (Proverbs 9:10).

Tara's story is a disaster that could have been avoided. Thankfully, when
Tara was warned, she listened to counsel and avoided the tragedy that could
have been.

Many girls go from disaster to disaster and think they will someday find
their Prince Charming and live happily ever-after with no complications. It is
a sad fact that disasters leave scars, some uglier than others.

"Regret" is one of the ugliest words in the English language. Regret is the
reason psychiatrists are rich. Some girls, usually the sweet-hearted, trusting
kind, are the sad victims of disasters caused by going over the line into territory where there is no recovery. This is called tragedy.

Tragedies go a step further than disaster. Tragedies are relationships that
wreck the dream of the fine prince coming to find you. The next story is a
tragedy that destroyed two families.

When Disaster Leads to Tragedy

There was this really cool lady who published a homeschool magazine that
I really liked. You would think that a Christian wife and mother of many
children, wouldn't fall prey to tragedy, but she played with a possible disaster
and it took her down. This is how it happened.

> This is a very sweet but ultimately sad story. How terrible it is when we tell ourselves something is
> so when it is not. My younger sister has a similar story but did not go as far as this young lady. The
> mind is a very powerful mechanism and when you suggest lies to it, if not immediately combated
> with the truth, those lies can take hold and cause irreversible damage as actions based on that
> lie play out in your life. Possibly the best thing to be done after an experience like this is to pour
> Scripture into yourself and spend as much time as possible deepening your walk with the Savior.
> Stop lying to yourself. Replace the negative with the positive. Pursue the mind of Christ.

While at a large homeschooling convention where she was one of the leading speakers, she met a fine, spiritually-minded man who was also one of the main speakers. The two really hit it off. He was really cool. I am not being sarcastic; he was handsome, wise, and seemingly godly. Although both speakers thought they were being led of God and were walking in truth, in reality they had both just been caught up in the homeschool movement. As the Scripture says in 2 Timothy 3:5, they had **"...a form of godliness, but denying the power thereof"**.

When the lady went back home, the two leaders had legitimate reasons to text…and they did text. At first it was okay, until the day she had an argument with her "lazy, unspiritual husband". When she reached her lowest point, Mr. Cool knew just what to say to make her feel better. Thus they 'got to know' each other in a more personal way through sharing the pain and disappointments of her marriage. Then, of course, he began sharing some of his frustrations at his wife's lack of interest in homeschooling their children. In time he began sharing his wife's disinterest toward intimacy.

When God wanted one word to describe sexual intimacy he chose *know*. **"And Adam knew Eve his wife, and she conceived..."** (Gen. 4:1) When one opens the door of one's spirit and emotions to another of the opposite sex, the result is "knowing." The man and woman, without any physical contact, were indulging their emotions to their own gratification.

Mrs. Magazine Lady felt his pain. At the next homeschooling conference they went out for coffee. The sweet, spiritual intimacy they had come to share through texting had taken their consciences to places neither of them would have allowed in a social context. At this second meeting the energy between them caught both by surprise. They were amazed at how attracted they were to each other. It felt so good, so fulfilling–love like they had never known. "It must be of God!" they thought. "Surely both of them had made a mistake and married the wrong person. Our love was meant to be." The Bible says in James 1:15, **"Then when lust hath conceived, it bringeth forth sin: and sin, when it is finished, bringeth forth death."**

"Stolen waters are sweet, and bread eaten in secret is pleasant" (Proverbs 9:17).

People often think the forbidden boundary is the act of fornication. Not so. These two crossed the boundary the day they met at the first conference and decided the other person was of such interest that they wanted further contact through texting. Each act of texting was foreplay. When they finally met in person the second time they were already turned on to each other. They left their consciences further in the dirt every time they advanced their emotional intimacy through their digital communication. When they agreed to going together for coffee, it was just the next to last of many steps away from virtue.

They divorced their spouses and the two "hot lovers" married. After a few weeks of bliss, they lived in a state of constant stress and unhappiness. Now, years later, they both know that their wild attraction was just Pie In The Sky.

> *"How weak is thine heart, saith the LORD GOD, seeing thou doest all these things, the work of an imperious whorish woman...as a wife that committeth adultery, which taketh strangers instead of her husband!"* (Ezekiel 16:30, 32).

As a young unmarried girl, do you think you would have to be married in order for your texting "love affair" to be soulish adultery? Think again. In the next story the girl had never even been kissed.

This is not a story I read in a book or got from a letter. I heard this sad tale sitting at my own kitchen table. I watched the tears flow down the faces of those who knew her. Her parents were shocked senseless for days because it never occurred to them that their clean, wholesome, homeschooled girl might have done this thing by her own volition.

Young Bride-to-Be's Pie in the Sky

Jane was 23 years old before Rodger asked for her hand in marriage. It came as a total surprise to her. He was a friend of her brother, but had never really shown her any special attention. Rodger was shy and awkward around her, and she was so nervous around him she couldn't say a word. He was a nice guy, and she would have swooned over him if he had asked for her just three months earlier, but now she wasn't sure.

Jane had been secretly texting and emailing a guy from Florida for several months. Through a mutual friend he had asked to be on her Facebook page.

She had never actually met Mr. Florida, but they had discussed everything while texting. As soon as Rodger left her family's house after asking for her hand in marriage she rushed into her bedroom to email Mr. Florida of Rodger's proposal and then shared with him her nervousness, fears, uncertainties, and doubts. Mr. Florida totally understood. Every evening for weeks Rodger came over to visit her, but she never could open up to him like she could to Mr. Florida. But, the wedding was scheduled anyway for Jane wanted to get married. Mr. Florida never mentioned marriage. She knew her parents would never approve of him anyway, as they had narrow expectations of a suitor.

Two weeks before the wedding, Jane was getting very nervous. She emailed Mr. Florida saying she wished Rodger were like him. She felt like she was marrying a stranger. Mr. Florida said he wished with all his heart they could be together, just to talk this out and make sure she was doing the right thing. In confused desperation she bought a bus ticket and slipped out of the house. Mr. Florida met her at the bus station and took her to a motel, where she fell into his arms weeping. They didn't mean for it to happen…they just felt so connected…like it was meant to be. You do understand, don't you? After a week of sleeping together at the motel, the spiritual, Bible-quoting, deeply sincere Mr. Florida revealed that he was already married and had two kids. He explained that he desperately loved her and that she was so much more than his own pitiful wife, but he had a commitment to his family. She walked into the motel an unkissed virgin; seven days later she walked out pregnant. Jane got back on the bus and went home.

Her relationship with Mr. Florida was just Pie In the Sky. It felt more real than what she felt for Rodger. Why? Because Jane believed she knew Mr. Florida. They experienced intimacy as they texted. They became relaxed and confident with each other, which made physical intimacy hard to resist. Emailing, texting, and phoning was the sin that lead to her ugly tragedy.

She had skated close to sin every time she punched a letter on her keyboard, and God is not mocked. Every time she pushed "send" she sent him a part of her intimate self. She had already given herself away before she closed the door to a cheap motel room with the noise of the interstate in the background. **"Then when lust hath conceived, it bringeth forth sin: and**

sin, when it is finished, bringeth forth death" (James 1:15). Her texting brought death to her lifelong hopes, dreams, and the possibility of becoming a pure bride.

Rodger didn't want a candy bar that had already been licked, so he went elsewhere and found a nice chaste girl who didn't text. I must note, just a few weeks after this event someone found the charming Mr. Florida on Facebook getting to know another nice Christian girl.

Pie in the Sky—the very thought is tantalizing to the imagination, the first bite sweet, the afteraffect as bitter as Hell.

When you get to know someone online it is like getting to know a character in a fiction novel. That character is the product of creative writing. When a young man writes to girls, you can be sure of one thing: he is doing his very best to make a good impression. Have you ever seen one of those nature shows that feature the mating rituals of wild creatures? The male bird fluffs out his feathers, making him look three times as big as he really is. Frogs inflate their chests and make deep croaking sounds. Lizards expand the skin around their necks until they look five times bigger. Young men go online and become spiritual giants, with large hearts and magnificent goals and worthy ambitions, but it's all bird feathers and lizard skins. He describes himself as he would like to be, or as he thinks she would like him to be. He develops an online personality. None of his assertions are tested. His body language and mannerisms are concealed. Like an author writing a novel, he is known through his creative writing. Like the country song goes, "I'm so much cooler online."

So, am I saying texting is inherently evil? No, not at all; it is just a form of communication. Texting in itself is not sin, but then, neither is parking a car. However, if you are alone with a guy when you park, you have already accepted the slippery slope. When you text a guy, you are alone with him, it is just the two of you—soul to soul. Because your body is not there, you feel safe. But intercourse of mind and heart is 90% of the intercourse of marriage.

Are you in a Pie in the Sky relationship with a guy or, maybe, several guys? To get to know a man who is not your husband is emotional adultery. To exchange intimate knowledge with several guys is whorish.

A Warning:

Texting, Facebook and emails are not private. Husbands are checking up on wives. Employers are now paying computer gurus to find "web noise" information on people who are seeking employment. If you sent it, someone can trace it to you. Sin and foolishness will find you out.

In preparing to write this book I asked several young men if they had gone to the web to check up on any of the girls they have considered as potential brides. Many men felt the best way to really know what and who a girl is was to check out her past cyber traffic: What has she written? Who has she been in contact with? The guys had thus eliminated many girls that never even knew they were being considered.

You think, "Shame on a man who would violate my privacy." What privacy? I say, "You typed it; you or one of your friends posted the pictures; you went to that place and associated with that crowd." If you have already soiled your cyber image, now is the time to start over.

Just say never again, and proceed to reform your foolish tracks with righteous and sober-minded remarks. A man seeing the change will appreciate a healthy repentance and a lesson learned.

Great White Throne Judgment

There is a new rash of suicides among very young teenagers. The reason has been tracked to the embarrassing situation kids are finding themselves in due to foolish "sexting" and texting. These young teenagers tingle with excitement as they, in the secret corners of their bedrooms, point a small phone toward their bodies and push the camera button. It seems secret and it doesn't feel that bad.

The Scripture teaches that there will come a day when every thought, deed and attitude will be made known and each person will give an answer. Some of you will give an answer long before The Great White Throne Judgment. Some of you will have friends (at least you thought they were friends) forwarding your messages and your pictures to people who only want to hurt you. It might not be revealed until your wedding day, or at your first child's fifth birthday party, or maybe when your daughter is eleven. But it floats around out there waiting to come forth at the most embarrassing time.

Don't let it happen to you.

God says in James 4:17, **"Therefore to him that knoweth to do good, and doeth it not, to him it is sin."** Then in I John 3:9, **"Whosoever is born of God doth not commit sin; for his seed remaineth in him: and he cannot sin, because he is born of God."**

> Amen! We all need this reminder.

Your Treasure Chest

God commands women to be chaste in their conversation. If you are not chaste as a single girl then you will not be trustworthy as a wife. You are what you do!

♥ Some of you are conceiving sin by participating in activities that will one day bring forth the death of your marriage. Are you NOW involved in an unchaste conversation with a guy, or maybe several guys?

_____

♥ If you knew every single week the preacher would read to the whole church your emails or texting, and show over the large screen every picture you sent or received, would you feel ashamed, embarrassed, or outright horrified?

_____

♥ Are you ready to honor God in this area of your life?

_____

♥ Are you willing to flee the temptation by removing from your chat list any person that you have written or who has written you in an unwise manner?

_____

♥ Are you willing to do whatever it takes to completely free your heart from attachments that dishonor God?

_____

They That Wait Upon The Lord

MORAL TO THE STORY: One of the sweetest things you will ever know will be those intimate things you first learned together.

A CAUTION: A first time is the only first time. Once lost, it is forever gone.

Enough with the sad stories. Now let's consider a girl whose love story is so special she calls herself Cinderella.

Are firsts important to men? What do I mean by first? Your first kiss is a first. Your first true love, the first guy you take home to meet Grandma or maybe your first night in bed with a man. Every first is a moment of awakening. The man who truly loves you will treasure these first moments you gave to him and him alone. Will you save your firsts for him? God told his people to bring the first fruits to him (Exodus 23:16-19). Why? Because they are very, very special. When you save yourself for your man, he will know you are giving him your best.

CHAPTER 12

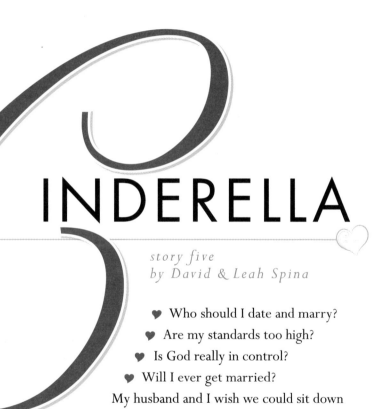

CINDERELLA

story five
by David & Leah Spina

❤ Who should I date and marry?

❤ Are my standards too high?

❤ Is God really in control?

❤ Will I ever get married?

My husband and I wish we could sit down
with each of you over a cup of coffee, look you
straight in the eye and answer these questions with zeal!

Being the Right One

Growing up, I had a beautiful blonde friend that had a
new guy every time I saw her. On one hand, I wished I
had a guy by my side. On the other, I wondered what

the single guys thought when they saw her with so many guys. My mother had me read a book called *Beautiful Girlhood* when I was a girl, and I always remembered one sentence about boyfriends: "Be reserved and careful, and though you do not seem to be so popular as the forward, giddy girl who is always 'cutting up' with the boys, you will have the respect of the best boys and young men, and she will not."

From that moment on, I started to realize that I was building my reputation as someone's future wife. Someday my husband would either be honored or dishonored by my conduct as a single woman. **"She will do him good and not evil all the days of her life"** (Proverbs 31:12). Did you realize that during your single years you are building your reputation as a wife? It was always hard for me to picture a flirty guy as a faithful husband. Remember that "dating around" for fun affects the way people view you–they will associate you with those you date. Even if you have no serious intentions, you are giving signals about who you are.

When I was single, I heard a teaching by Tommy Nelson on how to find a godly spouse. He asked how we expect to find a wonderful Christian spouse when all we do is go to church, go to work, and go to an occasional happy hour. He said run fast and hard after Jesus and look to the left or the right and marry the person who is at your side. That made sense to me. **"In all thy ways acknowledge him, and he shall direct thy paths"** (Proverbs 3:6). Most girls tote a fat list of credentials and want to marry a sold-out godly man, but few of us have taken the log out of our own eye. What kind of girl would he marry? I spent my time before meeting David finishing my degree, going on mission trips, Bible studies, and working with pregnant teenage girls. Remember, you will never regret any time you spent on your relationship with the Lord and ministry for the Lord. You are building faith and character to take into your marriage to bless your husband and future children. And your husband will be thankful if you don't bring debt into your marriage, so work as unto the Lord!

David flew to Papua New Guinea for a two-month mission trip with orphans when he was thirteen years old. He felt directed to start building businesses to support and serve orphans worldwide. He graduated with a finance degree, started his business and also volunteered with the youth at his church. As far as dating, David didn't look to the left or right. "If she wasn't marriage material, why date her?" He was already honoring his future wife while many of his friends were dating around all through high school, college and afterwards.

After 27 years of waiting, David was the first guy I took to church, the first guy I took to a wedding and the first guy I brought home to Thanksgiving dinner. Each "first" was like a special present I had saved for him. Once you realize a man is going to be your husband, you will wish you had not given any guy in your past any attention at all.

When I met David's friends, they all said the same thing: "Leah, you have the greatest guy in the whole world! David has waited for you a long time—we tried to set him up, but he wouldn't even give other girls the time of day. You must be one special girl!" How awesome that David honored me all those years! I felt like a celebrity.

"Draw nigh to God, and he will draw nigh to you" (James 4:8). Your single years are a unique opportunity for you to grow in your relationship with the Lord, preparing you to enter marriage with a solid faith, so you won't have to totally depend on your spouse for your faith. Some of my sweetest times with the Lord were during my single years. Once you marry, you will never again have that complete, utter dependence on the Lord. We all have friends that "cannot" be single—they must always have someone. But I would encourage you to relish these times with just you and the Lord. **"For since the beginning of the world men have not heard, nor perceived by the ear, neither hath the eye seen, O God, beside thee, what he hath prepared for him that waiteth for him"** (Isaiah 64:4). When it is time to enter a relationship, you will know Him and be able to discern if this is His will!

Waiting for the Right One

"They that wait upon the Lord shall renew their strength; they shall mount up with wings as eagles; they shall run and not be weary; and they shall walk, and not faint" (Isaiah 40:31).

I, Leah, grew up in Texas, the oldest of five home-educated children. I loved to play golf, tennis and chess. I graduated from the Culinary School of

Fort Worth and Thomas Edison State College with a Bachelor's in Business Administration. I worked as a reporter for a national political magazine and then at an adoption agency with young mothers-to-be in the residential program. I told my parents I was looking for three things in a future husband: a man of God, a man of character, and a man that commanded respect. If he sought the Lord, I could trust him when our views differed because I knew he was praying. If he had character, I'd never wonder where he was at night or what he was doing on the computer. If I respected him, honor and submission would be easier.

David was born in San Diego and moved to Texas when he was 13 years old, the second-oldest of four children. He played baseball and graduated from Oral Roberts University with a degree in finance. David was looking "for a woman with godly character that had a heart for the Lord with a strong foundation in the Word."

From David:

A lot of the girls I met had no substance or character. I would ask them questions about the Bible and marriage roles, but their answers were light and shallow. Although many loved the Lord, they didn't know the Bible well and had little moral fiber. It seemed they had no strong, secure relationship in the Lord. I wanted a girl that was so steadfastly grounded in the Lord that she would continue to seek Him even if the relationship didn't work out. I wanted a girl that had built character through turning to the Lord through trials. I also watched to see if she respected her father.

The waiting period can be difficult if you do not put your trust in the Lord. It may be short, it may be long. But once you meet the one God has for you, all of that waiting will not matter at all! Stay patient. Seek the Lord with all your heart, soul and mind. How can we believe that God can create the universe and send His Son to save us, yet we question whether He can bring the right person on His timing, not ours? My advice is to love the Lord your God with all your heart, soul and mind—to seek Him in everything. No matter what trials come, if you are seeking the Lord, He will direct your steps and lead you. Don't have a fairytale mentality of sitting at home, waiting for your prince. Anytime God did something in the Bible, it required action. If you want to marry a godly guy, get involved in ministry and places where there are godly men. Be active in church. Also, you must not try to compare your past, failed relationships to what God may have for you in the future. Even if you've experienced unsuccessful relationships, you shouldn't become cynical about future relationships. When you find the right one, there will be a peace.

Cinderella picks up here:

We both had well-meaning friends that tried to set us up. But for both of us, it usually took only one date for us to determine if this was marriage material or not. One thought always helped me weed out potential spouses: Is this the kind of guy I want to bring home to Thanksgiving dinner to meet all my family? Is this the kind of guy that I want to be seen and known with?

David and I met at his work. He was giving a presentation and I was sitting on the front row. After the meeting, we talked briefly but we both thought the same thing, "What are the chances they know the Lord?" I later called David with a work question and suddenly he was talking about God. I remember hanging up the phone and thinking, "I totally misjudged this guy!"

We talked for a good three months over the phone. No flirting, just theology, ideals and life. I grew frustrated and complained to my parents, "He never says he likes me. What kind of girl does he think I am? I don't continue a relationship with a guy if it is not going anywhere." My praying mama soothed, "Honey, he is studying you right now to make an informed decision."

David says, "Although Leah was beautiful and attractive, the biggest draw for me was finding out that we shared a common passion for the Lord and that we both had a strong, personal relationship with Him. She knew all the Vacation Bible School songs I grew up with—and the Bible stories. She was grounded in the Word and most importantly, you could tell she had built

No matter the circumstances, you can ALWAYS turn to God and seek Him in prayer. Maybe you're hopeless or confused, guilty or upset, you can ALWAYS turn to God. He is sufficient. No matter the mess you may find yourself in, He is sufficient. His wisdom is greater than any of our foolishness, His mercy greater than our shame, and His forgiveness greater than our iniquity. Trust in His sufficiency and though you may not see a way, know He can make one.

character and faith from years of walking with God as a single woman. She had truly established a strong relationship with God."

Seek the Lord while making the biggest decision of your life

During that time, another young man approached my dad about courting me. He was forward and flirty. Dad unveiled his hesitations and reservations, but said the ultimate choice was mine. I am so thankful I was seeking the Lord during this season and knew His voice from years of Bible study and prayer. As soon as Dad told me it was my decision, I felt a huge check in my spirit. This wasn't my husband. I told the young man "no" and the next week David asked me out on our first date – dinner and a comedy show. David still wasn't flirty, and the next morning I wondered if I had done the right thing. But in my prayer journal I wrote in all capital letters: LEAH, THE MOST IMPORTANT THING TO YOU IS A MAN AFTER GOD'S HEART AND THAT IS WHAT YOU HAVE ALWAYS ADMIRED IN DAVID.

My relationship guideline was a few dates, then the suitor meets with Dad. After two more dates, David didn't have to be asked – he called Dad up and they met at Starbucks. Dad was prepared with questions he had gathered for years. Dad even called some of David's references. The outcome: "Leah, you should be very honored that a man like David wants to pursue a relationship with you."

After Dad blessed our relationship, David blossomed into the romantic every girl loves. While we dated, I tried to think ten years down our marriage—if I felt like leaving, what would keep me in? The thought kept coming back that God called David and me into this marriage. I leaned on this reflection heavily as it was confirmed through parents, friends and prayer. It was hard to hear my parents analyze David, but I stood fast in the thought that if it was God's will, it would work itself out. David and I both told each other that God was more important than the other, and that if God called us in or out of this relationship, blessed be the Lord. It was such a peace—we were merely discovering God's will.

I remember the day David told me "I love you" for the first time. We took a walk with his dog and on the top of a beautiful hill he said, "I love you, Leah." He then shocked me by saying, "And I've only said that to two other girls." Immediately I started thinking, who else? Man, way to ruin the moment. David finished, "My mom and my sister." Do you have any idea how much that meant to me? I went home and implored my brothers to do the same for their future wives.

After a year of courtship, David proposed to me in front of 1,100 people at a work convention. We had never gone ring shopping and Dad had cautioned me, "Let David lead; don't push." I had no idea what was happening. Suddenly David was pushing me to center stage and getting on one knee. The crowd went wild and stood to their feet. David looked up, "Leah Grace Driggers, you are a godly woman of character. I love you with everything I have within me. I would be honored if you would be my wife. Will you marry me?" I couldn't say anything. I just sobbed and nodded yes. It was worth the wait.

After a seven month engagement and intense pre-marital counseling, we married a year ago. Marriage is the greatest gift the Lord has given me. No one told me how awesome marriage is—waking up next to my love every morning, watching him take a second helping of my cooking and just realizing I get to spend the rest my life with my best friend. That is my Cinderella story that I waited for, shaped in heaven. Girls, don't give up and don't settle for less.

Become the girl of a godly man's dreams. And don't mess around with any guys that aren't your godly prince. I can't wait to hear your story!

Post-marriage thoughts

No Regrets

Do you know how nice it is when we look through family photo albums at Christmas to never see David with another girl? Do you know how wonderful it is that David doesn't have to hear about my past boyfriends? Do you know how many times I have thanked the Lord while falling asleep that He helped me wait for a guy like my David? When you are single, sometimes it is hard to picture yourself married. But if you can, try. Try to think about the way you will feel when your spouse is proposing, looking in your eyes, and understand it's not worth messing around with other guys. Try to think of how happy you will be on your wedding night, when you are giving the ultimate gift with no hint of regret. Try to remember that you are building habits of faithfulness or distrust that will affect your marriage. What will you tell your children someday? What you are doing now will affect your future!

Learning to be a help meet before and after marriage

I never appreciated my mother's example of a biblical help meet until I got married. Shortly after getting married, I remember meeting with about ten other young wives. We were discussing respecting our husbands. The question was, "Is this something you were taught growing up?" Every single woman said it was the first time they had heard these concepts. Most said they were brought up the opposite. "I was taught I was a princess and to be independent. I didn't need a man." They agreed with the truth and the principles, but they struggled to tear away from years of wrong training and examples.

It was then that I started to realize the power of my mother's example. Of all the areas of conflict in our marriage, unconditional submission, respect and honor was never in question. Of course, the first year of marriage, I was learning by trial or error what came across as respectful. But I never struggled with should I respect him, should I honor him, should I submit to him? I knew the answer from my mother's example and years of my parents training me in the way I should go with a husband. Now that we are expecting a baby, I am so excited about modeling these same truths and principles because it not only affects your child's marriage, but so many other marriages by example! Marriage is an exponential ministry; what your example teaches now will multiply across the generations.

When I started dating David, I asked my mother to give me her top three books on being a good wife. One of them was Debi Pearl's *Created To Be His Help Meet*. I read all three, but I read Created four times during our courtship and engagement. I then read one chapter a day through the first several months of our marriage. The concepts changed my life so dramatically that a friend and I are planning to start a group of young wives to go through the book.

Find a marriage mentor

David and I purposed to never seek marital advice from our parents or friends after marriage. We wanted to honor and respect one another publicly. We do, however, believe in mentoring and accountability. I started meeting for marriage mentoring with an older, godly woman once a month after we got married. **"The aged women likewise…That they may teach the young women to be sober, to love their husbands, to love their children, To be discreet, chaste, keepers at home, good, obedient to their own husbands, that the word of God be not blasphemed"** (Titus 2:2-5). I had never met her before, but a friend I trust recommended her to me. Every month, I keep a list detailing areas where David and I had conflict or just general marriage questions. Usually the first Thursday of each month I drive to her house. We pray and then I ask her the questions on my list. Each session lasts two to three hours. We always end in prayer. She is the only one I open up to about conflict in our marriage. I cannot tell you how much it has helped me to have an older, godly woman telling me, "Good job—that was hard, but you did the right thing," or "That is very normal—welcome to the club," or "I understand how you're feeling; however…." I praise God for the priceless hours of biblical counsel.

If we invest time and energy in other areas of life, shouldn't we be devoting time to our coming marriage?

~*David and Leah*

Key phrases from Cinderella

💜 "I realized that I was building my reputation as someone's future wife. Someday my husband would either be honored or dishonored by my conduct as a single woman. **'She will do him good and not evil all the days of her life'** (Proverbs 31:12)."

Did you realize that during your single years you are building your reputation as a wife? What have you learned that will change the way you conduct yourself?

_____

_____

_____

💜 "Most girls tote a fat list of credentials and want to marry a sold-out godly man, but few of us have taken the log out of our own eye."

Think about and write a list of what kind of girl the man of your dreams would want to marry?

_____

_____

_____

💜 "You are building faith and character to take into your marriage to bless your husband and future children."

Make a list of some character traits that you can be strengthening now.

_____

_____

_____

💜 "Each 'first' was like a special present I had saved for him. Once you realize a man is going to be your husband, you wish you had not given any guy in your past any attention at all."

Make a list of firsts you will present to your Prince.

_____

_____

_____

♥ "My advice is to love the Lord your God with all your heart, soul and mind, to seek Him in everything. No matter what trials come, if you are seeking the Lord He will direct your steps and lead you. Don't have a fairytale mentality of sitting at home, waiting for your prince. Anytime God did something in the Bible, it required action."

We have discussed getting involved in activities of serving in previous chapters. After reading this story, do you have further ideas of what you could be involved in to put you into real action?

_____

_____

_____

_____

♥ "One thought always helped me weed out potential spouses: Is this the kind of guy I want to bring home to Thanksgiving dinner to meet all my family? Is this the kind of guy that I want to be seen and known with?"

List things you see in men that you know you would not want to introduce to Grandma (for instance: purple-haired, smoker, etc.).

_____

_____

_____

_____

❤ "I grew frustrated and complained to my parents, 'He never says he likes me. What kind of girl does he think I am? I don't continue a relationship with a guy if it is not going anywhere.' My praying mama soothed, 'Honey, he is studying you right now to make an informed decision.'"

Mom might have saved her from being Antsy or even a Grabber! Think of a time when you wanted to grab. Record it in your notebook.

_____

_____

_____

_____

❤ "I tried to think ten years down our marriage—if I felt like leaving, what would keep me in? The thought kept coming back that God called David and me into this marriage. I leaned on this reflection heavily as it was confirmed through parents, friends and prayer."

Notice her list of how she felt confirmed. What would your list be?

_____

_____

_____

_____

❤ "Girls, don't give up and don't settle for less. Become the girl of a godly man's dreams. And don't mess around with any guys that aren't your godly prince."

What you are doing now will affect your future!

_____

_____

_____

_____

♥ "We purposed to never seek marital advice from our parents or friends after marriage. We wanted to honor and respect one another publicaly. We do, however, believe in mentoring and accountability. I started meeting for marriage mentoring with an older, godly woman once a month after we got married. **'The aged women likewise… That they may teach the young women to be sober, to love their husbands, to love their children, To be discreet, chaste, keepers at home, good, obedient to their own husbands, that the word of God be not blasphemed'** (Titus 2:2-5)."

Think of someone you might be able to seek out for counsel. Pick a quiet, unassuming lady whom others might pass by. Remember that when you seek counsel you will actually be helping the older woman stay focused on God's will in her marriage, too. Start praying for God's blessing and wisdom for that lady. She will need plenty of God's understanding to be a good counselor.

Learning Moderation

MORAL TO THE STORY: Your wedding day is the first day of *ever after*. Start it with joy.

A CAUTION: The more details you try to control, the more stressed you will get. Don't let your nervous tension be what you and everyone else remembers about your wedding day.

CHAPTER 13

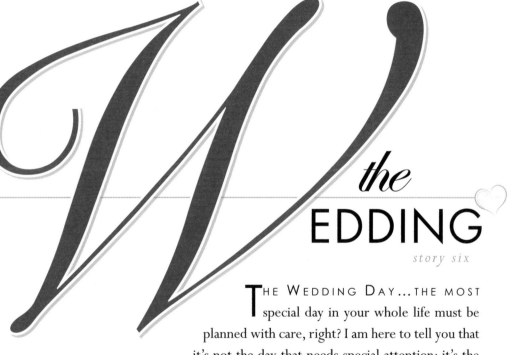

the
EDDING

story six

THE WEDDING DAY...THE MOST
special day in your whole life must be
planned with care, right? I am here to tell you that
it's not the day that needs special attention; it's the
night following. Most girls and their mothers get
so caught up in the Big Day that they overextend
themselves physically and emotionally. In this chapter I want to encourage you not to plan an elaborate
wedding.

Today's weddings often foreshadow the coming marriage: stressful. All the extra details are added to impress all in attendance and those who hear about it with the magnificence of this glorious event. Many girls look back on the days before their wedding and wish they had spent less time and money on useless pomp and staging and more time getting rested and refreshed for the days that followed the wedding. When a girl drives away from her wedding and feels like sleeping three days just to recover, it sort of defeats the purpose, doesn't it? Believe it or not, it takes a lot of emotional and physical energy to be a wife during the first week of marriage. Your firsts are going to need all your strength and focus. If you falter there, it can attach a negative association to the experience. Not a good thing. Think about it: if you were going on a ski trip, would you exhaust yourself beforehand?

Of course, what no one takes into consideration is that extreme stress throws a girl's hormones into chaos, so many wedding nights start out with the bride on her period—two weeks early. You do not want this to happen to you. Yet almost everybody makes the same mistakes. It is time to step away from tradition and be wise in your wedding planning. Work from the premise that the week before the wedding is all about being your very best relaxed and energized self on your honeymoon. Here is what one wise young woman did for her non-stress, joyful wedding.

When I attend Yetta's wedding, I was struck with its personal style and sheer simplicity. It was clear that everyone, including the bride and groom, was relaxed and having a good time. The people attending will look back to this wedding and think, "Wasn't it wonderful? They looked so happy."

What a testimony! So Yetta's wedding was chosen to gain notoriety in the pages of this book.

Debi's words to the bride about her observations of the wedding:

"Your wedding was so joyful. I saw several people crying and laughing with absolute delight."

"Even though it was a simple wedding, it had a touch of pure grace."

"Your dress was wonderful, so becoming. It was so regal, yet very modest."

"Often brides dress in such sexy looking gowns no one would think she looks virginal. It is in such poor taste to dress scanty on the most special day of your life. I say, save the sexy for later in the evening, when it will be appreciated! Anyway, it was refreshing to see your choice was one of a born-again believer with fine style."

"Another thing I liked was that the entire focus was on the bride and groom rather than on elaborate flowers, lots of extra people, and fancy details. I thought not having a maid of honor or bridesmaids was an excellent idea. Just the bride and the groom up front seemed to make the whole affair simply elegant. Plus, I didn't hear the usual conversation at the reception about the quality of the girl's dresses or the nonsense chit-chat of who was the best-looking bridesmaid."

Interviewing the bride:
"As I sat there, I felt your wedding really gave glory to God, more than any wedding I have attended in a long time. I tried to put into perspective why… what was different? Then I thought, maybe it wasn't the wedding day as much as it was the year that led up to that special day. That is when I decided to feature it in this book. You have only been married two weeks, so I expect to get some really fresh answers. Are you ready?"

Q. **I have to start with this question first because it is so unusual: How old are you?**
A. I am 34 years old.

Q. **That is pretty old to be just getting married. Do you want to explain to us why?**
A. I had other men interested in me from time to time, but I never was interested because I knew I needed to respect and honor my man. Until Kent, I never met a man I truly wanted.

Q. **So how did you meet your man?**
A. When he moved into our community, he started coming to our church. He joined the church music group and I was a part of that small group.

Q. **Did you immediately set your sights on the new man in town?**

A. No, I liked him, but never gave him a thought as a possible husband because he is seven years younger than I am, and I always said I would never marry a man younger than myself.

Q. **So, what changed your mind? How did you become a couple?**
A. First we became good friends. For months, after music practice, he would walk me out to my truck and we would talk. I saw that he was really growing in the Lord. I learned to respect him. I thought, he is such a cool guy, but he is too young.

Q. **He seems a little shy to me. He is a true priest-like Steady Man. How did he first try to get your attention?**
A. He picked (teased) on me, that's how! In our community, usually once a month, someone in our area will plan an evening (for adult singles) of playing board games. They always invite people from other churches and groups to come. It is a way to step out of our little world and invite others in. We play games like, What Would it be like if _____ were President? Kent would always stick my name in. Like, "Would Yetta rather be president or in prison?" I kept saying, "Why do you always put my name in these crazy things?"

Q. **That was pretty bold, yet you still didn't notice he was singling you out?**
A. My family (I have several sisters) started telling me they thought he was showing me a lot of attention, but I still wasn't so sure.

Q. **When did you start to feel he might be trying to get your womanly attention?**
A. Well, I was involved in a car accident. It wasn't a terrible crash; I just had a busted lip and was sore all over, but he came over as soon as he heard. I could see he was truly concerned. It was then that I began to suspect that he cared for me more than just as a friend. But still I wondered, because I was friends with his sister for a long time before I met him, and I had told her plenty of times that I would never marry a man younger than myself. I knew she must have told him.

Q. **Why were you so sure you would not consider a younger man?**

A. A couple years before I met Kent, I had this other fellow ask if he could get to know me. He was 30 and I was 32. After only a few months of correspondence and two dates I knew he was too young for me, so I cut off the relationship. He seemed to lack maturity, which I figured was due to him being two years younger. It was a good experience for me, because when I got to know Kent, I saw that he was mature, wise, and sober-minded. I was able to reflect back and see that age didn't have anything to do with that level of maturity. Sometimes the only way you can know what you want is to find out what you don't want.

Q. **Do you remember the first time you felt that you and Kent might become a couple?**

A. Over time I saw he was really very genuine. Like I said, after music practice he would often stand at my truck and talk. As my respect grew, I knew I was seeing him as the man he was…the kind of man I wanted. He was slowly winning my affections.

Q. **Everyone knew you and Kent were friends. What rocked the boat into the love boat?**

A. Well, one night his sister invited me to eat dinner with her family, and Kent was there. After dinner he walked me to my truck. While we stood talking at my truck he told me straight out that he wanted to be more than friends. We were both adults; there was never a boy-likes-girl crush thing. We both knew that when he said "more than friends" he meant we were considering our future together. He had already won my respect and admiration. I gladly said yes.

Q. **After that you were a couple, people knew. How did everyone react?**

A. Everyone was really happy for us.

Q. **Would a negative reaction from family or close friends have made a difference?**

A. Yes. If someone we loved and respected had questioned either one of us, we would have listened and considered. We both have seen many couples make bad decisions and live to regret it. We wanted to do it right.

Q. **So you went places together and were known as a couple for several months. Why wait so long?**

A. We both were cautious, knowing this was the rest of our lives, and we wanted to talk out everything before we married. All our convictions, all our family ideas, all our little whatevers were addressed. There would be no surprises to mar our marriage. It takes time. We didn't beat around the bush about anything. He knew exactly what I thought about every major issue, and I knew what he wanted. We agreed on issues ahead of time.

I'm not sure what "wait so long" means here. Several months isn't very long by most people's standards. This seems to be implying that couples should get married really fast. I'm not a proponent of long, drawn-out relationships, but not everyone is going to feel comfortable being proposed to after dating for only a few months.

Q. **So when did he pop the question?**

A. It wasn't like that for us. Love came softly, so we both knew it was right. We just set the date.

Q. **How did you decide on the date?**

A. We wanted to spend our honeymoon in Colorado when the aspen leaves were changing colors, so we set our wedding for that time. Besides, I wanted my special day to go smoothly, so I had a lot of planning to do.

Q. **I have to say, over the years I have been to scads of weddings, but your wedding dress and veil had a simplicity and style that looked modest and virginal and still made you look so good. I thought your veil was beyond beautiful. Where did you find such a beautiful dress and veil?**

A. Thank you so much. I did love the dress and veil as soon as I put it on. It was mail order. Can you believe it! I just got on the computer and did a search by typing in Modest Wedding Gowns. This site came up with hundreds of choices.

Q. How about the veil?

A. Actually, I didn't pick it out. The lady where I bought the dress picked out the veil and added the shimmery effect to match the dress. When it came in the mail, I just loved it.

Q. Your flowers were great, too. I liked the fall colors. They must have cost a lot?

A. I have a story about the flowers. When Kent and I first began to see each other we both started saving money for our wedding and our honeymoon. Together we decided how much we would spend for each part of the wedding. We had decided to do very basic flowers; then God blessed us with the unexpected. For several years I had been going to the nursing home to pick up and do the laundry for an old lady who had had a stroke. When I knew I was going to be married, I called the old lady's son to tell him my sister would be doing the laundry from now on. The man said to me, "Yetta, I am a florist. I have my own shop, and I would like to do the flowers for your wedding as a gift for what you have done for my mother." All those beautiful flowers were a gift. He arranged everything. The color and style were his choice. After all, that's what he does professionally, so I figured he would know best.

Since I am telling my story, I would like to tell all girls reading this: if I were young and just getting started in a job, I would start right away setting back ten percent of all I made for my future marriage. I am glad I was able to save for a few months, but just think if I had saved for years! I really think young women need to know that it is not someone's job to supply all their needs and pay for everything for their wedding. If they come into the marriage like that, and if they expect to be provided for as a daughter, they will come into the marriage with that mentality. They will have little to give, and will be just a taker. Anyway, that's my opinion.

Q. Your reception food was fresh, beautiful, light and healthy. The colorful flowers and fresh fruit really set a beautiful mood. I liked that there were no heavy, hot foods that would have been prepared that morning. Who planned and prepared the food for you?

A. Having several sisters is a big blessing. They were such a help. The fresh fruits made a lovely and easy set up. The cheese treats can be made days ahead of time, and the many cakes came from several different friends. I didn't even have to think about the food.

Q. So now you have the flowers and food…how about the wedding pictures?

A. Well, that was settled right here at work. My two friends and co-workers, Elizabeth and Pat, are also aspiring wedding photographers. I asked them if they would do the pictures for me. Liz gave me a great price, and they did a wonderful job. They are such great pictures! Liz is making the wedding book now. (ElizabethStewartPhotography.blogspot.com)

Q. After being married for two whole weeks what do you want to tell the girls who are reading this?

A. Oh, I used to think everyone would just know who they were going to marry as soon as they got to know the man. I guess some do, but now I know some don't. For me, Kent's tender, constant love for me caused me to want to be his bride.

Q. Are you sad you had to wait so long before the magic day?

A. It's funny because I was happy being single. Even as the years passed and everyone around me married, I still felt my life was blessed and full. I stayed busy. I made myself useful to a lot of people. I didn't stay at home moping. Sure, I had days I was a little sad thinking I might not ever find My One True Love and have children. I think those down times are from the devil. I am so glad I spent my life working, reaching out to others every single day and loving life. I'll pour that same fullness into my man.

Q. Now for the moment of truth. What has been the one practical thing that has been difficult on you as a new wife?

A. I wouldn't say it has been difficult on me, but it has been somewhat of a challenge having a meal on the table three times a day, or at least breakfast, then packing him a lunch and then a good meal in the evening. A man likes his food, and I surely want to please my man. It is easy to forget to plan a meal which includes laying out the basic foods (like meat to thaw) and then walk in the house at the last minute and wonder what to cook. I have to make myself buy and plan ahead.

Q. You have an audience of thousands of unmarried young women wanting to be Mrs. Someone Special. How would you suggest they find that Mr. Someone Wonderful?

A. I didn't stay home waiting. I would tell them to fill every moment with giving of yourself. I was involved with a traveling music group, worked at several different places each week, went on outings with other groups, and did lots of other ministry projects. In the end, it was in our small country church and tiny community that I found the love of my life. He diligently pursued me. It was so precious having a man that wanted me enough to try hard to get my attention and respect. I needed to know he really wanted me, that I wasn't just chasing him down and winning him. I have a real man. He was worth waiting for.

Lessons Learned

In the next few pages there is space for you to make some plans. Make a record of how you want to start being more actively aggressive in preparing for married life. What are you going to do that will better prepare you to be a good help meet?

Your Treasure Chest

"Through wisdom is an house builded; and by understanding it is established: and by knowledge shall the chambers be filled with all precious and pleasant riches" (Proverbs 24:3 & 4).

💜 What training should you get? Think about what Ellie did to prepare for her Italian Prince. She went to school to learn floral arranging, taught Sunday School, opened her own business, traveled, did mission trips, and organized weekly Christian socials.

💜 Many girls could be helping full-time in a ministry doing photography or even using their cooking skills.

💜 What are you doing to serve?

_____

_____

_____

_____

💜 What training are you now engaged in? And don't tell me you are helping your mom around the house! You should have mastered that by the time you were ten years old.

_____

_____

_____

_____

_____

_____

_____

♥ Make some heavy-duty plans. Notice that the virtuous woman is physically fit. Add serious exercise to your weekly plan. *"She girdeth her loins with strength, and strengtheneth her arms"* (Proverbs 31:17). Make yourself accountable to a friend so she can help you stick with your plan. To whom will you be accountable?

♥ What are your Weekly goals?

♥ What are your Monthly goals?

♥ What are your Yearly goals?

♥ What are your Lifetime goals?

Examine Yourself

MORAL TO THE STORY: Do you really know Jesus?
A CAUTION: Don't take your eternal fate for granted.

"Wherefore the rather, brethren, give diligence to make your calling and election sure: for if ye do these things, ye shall never fall" (II Peter 1:10).

The next story is special to me. Sheila tells the story of meeting her future husband Shad at a club where he was a leading rock star musician. I remember sitting in a pizza parlor when Shad's #1 pop song came over the speakers. The heavy beat and sad words filled the air, "Come back when you grow up girl. You're still living in a paper doll world. Living ain't easy and loving's twice as tough so come back baby, when you grow up."
I recall smiling as I listened because I knew the man who had written and sung that song was now a child of the living God.
Living and loving is easy with a new heart full of God.

CHAPTER 14

ALL THINGS *new* & *beautiful*

story seven

MY NAME IS SHEILA and this is my love story. When I was young, I read every fairytale I could get my hands on. I dreamed of being a beautiful princess and having a handsome prince come and take me away on his white horse to a beautiful castle, where we would live happily ever after. The Bible says Satan is the god of this world, and in his world there are no loving princes. When I was in junior high school, I discovered that most boys were anything but chivalrous princes. It seemed I was inevitably attracted to the very guys who treated me with little regard and even less respect. I was always hurt and disappointed, because it seemed the more I loved someone, the less he loved me. But deep in my heart, I still held onto the dream of finding someone who would love me uncondi- tionally—someone who would love me for who I was, not what I could do for them.

When I was 18, my mother, my sister and I moved to Memphis so we could be closer to family and so I could attend college there. One night I was attending a frat party and there was a band playing. A friend of mine introduced me to the lead singer, and there was an instant attraction. We began dating and fell in love immediately. This guy was so cool, and he was crazy about me. Finally I felt like a loved princess. After only five months, we decided that we wanted to get married. To say that my mother was against this was the understatement of all time. My mother was a Christian, and she was appalled that her daughter was dating a rock-and-roll musician, much less that she was talking about marrying one. Shad and I did the only rational, reasonable thing to do—we ran away and got married. My white horse turned out to be a green Mustang and my castle turned out to be his mom and dad's house. As if that wasn't bad enough, I soon realized that my prince was a bit of a tyrant, but by then it was obvious that I was a shrew.

Shad was a typical artist with the stormy temperament that can come with that type of personality. There were very few breakable items that lasted for very long around our home. I knew he would never hurt me, but all my little knick-knacks were not that lucky! Even with all the chaos around our home, I never doubted for one instant that my husband loved me. However, all that love didn't change the fact that both of us were full of selfishness, and neither of us had any idea of what God intended in marriage. <u>Our idea of a perfect marriage was changing the other person into our idea of the perfect mate.</u>

That right there is the #1 marriage-wrecking mistake of all time, even for Christians. You marry someone first, then try to turn them into what you want your spouse to be.

You can imagine how well that was working out! Neither of us was being a perfect mate, and neither of us was able to change the other into what we wanted.

One day a preacher came to our house to visit. We fully expected the man to tell us how bad we were and how awful our lifestyle was, but he didn't. He simply talked about how Jesus loved us and died for us, and then he quietly prayed for us. He seemed to really care. Shad said that he didn't know if he liked the guy or believed everything he said, but he sure was impressed by the guy's humility. The preacher came two more times to share the love of Christ. A few nights after the preacher's third visit, Shad got involved in a nasty fight after his band played at a club. The next day he was still consumed with bitter anger toward the guys he had fought. In an effort to cool his emotions, he took his guitar and went out to sit in a swing in the backyard. As he sat there, he began to think about what the preacher had said. Shad began to sing/pray to God in the only way he knew. He told God he was tired of living with anger and he wanted to be different. He told God that if He could make him a different person and change his life, then that's what he wanted.

God is ever ready to forgive and reach out to us right where we are. He looked down and saw a man who hated where sin was taking him and just wanted to know the forgiving, loving Savior. Shad picked his guitar and sang to God, saying, "When I get up out of this swing, I want you to get up with me." The amazing God heard his song/prayer and got up with Shad. It was a couple of days before Shad told me what had happened, and even though I didn't say so, I was really concerned about what this would mean.

We began to go to church, and this rock-and-roll guy that I had married suddenly began to talk about becoming a preacher. I cannot begin to tell you how disappointed I was. I did not marry a preacher; I married an up-and-coming rock star! It seemed like my whole world was coming unraveled all because some kind-hearted preacher came to visit us. I tried to put on a good front and act like a nice little Christian girl, but it was really taxing the limits of my abilities. I had gone to church since I was a little girl, but I really didn't know what it meant to have a personal relationship with Christ. However, as I watched the change in Shad's life, I began to see that there was more involved in this Christianity thing than just going to church and being "good." Truth was hard to resist. Finally, God broke through the façade of my life and showed me I had no hope apart from really knowing Him. That day I asked Jesus to forgive me of my sin and come and be the Lord of my life. From that point on, my life changed dramatically – in every way.

God really did have a purpose for Shad's life; He called him to be an evangelist. And I began to realize that if God called Shad, He called me, too. A man trying to do anything with a wife who doesn't support and believe in him is hard enough, but being in the ministry is even harder. I never considered myself to be a strong person, but as I began to try to become what my husband needed in a wife, God was there, ready to draw out of me things that I didn't know I was capable of. When my husband saw my heart was to do God's will and honor him, he eagerly poured his life back into me. He drew me into the ministry with him more and more. Before long we were singing together and ministering to young people all over the southern United States. After we had our children, we would take them with us and share the gospel anywhere God opened a door. But there was another, larger ministry God had for us on the horizon.

In 1975 Shad and I went on a mission trip with our church to East Africa. While we were there, God spoke into our hearts in no uncertain terms that He wanted us to go into international evangelism. We didn't know anyone overseas, and we would have to trust God to provide for the finances necessary to do this type of ministry. We also knew, from the beginning, that this would involve being separated for three and four weeks at a time. My responsibility would be to hold down the fort at home and take care of the house and family so that Shad could travel overseas and do what God had called him to do. No one wants to be left at home doing chores while wonderful and exciting things are happening overseas. It was hard, but I knew God needed me to do my part even if my part was not so exciting. I saw it as ministry, so I was able to take care of family life, train children, manage our finances, make minor repairs around the house, paint, wallpaper, sew, mow the grass, and deal with ministry business while I was home without my husband. And when he returned home I knew he would be tired from the long trip, several weeks of uncomfortable surroundings, and strange food. I would dress extra nice when I picked him up at the airport. We didn't have much money, but I would manage somehow to have his favorite meals and a special dessert when he got home. I would have nice fluffy towels in the bathroom and fresh linens on the bed so that he could be especially comfortable. This might sound sweet, but it was really a miracle. If you could have seen our early married life, you would realize what a miracle it really was. But something had changed after we were saved, really changed. We had become new creatures. Our whole attitude toward life was different. We began to try to become what the other person wanted instead of trying to change each other into the "ideal" mate. It is God who makes true Princesses. They are not born; they are born again!

I wish I could tell you it all came naturally and easily, but that would be a lie. It was anything but natural; it was supernatural. It was anything but easy; it was hard work. As we yielded ourselves more and more to the leadership of the Holy Spirit, God made us more and more what we needed to be for each other. The more I gave of myself to my husband, the more he gave of himself to me. Ephesians 5 says that the wife is to "reverence her husband" (v. 33) and to submit to him **"as unto the Lord"** (v. 22). This will, in turn, cause the husband to **"love his wife even as himself"** (v. 33) and to love her **"as Christ also loved the church, and gave himself for it"** (v. 25). God enabled us to choose to put the other person first and, as a result, find ourselves as equal partners in a wonderful life.

Now that our children are grown and married, I travel with my husband everywhere he goes. In fact, we spend all day, every day, together and have for years. I have women ask me sometimes, "How can you stand to be around your husband 24 hours a day? Don't you need some time for yourself?" At those moments, I realize anew how God reached down and saved two hell-bound sinners, how he taught us how to really love and surrender our rights to each other, and how he used us to tell others about himself. Salvation is free, an unearned gift.

My husband is my best friend, the love of my heart, and the delight of my life. I would rather spend time with him than anyone else. When I look at him, I see that prince that I always wanted. And my husband tells me that I am the most beautiful woman in the world. He tells me I'm the perfect wife, his life is complete because of me, and that he is forever thankful that God gave me to him. He adores me in a million ways and makes me feel like that princess I always wanted to be.

My glorious marriage became possible as I turned my heart to honor my husband, but then, as a child of God I could do no less. So I really did end up with the fairytale after all. I married the handsome prince, and I am living happily ever after. God taught us that to have happily ever after you must be a giver instead of a taker. Then God gives and gives and gives.

You can follow Shad and Sheila's ministry at: www.wegotothem.com

~*Sheila*

The Queen of His Heart

God warns us, **"Examine yourselves, whether ye be in the faith; prove your own selves. Know ye not your own selves, how that Jesus Christ is in you…"** (II Corinthians 13:5).

In this study we will do just that.

The girl in this story *assumed* she was a Christian. If her husband had not truly been saved, then today she might be sitting in church every Sunday still thinking she is a good Christian. It was the transforming change in his life, the abrupt turn-about of his mind and heart that led her to doubt that she had a real relationship with God.

When you really know God it shows. When you really have a relationship with God you know him like a friend. When you walk with God your heart will be constantly filled with him. You will not try to please him… you will just do whatever he wants you to do. If you know him, you will love him. Do you love him? Do you really know him?

As you read the following story, I adjure you to stop and ask yourself, "Do I truly have a real relationship with God? Am I sure that I know him?"

Most of you have always assumed you are a Christian, but does God know you are? Two times God says to us, **"There is a way which seemeth right unto a man, but the end thereof are the ways of death"** (Proverbs 14:12).

Salvation is easy and hard at the same time. God made it easy through the free gift of Jesus Christ, but we make it hard by trying to earn what God has already given. It is foolish to assume that because you made a profession, got baptized, and joined the church, you are on your way to heaven.

This next story illustrates what God has done for you through his beloved Son, Jesus.

Parable of the king's son
(taken from *By Divine Design,* Michael Pearl)

In a faraway land and in another time, a benevolent king ruled his kingdom wisely, and all the people loved him. Well, not all. There was a small group of rebels who worked in secret, seeking to overthrow his rule. They wanted the freedom to engage in immoral revelry, which was not permitted under this righteous king. The usual punishment for treason was death, but the king passed a law saying that anyone guilty of treason would be allowed to live but would have his eyes put out. On several occasions young men were brought before the king to be tried for treason. After carefully hearing the evidence the king had regretfully pronounced the penalty of blindness upon some of these young men.

One day the king's sheriff brought a young man before the court to be tried for treason. It was rumored that he was the ringleader of the rebellion. The king was disturbed by the hood covering the upper body of the prisoner. But the court lawyers requested that the concealment remain in place to assure that justice would be accomplished. The king went along with the request, assuming that the accused must be an acquaintance or perhaps the son of some state official. He had heard the evidence that proved to be overwhelmingly incriminating. When it came time to pass sentence the lawyers removed the hood to reveal the king's own son. The king was about to pass the sentence of blindness on his only son. With great restraint of his emotions he announced that he would wait twenty-four hours to pronounce the judgment. Though it could not make a difference in the court's decision, the king used that time, to no avail, trying to bring his son to repentance. The son felt sure that the father could not forgive him, and the penalty of the law was unavoidable.

During the intervening time, word of the developing situation spread over all the kingdom. There was much speculation about what the king would do. Half the people characterized the king as a man who placed duty and the letter of the law above his own feelings. They supposed the king would not only take out his son's eyes but also have him executed as an example. The other half of the kingdom believed the king would yield to deep feelings toward his son and free him unharmed. Many believed that he would elicit from the son a promise of allegiance and then set aside the penalty of the law.

The king found himself in a dilemma, with two conflicting compulsions. He desired to save his son, and he desired to remain a just and lawful king. Having blinded others for the same offense, could he make an exception with his son and still maintain the public perception of justice? How could the public continue to respect his rule? Furthermore, if he should withhold the punishment, how could he command respect or control of his son? The offense would forever stand between the king and his son. If unpunished, would the rebellious son not be even bolder in his rebellion?

On the other hand, how could he pass sentence on his own son? Could a father who begat a son of his own body, and invested so much in rearing him, suddenly shut off all feelings? Could he just blind his son and forget? Would life have any further meaning for a father?

Twenty-four hours later the court was reconvened. The royal city was packed with expectant, solemn onlookers. The prisoner was brought into the court. His face not being covered, his bitterness was clear for all to see. Looking at his countenance, one would think he was holding his father responsible for his rebellion.

The king was the last to enter the chamber. With expectancy running high, he was led into the chamber wearing the hood his son wore the day before. Feebly, he was steered to his place on the throne. He immediately commenced to recount the incriminating evidence. Then while the crowd stood in hushed wonder, just when he was preparing to pass sentence he reached up and slipped the hood from his head. The audience fell back in revulsion as they saw the two gaping, bloody holes where royal eyes had once been. The crowd gasped as the king addressed the general public. A servant placed before the people a tray containing the king's eyes. The king asked the general

public if common justice could be served by the substitution of his eyes for his son's. The people unanimously agreed that justice was served. The king had found a way to be faithful to his law, thereby maintaining its integrity, and a way to satisfy his love to his son.

One problem remained; the son's rebellion. If the father had been able to elicit prior repentance from the son, the sacrifice would have seemed justifiable. But the offering was made when the son was still a self-proclaimed enemy of the king. That too was resolved in the king's bloody sacrifice. Seeing the father's love and forgiveness, the son was moved to repent toward his father. All doubt as to the father's love and wisdom involuntarily vanished. The son fell at his father's feet and begged for the forgiveness that he had already received. He was placed at the father's right hand where he forever thereafter faithfully and benevolently assisted in all affairs of the kingdom.

The dilemma was solved. Sacrificing neither his love to his son nor justice, the law had been honored in a way that elevated it as never before. The king had not only expressed his love to his son, but had brought him to humble repentance. The integrity of the kingdom was maintained and the son was saved—all at the father's expense. **"That he might be just and the justifier…For God so loved the world that he gave…."**

Your Treasure Chest

♥ Write your testimony of when and how you came to understand God's amazing sacrifice for you in your notebook. If you are not sure about your relationship to God, then write out a prayer asking God to show Himself to you that you might know him. He will answer such a prayer.

♥ In the Teacher's Guide at the back of the book is a list of questions and verses to help you learn what God says concerning salvation. His WORD is effectual. There is life-giving power in just knowing what God says. Go through that lesson.

Reverence

MORAL TO THE STORY: Who you are as a single girl will be who you are as a married woman. If you are lazy, you will remain lazy. If you are rebellious, you will carry it into marriage. <u>If, at present, you are obedient and cheerful and a servant to others then your marriage will be blessed.</u>

A CAUTION: Beware of spiders, fleas, snakes, bats and mice, in addition to any other small terror that might come your way.

It's time for a few basic lessons that will help you transition into becoming a wife. You will learn that God expects you to honor and reverence your husband even when he quietly allows you to continue your disobedience. If you do not learn, God can and will come to your husband's aid if you ignore your husband's wishes.

In this chapter Patricia tells us how God used Fleas to help her come to understand that quiet disobedience would not be tolerated. Over my lifetime I have observed that God uses all manner of things to get his children to conform to his will. Knowing that God is thus working to mature us is comforting and, at times, scary.

CHAPTER 15

*F*LEAS

story eight

Spiders

BEFORE PATRICIA'S FLEA story, I want to tell you one of my own insect nightmares. Years ago I got mad at my neighbor for being offensive to her husband. I stewed, fumed, and even fussed about it to some friends. I knew I was acting ugly, but I kept my grudge. One night I grabbed a house coat to put it on and out fell a dangerous spider. I freaked! Spiders are the worst scary thing! For the next week or so I thoroughly shook every piece of clothing I put on. Somehow I knew God was rebuking me for badmouthing my neighbor. Several other times I had a spider jump out of my towel or coat. I lived in tension, nervous for the judgment I knew God was waiting to give me the first time my guard was down. I was right. Early one morning I heard someone beating on my door. I jumped out of bed and grabbed my jeans off the floor. You guessed it. I had one leg all the way in and was hopping around trying to shove the other leg in when out popped the biggest, hairiest, most terrible-looking spider this side of Papua New Guinea. I fell on my rump kicking and screaming and fighting with those jeans. I never did find the spider, but I tell you I shut my mouth about my neighbor and have kept it shut. Furthermore, I gave up jeans. They are too hard to get off.

If you continue in the sin of bitterness or speaking badly of a fellow believer, and you don't have any fear of God doing weird or scary things to you, then you'd better check your relationship with the eternal God. Chances are you don't have one…a relationship, that is. He does not let believers continue in sin.

"What shall we say then? Shall we continue in sin, that grace may abound? God forbid. How shall we, that are dead to sin, live any longer therein?" (Romans 1:1-2).

Here's something to consider:

Do you believe God leads and guides people before they get saved? Maybe even guides them in who they should marry?

Here is what God did to my friend, Patricia. She should be thankful; her rebuke was not nearly as bad as spiders. So get ready to start scratching. This is Patricia's flea story.

God Knew Me Before

Jesse started checking me out my first day at work. For some reason he unnerved me. When the people in my department would go on morning break, Jesse would stop by my table to chat. I would jump up and go back to work. I never knew what to say when he was around, so I would flee. I think he is a King…bossy, dominant, forceful, and I don't know…he just seemed so classy that it scared me.

Young men do well to bear in mind that a girl is who she is when she's not trying to impress a man. A wise man observed, "Someone who is nice to you, but rude to the waiter, is not a nice person."

Everyone in our circle of friends dated. It was expected. It was during the early 1970s and neither of us knew the Lord. People I worked with encouraged me to get my own apartment so I could do my own thing. To my regret, I listened to the troubled people who prodded me. Once alone, I stepped into a new foreign world, a world filled with peers who pulled me far away from those who loved and cared for me. My parents were very upset about my new life. I soon learned why.

One day a girl at work told me, "You have to get with it, you need to get on the birth control pill...everyone is." She escorted me to Planned Parenthood. Because I didn't want to risk losing my new friend, I went ahead and accepted the pills. I felt sick, pushed into a life I didn't want.

During my youth I had disdained my parents' religion, but now I felt a need to try again. I didn't want my rebellious friends leading me down paths I didn't even like. I wanted to think for myself. One Sunday I went back to church but left in the middle of the service; I knew I was being rude, but it seemed so dead.

The more I was with my new friends the less I thought about God. One night I went to a party. Jesse was there. I was still nervous around him, but since he was there I was forced to talk to him. Then he asked if he could call me and maybe we could go out sometime. I said; "Sure!" I really didn't think he would ever call me.

Not long after that Jesse asked me on a date. After just a few dates, somehow I felt that I would be his wife. My relationship with my parents began to improve, so I moved back home. Even so, I would not have admitted to my parents or even to myself that I had been willful and rebellious toward my parents in my recent lifestyle. I still felt they had just not understood me. I had a lot of baggage (self-centered will, that is) in the attic of my life, and it would come back to haunt me, but at that time all I could think of was Jesse.

One evening while having dinner with my family I announced that I might marry Jesse. I didn't know for sure, but down deep in my heart I felt peace. Jesse made a similar announcement to his family. Neither of us knew about the other's declaration. A month later, in January, he proposed.

After our engagement, I realized that Jesse was Jewish. Wow! Was I excited! As a young child I had a deep love and respect for the Jewish people.

I felt that Jesse was a gift from God. Six months later we married. I thought that such a fairytale romance would surely lead to happily ever after.

If you think for one second that you can enter marriage with your past behavior stuffed out of sight and out of mind in a trunk in your attic, think again! The attitudes you have before marriage will resurface. They will grow and become monsters that tear into your marriage.

If you resisted authority in your youth, once you marry you will feel just as trapped by your husband as you did by your parents. The worst of it is, you'll blame your pitiful existence on your husband. In your youth you can look forward to getting married and leaving the situation. Now that you are married, to leave the situation is to divorce.

Thankfully, God used fleas to wake me up to honoring and obeying God and my husband.

Fleas To the Rescue

My husband was…how would you put it…he was different. I was horrified to realize he did not agree with me on much of anything. I began to wonder how I could have fallen in love which such a cold-hearted, unromantic man. The man had no feelings!

About seven years into the marriage God reached his loving hand down and found us. We both, Jew and Gentile, husband and wife, came to understand the love of Jesus Christ. But becoming a Christian did not change my zeal for independence. I now wanted God's way in my life, although I had no clue as to what God wanted from me as a wife. I was to learn.

The years rolled on, and three children later, bitterness and resentment were my daily companions. Under my breath I would murmer things like, "I'll show you!" or, "I can't believe I married such an insensitive person." I would need a lesson from God if my marriage was going to survive and flourish. Even in my rebellion toward my husband, God knew I really wanted to know and honor God and my husband. God sent fleas to the rescue.

One day, as I was helping a friend pack up her home to move, she offered me several of her houseplants. I chose one, a beautiful healthy asparagus fern that hung just above where her cat slept. I excitedly took my prize plant home and hung it in our bedroom.

Several days later my dear husband suggested, "I'm beginning to get itchy. The plant must have fleas. You better get rid of it."

I gave him a look signifying how stupid he was. "Plants don't have fleas!" I conveniently forgot his suggestion to throw the plant out. Days passed, and he warned me again, "You need to get rid of that plant, because the fleas are getting worse."

Has your dad or mom ever given a command you thought was stupid? The same Bible that teaches we are to honor our parents also teaches that a wife is to reverence her husband. **"…and the wife see that she reverence her husband"** (Ephesians 5:33).

I had no idea God expected me to reverence my husband! He is just a man and is often wrong. Reverence him? But God gently continued to teach me.

By the next day it was clear that my husband was right. The fleas were multiplying so fast that they infested the whole house, including Spike, our long-haired guinea pig. My husband treated Spike with flea shampoo—over-treated, I should say. Poor old Spike looked like a mop gasping for air. I think he went into a mild cardiac arrest. What a mess! Getting rid of the fleas was quite an ordeal. My disobedience caused my husband and family a lot of frustration. The big question is: did I learn anything?

The Case of Fleas the Second Time Around
Remember, the baggage you accumulated as a single woman will come with you when you marry. I still assumed I was smarter and my way was right. God sent Lesson Two.

My husband felt God telling him to get out of debt, so we sold our home and started looking for a rental. I found our first rental. It had everything I wanted in a home. Jesse looked at it and didn't feel comfortable about renting it. I put my charm to work, convinced him what a great house it was, and *voila!* He signed on the dotted line.

Several nights after we moved into the house Jesse woke me up and announced, "We have fleas!" I rolled over and thought to myself, "Get a grip. We don't have fleas!" (Hmm…do you see a pattern here?) Yep! The house was infested. We discovered that the previous occupants were cat lovers.

It took months to get rid of the fleas. By then Spike had gone to the happy hunting land, so he was spared my flea lesson.

Evidently I am a slow learner. Maybe from this story you would think I should just start cleaning my house better, but I am and have always been a clean freak. Fleas are for the unfit and unclean, right? For a woman who prides herself on being a wonderful housekeeper, an infestation of fleas is very humbling.

I ask you, do you think God has a sense of humor?

Please, Please No More Fleas…PLEASE

That brings us to Lesson Three. In the back of my mind I began to wonder if the fleas might be God's way of getting my attention concerning my lack of honor toward my husband. But I reasoned that at this point the flea thing might still, maybe, be a happenstance—just a fluke.

We had friends who put a lovely house on the market, but it was not selling. We decided to exchange fixing the house up for a decrease in the rent and live there until it sold.

During the hot, dry month of August I decided to try growing grass in the dustbowl of a back yard. I asked my husband to help with the work. He agreed after some hesitation, but cautioned, "Don't you think it's too hot to plant grass seed?"

I chided him, thinking, "Why does he always drag his feet?" I am sure he read my thoughts, as my face must have reflected my dishonor, but he went along with me…again. We purchased the seed and then went to a local farm to purchase bales of hay. We prepared the ground, planted the seed and spread the hay.

While sitting in church the next day I noticed one of our sons scratching. He leaned over to me and said, "I think fleas are biting me." If he had said he had leprosy it would not have affected me more than the word fleas.

It was fleas from the hay which my husband had said was a waste of time to spread. Once again my family had to endure the consequences of my stubbornness in not listening to my husband's gentle caution.

Did I better understand submission by that time? You better believe I did. Did the grass grow? Of course not!

Disobedience is often disguised.

You may wonder why it took me so long to submit to my husband. The answer: disobedience is often disguised. I basically didn't know I was that disobedient. God makes it clear what he thinks of sin. James 2:10 says, **"For whosoever shall keep the whole law, and yet offend in one point, he is guilty of all."** Most of us never think we are being disobedient. Our first thought is that we are right in how we think, feel and do, and that the other person is insensitive, dumb and lazy.

I had developed the habit in my youth of doing my own thing. I thought I was smarter, more sensitive and caring, and surely harder-working. Remember the baggage that I thought I had stored in the attic? It was right on my back all the time.

It was easy to dismiss my husband's wishes without feeling rebellious because he never actually commanded me in anything. He never lorded his authority over me; he suggested. Even though he is a strong leader, he has what some would call "a quiet voice". He clearly wanted me to honor him, but he wanted me to honor from my heart, not from his demand. I knew, and he knew that I knew, what he wanted me to do. He wanted me to *want* to obey him.

I had spent years pretending to be the sweet, obedient wife to the point of deceiving even myself, but God knew my heart. He caused me to see my dishonor and disrespect—even contempt—toward my husband. Once I was willing to acknowledge that my attitude was sin against God, my heart changed. When my husband speaks I no longer take what he says as a suggestion, but as a word that God means for me to obey. It seems strange, but I no longer feel irritated or frustrated when things don't go the way I think is right. I guess I've stopped seeing myself as all-wise, all-feeling and caring. I no longer see him as insensitive; he is just different from me. Peace, both in soul and in daily living, flood my life. And I've stopped dreading fleas because I know where they come from. Needless to say, they have never returned. Many years have passed since my last flea lesson, and since then my relation-

Haven't I read something about swarms of insects coming upon people who wouldn't obey the Word of God? It's best to learn before the tenth visitation.

ship with my man has flourished into a thing of great glory both to God and to us as husband and wife. I just want to end with a praise of thanksgiving, "Thank you, God, for sending fleas, fleas, and more fleas."

~*Patricia*

Statistics

Some fathers lay down the law. Everyone knows that he means to be obeyed "or else." Other fathers gently entreat their grown daughters to listen and obey, hoping they have her heart to the point that she wants to do what he thinks best. Life is easier for girls raised by dominant, forceful fathers because they are accustomed to obeying. They were never given any other option and grew accustomed to strong authority. In contrast, girls raised by kind, gentle fathers often get bitter toward their husbands if they are demanding. But regardless of our predilection, all of us help meets are responsible for obeying God's guidelines.

God expects those who know him to follow his directions. God gives clear law that we are to honor our parents, and reverence and obey our husband.

"And hereby we do know that we know him, if we keep his commandments. He that saith, I know him, and keepeth not his commandments, is a liar, and the truth is not in him" (1 John 2:3-4).

Obedience can be difficult to ascertain when a husband drops suggestions rather than gives commands. But God commands wives to reverence their husbands, which would entail <u>discerning his will as best you can</u> and then treating it as a command.

It took three lessons of fleas for Patricia to finally come to realize that God expects her to honor her husband's wishes. Just as fathers come in all shapes and styles, so do husbands.

The way you as a single girl respond to your father is the way you will respond to your husband. Sometimes you might obey your dad while silently thinking he is out of touch and off the radar. Watch out—you will transfer

If you're not clear on his true wishes, ask him to clarify.

this attitude to your husband. Ask God to teach you wisdom. Ask him to show you where you are lacking understanding.

The word *reverence* means: respect, admiration, worship, awe, esteem, veneration, astonishment, and amazement.

An antonym (opposite) for reverence is contempt, which means: disdain, disrespect, disapproval, scorn and condescension.

The Scripture has a dire warning for a daughter who dishonors her father: **"For God commanded, saying, Honour thy father and mother: and, He that curseth father or mother, let him die the death"** (Matthew 15:4).

As daunting as that curse of death is, the admonishment for women to reverence their husbands is even greater because God chose marriage between a man and a woman to be a picture of Jesus' relationship to us, the church. We are to be the bride of Christ. The Scripture calls this a **"great mystery"** (Ephesians 5:32).

Amazing as it sounds, marriage between a man and a woman is what God chose as the closest example of Christ's relationship to his bride, the church. Submission, reverence, and honor are virtues God seeks to establish in his Son's bride.

Are you preparing to be that kind of wife? How?

1. *Obedience* is doing what you know your husband wants you to do.
2. *Submission* is giving your heart over to your husband's will.
3. *Reverence* is more than just doing what your man expects or demands. It is the attitude that results from truly believing your husband holds a divine position of leadership, and regarding him with a high degree of awe.

   Reverence: to revere, to be in awe; fear mingled with respect and esteem.

Obedience, submission, and reverence are all acts of the will and are not based on feelings. Showing deference toward one's husband is an act of reverence toward the God who placed you in that role.

Deference: deferring to his will, command, or authority.

Your Treasure Chest

*It is a sobering moment when a woman makes a
commitment to honor, obey and reverence her husband.*

♥ Write your commitment here. When you're married and are having a
bad day, come back here and read your commitment to God and to your
husband. If you really mean it, then God will begin to work in your heart a
change that will lead to beauty, glory and honor.

Contempt Instead of Honor

MORAL TO THE STORY: We are what we think, say and do. If we occupy our minds with thankfulness toward other people, we will be thankful in spirit and in deed.

A CAUTION: If we give our mind to doubt, mistrust, and accusation, it will destroy our mind as well as our life.

Are there really any spiritual consequences to living loosely in self-will and independence? Could devils be busy planting in us unhealthy thoughts, making us agitated and depressed, or worse, accusing of others?

Years ago a book about "the power of positive thinking" took the market by storm. The book continued to be a bestseller because there is power (both healing and destructive) in how a person thinks. This story was written by a woman who has learned the hard way.

CHAPTER 16

the
OWER
of
STINKING
THINKING

HE CAME AT A MOMENT in my life when I was really lonely. I had moved to a college town to be a volunteer for a thriving ministry. We were busy with lots of Bible studies, meetings, memorizing Scripture, conferences, and friends eating together and talking. Then one day, out of the blue, I was dismissed from the ministry. I was several hours from home, had expenses to pay, and a job I had just begun, so I decided to stay put for a while to get my bearings and give myself time to decide how to move forward. I was more than just a little lonely; I had a great big need to be needed. I thought a lot about the kind of man I wanted to marry. I knew he would have to be real, not a Christian automaton. Being outside my group now, alone in the world, I wondered how I would meet him.

Then one day it happened, while I was running an errand. On impulse I shot into the coffee shop, ordered a latté, and sat down by a friend who was having lunch. She poked me in the ribs, "Don't turn around now, but you should know that a gorgeous man sitting at your right is checking you out. He looks Middle-Eastern or something, but I've seen him in church, so he must be a Christian." When she gave me the word I turned to look. He was beautiful, with black curly hair and a big moustache. He suddenly turned my way so our eyes met. I could feel my face blushing. I saw him grin before I dropped my eyes.

A couple of days later I was running another errand when suddenly there he was right in front of me. It was one heart-stopping, magnificent moment. We both just stared into each other's eyes and laughed. It was one of those moments when it seems something was meant to be. Jude started dropping by work, we took walks, ate ice cream or visited some out-of-the-way restaurant. I loved his voice. He was charming, spontaneous, people-oriented, fun and independent, which balanced my methodical, steadfast personality.

I lived for the times we had together. Jude was so full of adventure and made my life so full and worthwhile. It was thrilling, heady, and wonderful; love has a sweetness that makes everything beautiful.

Jude was so courteous and thoughtful. He would leave me breakfast in a bag on my car seat early every morning. That meant he went into work about 5 a.m., baked the spinach rolls, made the freshly-squeezed orange juice, drove to my place a half-hour away, dropped the bag off, and got back to work. Waking from sleep, I would hear his van drive into the parking lot, and I knew it was him!

Something about love gave me energy I never had before. Always given to depression, this was a welcome contrast, energizing and life-giving. I could talk with him until the wee hours of the morning and then get up early with a spring in my step. Work didn't seem so hard, and everyone seemed grumpy compared to me. Sometimes there would be a card or some other cool thing he left on my desk.

After dating for a couple of months I took Jude to meet my parents. They really liked him. The second time he came to visit my parents Jude asked me to marry him.

Our wedding took place on a cold, clear day just after a blizzard in beautiful New England. I was so excited. His father married us, and before pronouncing us man and wife, he wrapped his priestly stole around our hands, binding them together, just like in a movie I saw.

After we married, we kept up our walks and talks, which I loved. We would buy one expensive dinner and split it; we did the same thing with a piece of gum—always splitting it—it was our thing. People could see how perfect we were for each other. We cooked together, laughed together, enjoyed our friends together, and were full of the joy of the Lord together.

It happened so slowly I never even noticed until one day, it seems out of nowhere, fiery darts started flying at my soul, like a bad dream from who-knows-where; accusing thoughts, irritated feelings, doubt and insecurity nibbled at my soul. Things in our courtship I could overlook now invaded my mind, not allowing me to think clearly. Baggage from my youth clouded my soul like a foul odor.

Being taught to submit as a wife, I knew there was no way out except to obey, but it was with a heavy heart and a bitter grudge. Then my Prophet-type Jude decided to go to Bible college 3,500 miles away…in another country! His grand ideas were foreign to me. I harbored continual disapproval of him. I began to question his motives. I talked down to him because I felt he was stupid in the way he handled our money. He seemed to lack spiritual clarity. I wanted to start a family; Jude wanted to wait five years before having children! Why should he be the one to decide? I have my convictions. I have to do as I know God says, not him.

All day at work my mind churned over and over with insecurities and doubts about his motives and his leadership. Did Jude hate me now? Did I displease God somehow? Did I marry the wrong man? My brooding thoughts constantly blamed him for my unhappiness. And so the sweetness vanished.

He said that I would only have to work while he finished a one-year degree, but his schooling lasted longer. I kept hoping I would get pregnant so I could at least take a break from the demanding job at the ad agency. Then the biggest blow came; a doctor told us that we were not able to have children. It felt like death. My dream of motherhood was shattered. Depression called my name daily.

His management of our finances, which resulted in accumulating debt, really made me fall apart. I was a nervous wreck, and he avoided dealing with it. Remember what I loved about him when we met? He was so spontaneous, so he balanced out my methodical personality. Jude was still Jude. He had not changed. After awhile he just stopped talking to me. He stayed away for hours. When he was home he would sit and stare at me with confusion on his face, as if trying to piece together what had happened to bring us to this place.

Then one day, after six years of marriage, I came home and he was gone. It wasn't like he just packed a bag; his clothes, his clutter, his stuff... everything that said "Jude" was just gone. It had never dawned on me that he might actually leave me. We were Christians. We were preparing to go into the ministry...right? I mean, that was why he was going to Bible College, so surely he would come back, and I would forgive him and we would be lovers again and go on into ministry. He had a reputation to uphold; this would disgrace the Savior. Jude had vowed to love and protect me; divorce was not an option...ever...right?

But he was gone. I had slowly but surely eroded his spirit with my contempt, condescension, and disapproval. But never would I have believed this would have led to his leaving. He loved me...I know he loved me. We were perfect for each other. Everyone said so. Why would he leave? We could work this out with a little counsel if he would just...

Now I was terribly, terribly alone. It was not like being single again; it was like being ripped into pieces. Visions of camping out on his doorstep to bring him back whirled around in my mind; maybe that would make him love me again. I prayed earnestly that he would come back, but he never did.

So what is it like to lose the love of your life? You are a tangled mess of needs that cannot express themselves properly—the need to deal with the loss of a relationship without a funeral or comforting friends or family; the need to feel a sense of purpose again; the need for a way to provide for yourself; the need to keep a lid on your hormones; the need for legal and financial advice; these are some of the many things you face. Add to this the shame of being a Christian with the black letter "D" on your résumé. So after three miserable months of being alone I went back to my parents' home a dismal failure. The vision that kept coming up before me was of a Treasure Chest turned into a coffin with all my hopes and dreams inside. At age 31, my life was over.

I clung to a dream that God would bring our marriage back to life. I desperately prayed and hoped for Jude to repent, humble himself and come back to me as the man I thought he should be.

The same mental foothold I had given the devil that destroyed my marriage still controlled me and kept me alone. It was the same attitude that had made me depressed before I ever married and the same problem that caused the ministry I was involved in before Jude to dismiss me. In my mind everyone was insensitive and unspiritual. I alone sought the Lord. I could not see my fault. **"All the ways of a man are clean in his own eyes; but the LORD weigheth the spirits. Commit thy works unto the LORD, and thy thoughts shall be established"** (Proverbs 16:2-3).

I eventually came to believe that I in fact married the wrong man. I played spiritual gymnastics in my mind. It caused serious depression to come back into my life. It seemed that God Himself was punishing me. I became more "conservative," applying the Old Testament law to my life. I tried to "keep the Sabbath." I became a "poster child" for standing on, "What God hath joined together let not man put asunder." Jude's lawyer contacted me over and over saying my husband wanted a divorce. I refused.

This mindset would continue to control Jude for the next nine years. He would not be allowed to continue his life. I had heard Jude was with a woman that he truly loved and wanted to marry. I thought if he didn't repent and come back to me then he could just be forced to live in sin if he wanted a wife and family. For me it was a martyrdom of sorts.

But, divorce is just a word. Divorce in the Bible means "not living together as one." The reality was…I was already biblically divorced.

About eight years after my husband left me, I began receiving the No Greater Joy magazine. With each issue I began to see grace versus bondage. A small crack began to form in the unbearable Jezebel fortress that I had built. I could not put my finger on it, but something was changing in me. For over two years I listened to Michael Pearl's Romans series. The Word of God was giving me light. I was beginning to see myself for the self-righteous controller that I was.

Finally, I was willing to admit that the man I was married to many years earlier was no longer my husband. It was at last clear to me that I had to let him go if that was his wish. I wonder what might have happened if I had, with a free heart, let him go years earlier? Would he have changed his mind in the process? Would he have forgiven me? It is too late to know.

Over the years my bitterness had made him distrust my intentions. When he heard my voice over the phone his answering tone was angry. I told him in a matter-of-fact-way, "I am truly sorry. I will sign the papers." As we talked it was like a window shade came up on his soul. He sounded more and more friendly, like the man I had married. Was God giving me a second chance to be the person I should have been toward this man? I didn't know, but regardless of the outcome I would be thankful. We talked five times that day. It was my 40th birthday. It was one of the happiest days of my life. In the end he sent me 'the papers'. I had to accept his decision with grace. I finally, after all these years, obeyed my husband.

It was over. But God did not leave me in the ashes to squander my life away. I am his. He will never leave me nor forsake me regardless of my Stinking Thinking. Well, this is the rest of my story and you can read for yourself that some lessons are difficult.

Alone but not Alone Ever Again

For the next couple of years I spent a lot of my free time taking long walks, talking and crying. I found myself back in a spiral of stupid thoughts when I finally said, "God, I know you have some kind of plan for me, please show me. I need to give out to people. I need a life with purpose." Remember the verse I cited earlier: "Commit thy works unto the LORD, and thy thoughts shall be established."

That morning as I walked and prayed it was as if I heard a snippet from a message by Elisabeth Elliot, "Just do the next thing." Not a minute later, I heard a little boy calling out, "Hey! Wait for me!" He came running to walk with me and my dog. He started walking with me every day and afterwards came to my house. Now there was no time for moaning and groaning, because I had a pestering little boy that demanded my attention. It was wonderful. I loved his company. That long-buried need for a child was suddenly finding an answer. I taught him to do all the things I was doing in the garden and in the house. He was as starved for a friend as I was. We became great friends.

Soon, other children whose parents were too busy to spend time with them began showing up at my house. One day I was folding a baby quilt that I had made years earlier when one of the older girls who dropped by asked, "I wish someone would teach me to do that!" Wow! I had a ministry and it was really fun. I made invitations and put them in the kids' mailboxes on my daily walk. Every Friday night I would teach anyone that wanted to come how to make one easy quilt block. I only had one sewing machine, and so I expected only one or two girls with short attention spans and yawns. Well, they came, eleven of them, girls and boys. We had teacups, a silver tea pot, leftover baked goods from a board meeting, an ironing board and iron, fabric scraps, one rotary cutter and a ball of nerves in my stomach. I knew the Lord was using me. Months and years passed; the children grew and gained other interests, but I had left God's mark in their lives. Like the Psalmist said in Psalm 30:11, **"Thou hast turned for me my mourning into dancing: thou hast put off my sackcloth, and girded me with gladness."** While I ministered to these needy kids God turned my ashes to beauty. Then God moved me to the next ministry.

I am now working in the graphics department for a worldwide ministry. People are being drawn to the Savior and marriages are being restored and I am a part of it!

It is true that my ugly sinful attitude brought me down to disaster. But only sin (more Stinking Thinking) would keep me there. God is ready and able to pick up broken pieces and forge them together to create a fine picture. Yes, the lines are there showing that life is a puzzle of put-together pieces, but step back five feet and even those lines disappear, showing only the beautiful workmanship of the Master.

This is my story, one of tragedy that could have so easily been avoided. Jude was not unlike many young men. He was full of crazy ideas and not wise in the way he spent our money, but, doubtless, he would have matured. If I had only obeyed God's command to wives and kept my vows to honor, obey and reverence Jude, then today I would be a greatly loved and cherished lady.

Don't take for granted that you can pitch a fit, treat a man with contempt, demand control of the money, and still have your man desperately in love with you. Learn from my mistake.

~*Mary*

"Brethren, I count not myself to have apprehended: but this one thing I do, forgetting those things which are behind, and reaching forth unto those things which are before, I press toward the mark for the prize of the high calling of God in Christ Jesus" (Philippians 3:13-14).

Pure thoughts

Pure, thankful thoughts can arise from many acts of the will. Years ago I had a friend that developed a strange habit. Her youth had been spent in sex, drugs, and bitterness. She thought evil toward a lot of people. After she was saved she said her mind was a rotten sewage pool and she hated the constant bombardment of evil thoughts. One day the ugliness of her bitterness hit her in the face and she decided she hated it so much she would stop regardless of what it took. She decided every time she spoke evil of someone, even if it were true and the person deserved it, every time an angry response came to her, and every time she had a negative thought or a sexually impure thought or depressed feeling she would call out loud the name of Jesus. Having a conversation with her was….how can I say…startling. Almost every time I spoke to her face-to-face or on the phone she would without explanation or pause suddenly exclaim, "Oh, Lord Jesus, help me."

Her constant calling on God was very effective for both of us, as I am sure it was for the rest of her friends. I was very careful what I talked to her about. She meant business before God. I admired her for it, and I am sure God blessed her for her desire to walk pure. A man has a propensity to sin with his body; a female's sins are more in attitude and words. Sin is sin, and will be judged the same.

"She openeth her mouth with wisdom; and in her tongue is the law of kindness" (Proverbs 31:26).

It is human nature to climb on someone's back if you are drowning. People, especially girls who are frustrated with their lives, have a tendency to want to bring others down. They rationalize to themselves that they are just telling what happened, just being honest, and so forth. This need to bring others down will follow you into your marriage, job, and life, for there will always be those whom you will decide need "telling on." It is a death trap of Satan's. Not their death trap; yours.

Only when a girl learns to control her need to tear down, when she lets people go unmolested by her "truthful" information, will she begin to grow as a person. Every argument, every misunderstanding, every hurt feeling— every black depression stems from someone "supposing" another meant evil toward them, used them, thought offensively toward them, or whatever else the mind contrives. Imagine being free from all these misapprehensions! You *can* be free.

"A wholesome tongue is a tree of life: but perverseness therein is a breach in the spirit" (Proverbs 15:4).

The word perverseness means unreasonableness. Everyone thinks they are reasonable and that the one they hold in distain is unreasonable. If you have conflict with someone, chances are you are unreasonable at least half the time.

If you have some irritation, scorn, or conflict with more than one person, then chances are you are the culprit in most of those relationships. No matter how sweet you think you are, it is you who lacks a wholesome tongue.

Some families, even some communities of people, seem to have a heredi-tary predisposition to bitterness and strife. Those raised in such an atmo-sphere come to accept jealousy, suspicion, and evil thinking as the norm. They just assume that everyone is critical of them. Believe it or not, there is another world where people love one another and there are no feelings of bitterness toward anyone, where one never imagines that another is thinking ill of them, a world of daily peace and contentment.

"Casting down imaginations, and every high thing that exalteth itself against the knowledge of God, and bringing into captivity every thought to the obedience of Christ" (II Corinthians 10:5).

Right now, as a single young woman, ask God to give you the wisdom to clear your soul of this plague of negative thoughts. Just as my friend called out to God, fill your soul with the beauty of a good thought-life. Expect good from people. Get busy serving others—not just your friends, but any-one who has a need. You may get treated unfairly (but probably not) and in the meantime your soul will be free to soar.

The Psalmist sung out in chapter 15, **"LORD, who shall abide in thy tabernacle? Who shall dwell in thy holy hill? He that walketh uprightly, and worketh righteousness, and speaketh the truth in his heart. He that backbiteth not with his tongue, nor doeth evil to his neighbor, nor taketh up a reproach against his neighbor."**

Your Treasure Chest

"Through wisdom is an house builded; and by understanding it is established: and by knowledge shall the chambers be filled with all precious and pleasant riches" (Proverbs 24:3-4).

♥ I put this tragedy toward the end of this book for a reason. All that we have covered in this book—prayer, courtship, finding God's will, chastity—everything can be done correctly and you can still trash your life and marriage if you are full of accusing thoughts or hurtful words.

♥ A pure heart and mind is one of the most important elements you will bring into your life and marriage. Most surely add it to your marriage Treasure Chest for the priceless gift that it is. Make a written commitment.

♥ Find a verse from the Scripture to claim as a promise. This is a Ribbon day! Make sure it is marked with bold letters on the table of your heart.

Preacher, Teacher & Farmer

When all is said and done, the final thought comes down to this: What do men look for in a mate? What kind of girl attracts their interest? What makes them happy? We must ask this question of ourselves: "What will make him proud to have me as his wife? What will make him want to be faithful, loving, and kind to me? What will make his love grow deeper with each passing day? What do I, his helper, need in me that will leave him free to respond to God and become all that God would have him be?"

So I have asked married men to give me the one thing they deem most important in a female. I will start with my own wise husband.

CHAPTER 17

WHAT SAY *the* MEN?

A Heart of Thanksgiving

Michael speaks:

WHEN I AM COUNSELING YOUNG men and they ask, "What is the most important thing we should look for in a prospective female?" My answer is simple and has been the same for many years.

I tell the young men, if a young woman thinks she is a real catch, then know she is not. If she feels she is doing you a favor marrying you, then know for a fact you are marrying trouble. Make sure she feels blessed that you have chosen her. Keep searching until you find a girl with the most valuable of all character traits: a thankful heart.

A lazy girl can be taught to do her share; an untrained girl can be guided into learning everything she needs to know; an ugly girl can wear makeup (and besides, as women age they all lose that youthful beauty); a fat girl can lose weight (although over time us married men come to appreciate a little extra to handle); even a mean-spirited, hot-headed girl can repent. But a girl who thinks she is better than you will not be open to correction; she is a dead end.

A girl that goes into marriage thinking she is quite the catch, beautiful, talented, kind-hearted or spiritually superior, will be a pain as a wife. Anytime her husband crosses her, her soul, mind, and occasionally voice will yell, "Why did I ever marry such a loser? I could have had anyone I wanted." No man wants to end up with a woman who feels that way.

A thankful spirit is the opposite of a prideful spirit. A girl that laughs and enjoys life, bubbles with joy, and just seems satisfied with her life—that's what I looked for in my wife.

After more than forty years of marriage, I still think the number one important trait to look for in choosing a wife is a joyful, thankful spirit.

~*Michael Pearl*

Attitude of Gratitude

There is a lot to be said of a thankful heart. As a matter of fact, the word *joy* appears 167 times in God's Word. Words like thanksgiving, giving thanks, gladness, merry heart, and praise are woven in and around the word joy, signifying that one begets the other.

And since many women have dreamed of marrying a perfect man but no woman ever actually has, a girl who thinks she's a catch will inevitably come to believe she could have done better, no matter how good a husband she married.

A wise mentor told me that spiritual pride always leads to bitterness. I've seen wives look down on their seemingly "unspiritual" husbands but it seems to be the case that the husband is spiritual but simply isn't meeting her expectations of him.

The Proverbs are full of contrasting a negative behavior to a godly trait. You can read how God views a merry heart. **"A merry heart doeth good like a medicine: but a broken spirit drieth the bones"** (Proverbs 17:22). Then, in Proverbs 15:13, God says, **"A merry heart maketh a cheerful countenance: but by sorrow of the heart the spirit is broken."**

Depression, bitterness, anger and frustration are not of God. They are not his will and way, and they will lead to an ugly face as well as an uglier soul. Face reading tells us that a woman's face is a road map of her thankfulness or bitterness. The tiny lines fanning out on either side of the eyes testify to much laughter, while the deep early furrow etched between the brows is the mark of a constant strained bitterness. The lines are unavoidable and something you will carry to your grave, testifying of the soul within.

Most women say they can't help how they feel. This is a lie which will keep you bound to a wretched life. God says, **"All the days of the afflicted are evil: but he that is of a merry heart hath a continual feast"** (Proverbs 15:15). <u>It is not that one woman has a wonderful life and the other has nothing but misery; it is that one sees life through the eyes of thankfulness and the other through a heart of discontentment.</u> A downcast attitude is a dishonor to God and your husband-to-be. Many of you girls have had only a few spats with your parents and an occasional crying upset, but when you are married and your insensitive husband hurts your feelings over and over, suddenly this challenge will become a real battle for your soul.

Commit to memory such great verses as Philippians 4:11, **"...for I have learned, in whatsoever state I am, therewith to be content."** Then I Timothy 6:6, **"But godliness with contentment is great gain. For we brought nothing into this world, and it is certain we can carry nothing out."**

Keep in mind that God listed the fruit of the Spirit. When a person knows the Savior, she will bear his fruit. **"But the fruit of the Spirit is love, joy, peace, longsuffering, gentleness, goodness, faith, meekness, temperance: against such there is no law"** (Galatians 5:22-23).

If you're not a grateful person or are prone to bouts of depressive loneliness, start giving thanks. Don't expect that depression to leave immediately, but it will if you make giving thanks a habit. I love Isaiah 61:3. He's given us the garment of praise for the spirit of heaviness!

Life is a choice. You choose to honor God by cheerfully going his way, which is the way of thanksgiving, joy, honoring and obeying your husband, serving others, showing kind responses, not taking offense, being chaste in your conversation and lifestyle, and having ears to hear and a heart to change.

A thankful heart spills out of a person, not with cards or gushy sentiment, but with service and delight. All of us reading this will think of someone whom we know is thankful. It is manifested in her speech; it is written on her smiling face, and it is expressed in the way she serves others. God loves thankfulness. He wants thankfulness in his heavenly bride, and your future husband will want it in you.

Thirty-one times in the Psalms, David cried out this thanks to God. David committed some very serious sins in his life, yet God called him "a man after God's own heart." David is the man God will set up to reign as king in time past and in time to come. Why? David had a heart of thanksgiving. Over and over he calls out his thankfulness. Nineteen times David exhorts us to joy. Joy is the result of thankfulness. Joy is visible. You can't keep a lid on it. It bubbles forth in praise and singing.

Are you bubbling with joy?

Does your face shine with thanksgiving?

The Case of Plumbing

From Preacher Tremaine (truthfromthebible.com)

Well, I would like to say the most important thing to me is that my wife does not have a critical spirit toward me. She does not keep a "weighed-in-the-balance" score card like some ladies do. What I mean by that is, she does not keep mental records of the household chores I do and then compare them to the amount she does. I see other wives making sure their husbands take their turn doing housework or babysitting, and if the husband does not jump into "his role," as she has determined it to be, then she is mad. I am so proud of my fine wife. Her serving heart makes me love her more and more every day.

My favorite photo of her is a shot of when she was covered with mud after doing some plumbing. There is a great story behind that picture which demonstrates her commitment to me.

I am a preacher of the gospel. One of my favorite places to preach is in prisons. I had put in a request to preach at a new prison, but months passed and they did not have any openings. Then one day the chaplain called and said someone had cancelled and I could come in. It was an opening which I knew could lead to a weekly time slot. I was dressing when I heard my son yell, "The water doesn't work." My wife went outside and looked under the house. She came in and told me there was a break in the pipes and water was pouring out. It was Sunday afternoon and there was no chance of getting a repairman even if we could afford it. I felt my heart sink. I knew nothing of repairing plumbing, so I dreaded to even try, and further, I knew if I missed going to the prison this time they probably would not call me again. My face must have reflected defeat as I sat on the bed to take off my dress clothes.

I felt my wife step up close to me and lay her hand on my shoulder. I looked up into her smiling eyes. As she spoke, her tone was full of encouragement and confidence. "I can fix the pipe. You go on to the prison. I know how much this means to you."

Late that afternoon I was energized as I returned from a really wonderful meeting of preaching to a bunch of sinners. When I pulled into the driveway my wife was just crawling out from under the house, muddy and tired but successful in fixing the plumbing. My son snapped a photo.

What kind of woman did God give me? The very, very best. She is the most willing servant I could ever imagine.

We have a house full of homeschooled kids, she is a great cook, and she keeps the house clean while always being cheerful. When I come home from work I feel like a king as she and all the kids crowd around to welcome me. I could not be the man I am today without her. Every time I stand to preach I know I am here because of her. I am free from the burdens of life and the turmoil of stress because she makes sure the household is running smoothly and peacefully. Without such a wife I would not be a successful preacher.

So am I a wonderful, sacrificing husband? No. I am distracted with thought, focused on ministry, and probably more selfish than most. But I am so thankful she does not measure my worth and service to her before she honors and serves me. Together we are a team working to honor and serve the Savior.

So what do I think is important in a woman? A willing heart.

~*One thankful Preacher*

Debi Expands

Add plumbing to your list of things to learn. Any trade a girl can learn will come in handy once married. Learn how to change the oil in your car, change a tire, care for animals, cook foreign food, treat and prevent common disease through natural means, and any other skill you have a chance to learn.

Remember the wise woman described in Proverbs 31. God calls her more valuable than rubies. She knew sewing, weaving, buying and selling property, street vending, cloth dyeing, planting of vineyards, dealing with the sick and poor, and many other things.

Preacher Tremaine values his wife because she is valuable. She proves her worth over and over. Don't get on a high horse thinking a man should value you because it is his duty to love and adore you even when you act like a miserable shrew. Be worthy. You will never regret learning how to do a wide variety of things.

Debi Interviews the Farmer

You and your wife seem to really have a good marriage plus really great kids. I would like to get your input. I guess my first question would be: What do you think are the most important traits for a wife to possess?

Johnny Answers: Of course, I would say what Michael has already said, that thankfulness is paramount in a woman. And as Tremaine said, a hardworking, willing woman can free a man to be more successful in any endeavor. Since they already covered those most important issues, I will speak of balanced relationships.

When a girl marries, her husband's lot in life is hers. This says a bunch. If a girl marries a farmer, like my wife did, then the girl will be a farmer's wife, which could mean milking cows, making butter, gardening, canning hundreds of jars of vegetables and a thousand other chores. If she was raised in the city this can cause real cultural problems.

Likewise, I suppose, if a man works in the city and must attend social engagements, then a country wife might naturally be a little uncomfortable in that environment. Regardless of how she was raised, she will just have to enjoy adjusting to his needs and be there smiling beside him when the occasion comes up.

A good working marriage can only happen when the family has one vision and works together to achieve it. A couple should not come to marriage with her wanting to live in New York City and him bent on working a farm in Tennessee.

A young man would do very well to consider this carefully when choosing his wife. He should not pull a fish out of its water unless the girl is sincerely enthusiastic about adapting her lifestyle to his.

I have a couple mules that I work with, and I have learned one thing from them: where there are two mules pulling the same wagon, there can be only one driver deciding where to go. Marriage is that way. Two mules with different minds can produce a runaway wagon—sure won't get any work done.

Bible says not to be unequally yoked (2 Corinthians 6:14).

Q. **I have heard you say that love is a choice. What do you mean by that?** Does that mean there is no such thing as falling in love?

A. The feeling of falling in love is nice, but a more accurate way of defining that experience is to say "highly attracted." A good knockout attraction can make you feel like you are falling. A good relationship starts like this:

First there is attraction. There needs to be a natural attraction. But in life there can be many natural attractions which never go anywhere, nor should they.

Next there needs to be evaluation. By that I mean a person needs to say to themselves, "I am attracted to this person, but are we headed the same direction?"

This would mean each person's walk with the Lord, doctrinal beliefs, preferences in work, stations in life, and hopes for the future

No such thing as "love at first sight." Attraction, yes. Love must come later as you grow into knowing the girl.

should be basically the same. Since a woman is the one who has to do all the giving over, it is important for her to think ahead and make a wise decision before she gets emotionally caught up in the relationship. This is where <u>good counsel</u> is very important. If a girl is open to wise counsel she can avoid making bad choices. The trouble is, most girls are mulish when they become attracted to a guy and think he is the one love of their life. Thus the little gals think themselves wiser than those over them. They destroy their chance and their future children's chance of a good life due to lack of waiting on God. This is important because love is a choice; even in the throes of love you can choose to take the wise path rather than the feel-good trail to perpetual conflict.

I wish I knew this several years ago before I gave my heart away to a girl who was going a very different direction than I was in life. She wasn't running headlong into sin but definitely not into the calling God had given me.

Love is a choice. When you are young you want to think that love is falling in love, because you do it so many times and it feels so good. When a young person is highly attracted to someone, they just naturally hope, or "know," this is "the one." But before you allow yourself to go further you need to step back and let your mind perform an evaluation. After you and those who care for you are convinced that you will do well in conforming to his life's goals, and assuming he is equally attracted to you, only then should you proceed with a courtship, or whatever you want to call the steps leading to marriage.

When I first met my wife I was highly attracted, and I knew she liked me. I went home and talked to my parents about her. She was like-minded to my lifestyle and doctrinal belief. We knew she would be a good match for me. Even though I was only nineteen years old and she was sixteen, our parents gladly gave their blessing on our marriage.

It has been a marriage forged in heaven, although it was also carefully orchestrated here on earth. Sometimes I look at her and wonder

"Where no counsel is, the people fall: but in the multitude of counsellors there is safety" (Proverbs 11:14).

how I could be so blessed. There have been financial hard times, and we have done without; but she stands by me, she works with me, she laughs away our trials, and she loves me oh-so-tenderly. I've got goose pimples just thinking about her. Lord, thank you for this woman. I am so blessed.

Your Treasure Chest

"Through wisdom is an house builded; and by understanding it is established: and by knowledge shall the chambers be filled with all precious and pleasant riches" (Proverbs 24:3 & 4).

♥ Will a man someday feel this way about you?

_____

_____

♥ What are the things the men value most?
   ♥ Thankfulness and appreciation of her man.
   ♥ A woman who does not keep score making sure her husband does his equal duty.
   ♥ Hard-working lady to walk along side him.

♥ Write down the areas of your life which you believe will bless your future husband. Add to the list things in your life that you want to refine for that special man. God sees your heart. He knows that you have turned toward him and his way as you have learned. He wants to bless you. Do you feel a tingle of anticipation?

_____

_____

_____

_____

_____

_____

CHAPTER 18

REFLECTIONS

IN CHAPTER 1 WE learned that the girl who ended up getting the preacher prayed *for* the man rather than praying to *get* the man.

We learned that prayer is a tool God commands us to use. We are commanders in spiritual warfare. God's military is standing ready, waiting for us to pray for laborers in the battle for the kingdom. The men in our circle should be on our prayer list as we obey God's command to pray for laborers.

♥ Record your thoughts on what God taught you in chapter 1.

_____

_____

_____

_____

In **Chapter 2** we read the story of Lydia having to decide whether she was open to her parents' advice to accept the proposal of a relative stranger. An important piece of information we learned from Lydia is **that we need to keep our options open.** If she had been secretly hoping on some guy she knew, then she might not have had an open heart to be willing to consider a man who had not caught her attention. We learned that if we are walking in truth and have an open mind to the will of God, then he will direct our way. I guess the key words are open mind and heart, which means she was willing to try to like him. Giving attraction a chance was wise, and lasting love is a choice based on wisdom.

♥ How did this story affect you?

_____

_____

_____

_____

In **Chapter 3** we learned that man was created in God's image, which is in three distinct persons: the Father, the Son and the Holy Spirit. We learned that the Father is King, the Son is Priest, and the Holy Spirit is Prophet. The three offices of Prophet, Priest, and King are found in every culture. Likewise, men come in these three natures. If we marry a man who is in the image of a Prophet (Holy Spirit) we would need to be flexible, encouraging and very chaste in conversation.

♥ Describe a guy you think might be a Prophet type.

In **Chapter 4** we learned that if we married a man who seems more like Jesus, he will be Priestly, kind and serving. He will want his wife to serve others as he will serve those around him. This will mean keeping a gracious home open for hospitality.

♥ What is godly hospitality? How would you use it as a ministry?

In **Chapter 5** we were taught how to be queenly if we marry a man in God the Father's image, a King. We learned how important it is to reverence this type of man. If this man will be used of God, we must learn our place as his helper.

♥ How would you react if you were at the dinner table having cooked a fine meal and were feeding a toddler while holding your infant, and your husband told you to add ice to his tea? Be creative in writing how you hope you will react.

In **Chapter 6** was a big surprise! We learned that guys and gals are different! God created us to fill different roles so as to picture Christ and the church, which is why it's so important to God that we maintain our place as females in his agenda. Our goal is to conform to being the type of woman our man needs, whether he is Prophet, Priest or King.

♥ Write a simple short guideline to a woman's role in marriage.

In **Chapter 7** we were taught to open the door to knowledge, understanding and wisdom. Every day of our lives should be used to learn something new and challenging. If we don't start learning today, then we have lost something.

♥ Make a list of things you have and will implement in your life in making knowledge a part of your being.

In **Chapter 8** we read the story of Ellie and her Italian Prince. Ellie showed us that using her youth to learn and serve made her the kind of woman the Italian Prince highly valued. We learned that the kind of woman we are when we're single will determine the kind of man we attract. Ellie's relationship to her man was more of a buddy-type courtship, which was the same as in the first chapter, the story of the Kid.

♥ List the new projects or studies you are going to embark upon after reading this chapter.

In **Chapter 9** we learned balance as females. None of us wants to be Grab-bers, nor do we want to languish away our life being Hidden Flowers. We learned how to show men we are open to their attention without being a come-on.

💜 Pretend you are quietly sitting in church and this wonderful young man walks in. Your heart starts thumping, you try not to stare, but you wonder how you will ever catch his attention. Give an interesting scenario.

In **Chapter 10** we read several stories about Antsy Babes and the funny or sometimes terrible places being antsy will take you. We are all going to learn to be content and patient until God brings us our man.

💜 Tell of a time when you were antsy...just a little too pushy in a possible relation-ship. Now how would you react?

In **Chapter 11** we had a sobering look into Pie in the Sky texting. Through several true stories we learned that texting can be used by the Devil as an evil weapon to destroy lives. We learned the story of a young homeschool girl who totally wrecked her life by believing in Pie in the Sky. We learned in this chapter that there cannot be an honest, clean courtship through texting.

💜 Write a commitment so that if you are tempted you can turn back to this page and remind yourself of your earlier wisdom.

In **Chapter 12** was a breath of fresh air. Cinderella taught us the preciousness of the firsts you will share with your lover if you walk in truth and purity. Two statements from Cinderella were profound:

> **The first:** As you run fast and hard after Jesus, look to the left and to the right and marry the man who is running beside you.

> **The second:** Don't try to find Mr. Right. Learn to be Miss Right, and the one who finds you will be Mr. Right.

Are you running hard and fast after Jesus, or are you just sitting around being spiritual? Running is doing. Get started in ministry and then become acquainted with those in your circle.

Cinderella's relationship with her man came from him checking her out and then taking her on two dates so he could get to know her before he asked her dad if they could pursue a possible relationship.

♥ What style of courting do you visualize for yourself?

In **Chapter 13** was the Wedding. We learned we have an obligation to prepare to be a good wife by learning trades, saving money, and buying things that will aid our husband when we marry. Our bride taught us that the wedding is the first place you can demonstrate that you are not in this marriage for yourself but for your man. Plan a wedding that will leave you refreshed for the honeymoon!

Our bride taught us that a man proving his honor causes a woman's love to bloom. He gently won her heart. For this bride, love came softly. She is indeed a blessed young woman.

♥ Have you started saving money for your marriage yet? Write down what you are going to do to start making money for your coming life.

Chapter 14 has the story of the rock-and-roll singer getting saved. His young wife could see that she didn't know Jesus like her newly saved husband. It was a wakeup call. We were admonished to make sure we truly know the Savior. <u>Until we are sure we are saved, all else is moot</u>.

♥ Write a note to God concerning how you feel about your relationship with Him.

Chapter 15 was about the fleas. We learned that God uses all manner of things to cause us to reverence our husband. We were also reminded that the rebellion of our youth will follow us into our marriage. We must beware.

♥ Do you think God has ever used anything "different" to get you to turn around? What would you dread most?

In **Chapter 16** was the most sobering of all. The Thread grew dim, so dim it seemed all color had been lost. Through this terrible story we saw how critically important it is for us to keep our minds and hearts full of thankfulness. Stinking Thinking can destroy your marriage and your life.

♥ All of us are guilty of mean, ugly thoughts from time to time. How has this chapter changed the way you think?

_____

_____

_____

_____

In **Chapter 17** we heard from the men. They told us all men are looking for a joyful, uncritical, supportive woman. Through them the bold ribbon found new meaning as we could see it in the lives of the women they love. They spoke highly of their hard-working and smart wives. Farmer Johnny told us that love is a choice. He taught us that just because we are "in love" doesn't mean we should make a commitment to marriage. We learned that we can choose to not love when it is clear that the love we entertain is not wise, and we can choose to love when it is a good choice.

♥ Which of the three men's messages stirred you the most? Why?

_____

_____

_____

_____

If I had to boil this whole book down to one sentence it would be this:

Walk in **truth** and *joy*, become a s e r v a n t, study and learn all manner of different **skills**, practice *honoring* those in authority over you, and *pray* for **every** man you know who seeks the Lord; **pray** that these men have the heart to labor for the harvest.

In all this you will become the kind of woman a man wants and needs. You will become a Miss Right. When you are that kind of woman…God will make sure Mr. Right finds you.

"Trust in the LORD with all thine heart; and lean not unto thine own understanding. In all thy ways acknowledge him, and he shall direct thy paths" (Proverbs 3:5-6).

For Your Final Treasure Chest

♥ I Corinthians 13 is known as the LOVE chapter. God uses the word charity because charity is the act of love–not passion, not feeling–but the deep giving of one's self. Charity is love without asking for an equal return.

If a girl becomes totally acquainted with this chapter, reading it often to wash and re-wash her soul in its purity, and if this girl makes a commitment to have this kind of love, then surely she will become a bride most noted. In the portals of heaven her marriage will be recorded as a glorious picture of things to come. Her husband will adore her, her children will rise up and call her blessed, and indeed, she will be of all women most blessed.

♥ For your Treasure Chest, rewrite this love chapter in your own words, making it your own.

> *"Though I speak with the tongues of men and of angels, and have not charity, I am become as sounding brass, or a tinkling cymbal. And though I have the gifts of prophecy, and understand all mysteries, and all knowledge; and though I have all faith, so that I could remove mountains, and have not charity, I am nothing. And though I bestow all my goods to feed the poor, and though I give my body to be burned, and have not charity, it profiteth me nothing. Charity suffereth long, and is kind; charity envieth not; charity vaunteth not itself, is not puffed up, Doth not behave itself unseemly, seeketh not her own, is not easily provoked, thinketh no evil; Rejoiceth not in iniquity, but rejoiceth in the truth: Beareth all things, believeth all things, hopeth all things, endureth all things. Charity never faileth…"* (I Corinthians 13:1-8).

♥ *"Surely goodness and mercy shall follow me all the days of my life: and I will dwell in the house of the LORD for ever"* (Psalms 23:6).

♥ *"And let us not be weary in well doing: for in due season we shall reap, if we faint not"* (Galatians 6:9).

I can think of nothing
I want more

than someone to *truly love me.*

Teacher's PRE-Guide

So, you want to teach a *Preparing To Be A Help Meet* class? Good for you. It is easy and you will enjoy the challenge. The girls in your class will do most of the work; they only need a guide to keep them on track. Your willingness to take on this endeavor could change the lives of many people and save countless marriages in time to come. A small pebble thrown into a pond continues to make ripples long after the stone rests at the bottom.

Here's how to get started: First, pass out invitations with date, time, place, and how much each girl needs to invest for her copy of the book. Get payment from each girl who wants to participate. Buy the number of books plus a couple more in case other girls join later. Have the girls get their own notebook or diary to record their journey.

▶ **At the first class** have hot tea and some eats prepared. The girls can volunteer to provide refreshments as the class progresses.

▶ **Open the meeting with prayer.** We are here to discuss the material in the book *Preparing To Be A Help Meet*. In this study guide we will be looking up verses and discussing what God says about each subject. You should read the chapter and become very familiar with it before each class. You will need to bring to each class your book, your KJV Bible (so we are all reading from the same translation), and a notebook and pen. Get the girls participating by asking them to share what they hope to learn from the meetings. Be sure to share what you hope to learn.

▶ **Now I will read** *Shalom's Love Story*.

Shalom's Love Story
By Shalom Brand

Since I am writing the *Teacher's Guide* I thought you might want to know my love story. It is truly sweet and grows sweeter with each passing year. My husband and I just celebrated our seventh anniversary. We now have two little girls and a wee newborn son. I am so thankful for God's goodness in our lives. This is my love story.

Every girl I know who has a desire to find a good man and raise a family has the same fear: Will I find the right one?

Is this the one, or what about him? That guy is nice, too. A lot of girls make a list of what they want, or what they *think* they need. I can tell you, we girls don't have a clue as to what we *really* need.

When I was at the end of my nineteenth year, I met the man whom I would come to love and call *My Man*, but at that time, I could not have picked him out in a group of five. He was just one of all the other guys who hung around our community. It was over a year later that I would come to see him as the man for me.

From the time that I was quite young, I knew that I would need lots of wisdom and my parents' guidance in choosing the man to whom I would say "yes." I am a very gullible person. It was this trait that eventually caused me to pray for wisdom and be totally open to counsel.

One summer my dad held a one-week men's Bible and missions training camp. All of us girls helped with the cooking. Justin Brand was there among the rest of the young men for that week. He was only nineteen, and just a boy at heart. His parents had told him that the Pearls had a daughter about his age and had hinted for him to check me out. He did, and he loved me from that brief beginning, although I never even knew who he was.

A year passed.

My brother Gabriel was planning a young people's June weekend camp, and he invited Justin to come down for it. He lived a couple of hours from us. Over the next few months, Justin found one reason or another to come down to visit. He worked in the children's ministry for his church. At that time, my sister and I were making puppets to use as a ministry tool, so he would use that as an excuse to come and borrow the puppets to use in his ministry. He got to know my family during that time.

I worked long hours helping with an old lady, and would come home tired and never really thought about him as a potential husband. I actually did not know a lot about him, but I knew by this time that he liked me a lot, because my brothers were always laughing at how obviously in love he was.

Gabe's camp that summer was on my parents' property. The girls stayed elsewhere, in homes, but the guys camped out down by the creek. We had lots of activities during the day, including volleyball, hiking, swimming, and canoeing. Every chance Justin could find, he was right there telling me what he wanted out of life, and what his goals were. I found it cute that he was so persistent; most guys would have given up. But he knew what he wanted, and he was determined to keep trying.

I had always prayed for wisdom so that when the right man came along, I would just know God's will. I also knew that when my parents finally said "Yes" to someone, that meant something, for they had said "No" to several good, godly men. My dad does not value what most men value. He is not impressed with appearances, money, schooling, houses, jobs, family ties, future possibilities, etc. I cannot explain to you exactly what it is that my dad looked for in a man, but I knew, without a doubt, that I could trust him to make a wise decision.

It was at the end of the camp week, while I was visiting my brother and just getting ready to leave, that Justin pulled up in Gabriel's driveway. I later learned he had called his parents and told them that he was going to talk to me about getting to know me, with the idea of marriage in mind.

I was in the car ready to leave when Justin came flying out of his truck and said, "I need to talk to you." I still had no intention or interest at this time to get to know him, but said I would walk with him so he could talk. He talked and talked about everything he was thinking. I had always thought I would marry someone who was in a ministry. But as he talked, he kept saying, "My family will be my ministry, no matter what I do or where I go; they will come first. My children will know that they mean the world to me. If I lose one of them, then I will lose my heart." He said this with tears in his eyes.

At that moment, God gave me peace in my heart about this persistent young man, and I knew that he was God's man for me. If he loved his children, then he would always do what was right for them and me. Nothing else really mattered. So, after about an hour of him talking with me, I told him, "If my dad says 'yes' then I'll say 'yes'." He turned to me and started to pray and thank God for his blessing, asking God to bless us as we were seeking to do his will.

The next morning, Justin showed up at the house before Dad was awake and waited outside for him to come out. All of us girls went to the herb garden to wait and watch. After about two minutes, Justin came running down the hill yelling, "Yes!"

God is such a big God, and he likes to bless those who want his will and seek after him. Three weeks later we were engaged. Two months after that, we were married. God knows what he is doing. All I had to do was trust him.

Learning to do a word study on **Prayer:**

During these classes you will be asked to do word studies. This is a simple exercise, but one that will greatly expand your understanding and knowledge. This week look up the word *prayer* in a regular dictionary. Record the definition. Select words from the definition (including antonyms, opposite of prayer) and look those words up to expand the definition. Use a concordance or a Bible program on the computer and do a search for the word *prayer* as found in the King James Bible. Find how many times the word is used. Read a few of the passages so that you can get the context of how God uses the word and come to appreciate God's perspective on *prayer*. Jot down a few key verses containing the word *prayer* or *praying*. Record all that you learn so you can share it with the class.

Use this same technique for each week's word study.

HOMEWORK:

1. Ask the girls to pray every morning and evening this next week that God will open their hearts and minds to His leading and will direct them in finding his will for their lives. Have them record it in their notebook, which they will bring to class.

2. Ask each girl to find three verses on prayer for the next meeting. Show them the concordance at the back of their Bible and how to use it.

3. Remind them to read the first chapter of *Preparing To Be A Help Meet* in preparation for the next class.

DISMISS WITH PRAYER.

TEACHER'S GUIDE FOR CHAPTER 1:
THE KID

OPEN WITH PRAYER:
I would like to start this class by thanking God for the opportunity to study his Word and by asking Him to open our hearts and minds.

ICE BREAKER:
Ask the girls the following question and have them write their answer on a small slip of paper and drop it in a box where they will randomly draw out one and read it aloud. Then everybody tries to guess who the author is. (Each week the teacher will need to provide a post-it note pad so all the girls' slips of paper are the same color and size.)

- If you could be the recipient of twenty pounds of anything other than gold, silver or jewels, what would it be?

ASK AND DISCUSS:
Ask the following questions, encouraging the girls to answer. Call on different ones if they hesitate to speak up.

- Did you read the first chapter? (Remind them to always read the next chapter before coming to class. Since this is the first class, you should review the contents of the chapter. Tell them you will call on two or three of them to do the reviews hereafter.)
- How did the Kid's prayers change her life?
- If she had not listened to God and prayed, do you think she would have married Mike?
- Why or why not?
- Could it be that you are missing out on God's best option for you right now because you are not praying?
- If God spoke to you, how would you answer?

READ:
God has spoken to each of us. It is our duty to pray for those who are busy giving the gospel to those who have never heard. We can and do make a

difference in eternity when we pray. If that were not true, prayer would be pointless. God's Word is straight from him. Every word is special.

▶ Have the girls take turns looking up and reading the following verses aloud and comment on them: Matt. 9:38, Luke 10:2, John 15:7, 2 Thessalonians 3:1&2.

READ ALOUD:

Call on girls to read aloud both of these sections in *Preparing To Be A Help Meet*.
- ❤ Why Does God Want Us To Pray?
- ❤ Called To Pray.

READ:

Matthew 18:18 says, **"Verily I say unto you, Whatsoever ye shall bind on earth shall be bound in heaven: and whatsoever ye shall loose on earth shall be loosed in heaven."**

Remember reading about Daniel and how his prayers started a fight between good and evil. Things have not changed. God is still God and we are still called to pray. It is up to us to start the fight. Don't leave the angels waiting while you brush your hair and put on your makeup.

LOOK UP AND READ:

Have the girls look up and read aloud these verses: Matthew 7:7, Luke 11:9, John 16:23

LOOK UP AND READ:

James 4:3-4

God tells us the kind of prayers he will not honor. Did you notice how the other young women that wanted to marry Mike were praying for their own gain? The Kid prayed for him as a warrior of God that needed to fight the war against evil.

ASK AND SHARE:

Who did a word study on *prayer*? Share with us what you learned.

A PRAYING TEST:

Try praying for someone that has made you mad or hurt your feelings, and you will see God answer your prayer by changing your heart toward them. Come next week and tell us what God has done in your life and in their life in answer to your prayer.

HOMEWORK:

Next week read Chapter 2 and pay close attention to how Lydia opened her heart in willingness to consider a man she did not know. She did so because those who were in authority over her felt it was right, so she was willing to consider that it was indeed God's will. She is an example of the verse we read earlier; John 15:7. Also, next time you come to class be prepared to tell why you think Billy chose Lydia over other women whom he might have found attractive. Do a word study on the word *stubborn*.

DO A WORD STUDY ON STUBBORNESS:

This week look up the word **stubborn** in a regular dictionary. Record the definition. Select words from the definition (including antonyms, opposite of stubborn) and look those words up to expand the definition. Go on a Bible program on the computer and do a search for the word stubborn as found in the King James Bible. Find how many times the word is used. Read a few of the passages so that you can get the context of how God uses the word and come to appreciate God's perspective on stubbornness. Jot down a few key verses containing the word stubborn or stubbornness. Record all that you learn so you can share it with the class.

TEACHER'S GUIDE FOR CHAPTER 2:
COURTSHIP TO WHOM?

OPENING:

Last week we read about The Kid and how she prayed for Michael. We learned she prayed for him to be a mighty warrior of God, a laborer of the gospel. This week the story was about a girl named Lydia who was asked to consider marrying a man whom she barely knew.

PRAYER:

Let's start the meeting by asking God to direct us. Who would like to ask God's blessings on this meeting?

ICE BREAKER AND DIRECTIONS:

▶ Ask the girls the 'personal view' question below and have them write their answers on the post-it notes. Then put all the answers in a box and have each person draw out and read the answer, trying to guess the author.

♥ Before we start, let's share our personal view on an important matter. Would you prefer to marry a man ten years older or five years younger than yourself? Why?

FOLLOW UP ON HOMEWORK:

Did each of you girls notice while reading about Lydia that she was not stubborn, but open to God's will? What other things did you notice she did to discover God's will?

ASK AND SHARE:

Who looked up verses on *stubbornness*? Have the girls share what they learned in their study.

READ AND SHARE:

Let's read some verses that tell us what to do to aid us in coming to a knowledge of God's will. Read each statement and have different girls look up the verses. Can stubbornness cause us to miss God's will and maybe even God's man for us? How does a girl know the will of God concerning the person she is to marry?

- She honors God in her youth. 1 Corinthians 7:34
- She is open to counsel. Prov. 11:14 and 12:15
- She proves herself hard working and willing to be a good wife. Proverbs 31:10-31
- She prays for wisdom. James 1:5
- She prays for those in authority over her so that they will be watching for any young man who might be a good match. 1 Timothy 2:2
- She waits with patience and joy. Colossians 1:11, Romans 5:3-4 and 8:25
- She looks for ways to serve others. Galatians 5:13
- When a man of honor asks for her, and those who have watched over her feel he is a good man, then she genuinely seeks the Lord for his direction. Proverbs 19:20-21

FOLLOW UP HOMEWORK:

▶ Ask the girls to respond to these questions:

- Why do you girls think Billy chose Lydia?
- If a good, godly man came knocking on your door, are there things you would not want him to see about you right away?

RESPONSE:

Some of you might say, "Well, if he does not like what I wear, or what I write about, or who I talk to, then I do not want to marry him anyway." If that is how you feel, then you need to lower your standards on what kind of man you want to marry. If you are not the best, then don't expect the best. Guys are watching you all the time to see what kind of girl you are.

- Have you ever noticed a good guy watching you and then one day he no longer does, and you wonder why? Could it be that you did not add up?
- Could it have been something you wore or the way you flirted with him or another guy?
- Could he have read something you put on the web that was off color? Remember what Billy wrote?

  "I searched the internet on anything she might have written to anyone. I found her blog and read all her posts. If I had read flirty nonsense, or noted anything that lacked chastity in her manner, or seen pictures that had alerted me to anything off color, then that would have dismissed her."

LOOK UP AND READ ALOUD:

Proverbs 3:1-6

God calls us to walk in righteousness. As we acknowledge God in our lives, so he will acknowledge himself in our lives.

HOMEWORK:

For the next four lessons we will be learning about the three types of men and which type you will best complement. This is going to be fun. As you read chapter three, think about the men in your life. Try to type them and be ready to talk about it next week.

Do a word study (dictionary and Bible search) on the subject *conversation*. Be prepared to share what you have learned from your word study.

TEACHER'S GUIDE FOR CHAPTER 3:
THE PROPHET

OPENING:

The first week we studied prayer. Last week we saw how being open and not stubborn allows you to be free to hear God speak through those that love you. This week we are beginning our lesson on the three kinds of men. You read about Prophet types in chapter 3.

PRAYER:

Let's start the meeting asking for God's blessing as we study. As we pray, girls, silently ask God to teach you to be open to his will. Who would like to open our meeting up in prayer?

ICE BREAKER:

Before we start, let's do an Ice Breaker to see who thinks they would like to be married to a Prophet/Visionary type.

♥   Be very honest. If you were married to a Prophet and one day he announced he was moving the whole family to Iraq to minister, how would you respond?

DISCUSS:

▶ To start this session, pick two girls to give a review of Chapter 3. What must a wife be and do to become a true help meet for a Prophet/Visionary type man?

READ AND DISCUSS:

▶ Have girls look up verses and read as you teach.

♥   Matthew 12:36

Good intentions don't always keep Visionaries from causing great harm. If they are not wise they can stir up pudding and end up with toxic waste. An unwise wife can add to the poison with negative words, or she can, with simple words of caution, bring attention to the goodness of the pudding and the wisdom in leaving it alone. Every Prophet type needs a good, wise, prudent, stable wife who has a positive outlook on life.

- 1 Timothy 4:12

  You can start learning right now how to have your conversation be coupled with fear. Then, if you are one day married to a Prophet type, you will have chaste conversation, and will not stir your man up in anger against you or others. Learn to be his calming waters.

- Ephesians 2:3, 4:22-32

  A reminder not to let our conversation be ruled by the lust of the flesh.

- Philippians 1:27, 3:20; 1 Peter 1:15

  A link between our conversation and the gospel.

- Hebrews 13:5

  A reminder to be content with what we have.

- James 3:13-18

  The link between wisdom and conversation.

- 1 Peter 3:1-2 and 16

  Conversation without words.

ASK AND SHARE:

▶ Encourage the girls that studied the word *conversation* to present what they learned.

DISCUSS:

Traits that the girls will need to learn to be the wife of a Prophet are listed below. Have the girls discuss these traits:

- Learn how to be flexible.
- Learn how to be loyal to your man.
- Go with the flow.
- Know he will need your support.
- Learn to enjoy the trip.
- One of his greatest needs will be for his wife to think objectively and use common sense.
- You will need to stay in a positive state of mind, yet never jump into his make-believe world, trying to be too much of a cheerleader on dead-end dreams.
- Every wife must guard against negative conversation about people. An idle conversation can create an angry husband.

- A Prophet's wife will need to be tough, not easily given to taking offense at things he says or does.
- She needs to listen, to be supportive, to be his cheerleader.

ASK AND READ:

Can any of you girls think of anything that you could add to this list? What about faith? Read Hebrews 11:1-40.

- You will need a good deal of faith to follow a Prophet/Visionary. Faith sees beyond the things you don't agree with or understand. Faith looks to God to direct your husband as you follow him.

PARTING COMMENTS:

Start now by searching your heart to discover your motive in what you say about other people.

- What is your intent when you speak?
- Do you criticize in order to build yourself up and make others think that you are perfect?

HOMEWORK:

Next week we will be learning about the Priestly/Steady man. Read Chapter 4 and be prepared to give a review. Do a word study on *shamefacedness* and *idleness*. Be prepared to share what you have studied.

CLOSE IN PRAYER

TEACHER'S GUIDE FOR CHAPTER 4:
THE PRIEST

OPENING:

Did you read chapter four in readiness for this class? I know you can think of several men who fit the Priestly type. Let's start this class praying for several of these men that God will cause them to be laborers for the harvest.

ICE BREAKER:

What idle thing do you do more than one time a week? Examples: Excessive reading, standing in front of the mirror, eating, sitting at the computer, chatting/gossiping with friends or excessive exercise.

READ AND DISCUSS :

▶ Now let's get started. Call on two girls to review chapter 4.

Read each of the following, then encourage the girls to respond:
Here are a few things we learned about the Priestly type man.

- ♥ If you marry a Priest, he will want you to walk beside him, yet let you grow in your own right before God and man.
- ♥ A Priest prefers his wife to show some initiative.
- ♥ A Priest likes his wife to be involved in business.
- ♥ He will be proud of your accomplishments. He will want you to use your natural skills, abilities, and drives. Your achievements will be an honor to him, but if you are lazy or slothful it will greatly discourage him.
- ♥ A Priestly man really values a resourceful, hardworking woman who shows dignity and honor. It is very important to the Priest that his wife be self-sufficient in all the mundane tasks of daily living.

ASK AND DISCUSS

- ♥ Do you know any man who is very much this Priestly type?
- ♥ Is your dad Priestly?
- ♥ What could you do as a daughter that would please him?
- ♥ What are some other qualities you think a Priestly type would want to have in his wife?

READ ALOUD AND DISCUSS:

▶ Encourage the girls to contribute what they have learned about *shamefacedness* and *idleness*.

Let's read a few scripture verses on *laziness*. The word idle means: inactive, lazy, useless, slothful, slow. If we are idle as singles, we will be idle as married girls. Let's see what God says about *idleness* or *slothfulness*.

- ♥ Proverbs 19:15 - slothfulness
- ♥ Ecclesiastes 10:18 - slothfulness
- ♥ 1 Timothy 5:13 - idle
- ♥ Proverbs 31:27 - idleness
- ♥ Ezekiel 16: 49 - idleness
- ♥ Romans 12:9-21- slothful
- ♥ Hebrews 6:9-12 - slothful

ASK AND DISCUSS:

▶ Get the girls talking by asking these questions:

- ♥ What are you doing today to learn skills for the future?
- ♥ If you could do anything every day for the rest of your life, what would it be?

SUMMARY:

A good wife will conform herself to her husband's needs and interests. She will use her time to make her home a pleasant place to gather. She will learn to cook for groups and become a gracious hostess. Her strength and ministry will be hospitality. This will bring him honor.

Start today and learn how to pay bills, make appointments, and entertain guests with a competence that will bring your husband-to-be satisfaction. Your hobbies should be creative and useful. Learn useful things that you can pass on to your children. If you are busy and productive now, then it will be who you are once you are married. Your skills and achievements will be your husband's résumé. If you are wise and competent, then he must be even more so, the onlooker will think. At the end of the day, your Priestly husband will enjoy weighing what he has accomplished with what you have accomplished and will rejoice in the value of having a worthy partner in the grace of life.

DISCUSS:

▶ Give the girls an opportunity to say what they plan on doing differently with their lives since reading this chapter.

HOMEWORK:

For next time read chapter five. We will be reading about the Kingly type of man. This week as we read, we will be learning how to serve others. Do a word study on the phrase, *in subjection.*

CLOSE IN PRAYER

TEACHER'S GUIDE FOR CHAPTER 5:
THE KING

OPENING:

This week we read about the Kingly type. Raise your hand if you think your dad is a 100% kingly type. How about your pastor?

Kingly types are not common. A group of people only needs one king, so God seems to limit the number of kingly types. Can anyone think of a young boy who shows kingly traits?

PRAYER:

Let's get started by opening in prayer. Who would like to ask God's blessings on us as we seek to prepare to become good help meets?

ICE BREAKER:

Describe the perfect boss in four words or less.

READ:

A King does not want his wife involved in any project that prevents her from serving him. If you are blessed to win the favor of a strong, forceful, bossy man, then it is very important for you to learn how to serve with joy. Today we are going to study how to serve with joy.

ASK AND DISCUSS:

Who studied the phrase *in subjection*? Share what the phrase means.

READ AND DISCUSS:

In subjection means, to put under or subdue to be in obedience, submitting oneself to another; to be enclosed or shut up in a place; to be bound by the law. This phrase is also translated: submit, subject, submitting, obey, obedient, obedience, put under, subdue.

▶ Read the next sentence and encourage the girls to talk. After a few minutes, stop the opinion talk.

Is it God's will for a wife to submit to her husband? Should a wife seek understanding from God before she obeys her husband? If a pastor tells a woman to do one thing and her husband tells her to do another, who should she obey?

READ AND DISCUSS:

Open your Bibles and read what God says concerning submitting.

- ♥ Philippians 3:21
- ♥ Colossians 3:18
- ♥ Titus 2:5,9 and 3:1
- ♥ Hebrews 12:9
- ♥ James 4:7
- ♥ 1 Peter 2:13-18
- ♥ 1 Peter 3:1, 5, 22
- ♥ 1 Peter 5:5
- ♥ 1 Timothy 2:11 and 3:4

SUMMARY:

When a Kingly Man, lost or saved, is treated with honor and reverence by a good help meet, she will find that her man will be wonderfully protective and supportive. In most marriages, the strife is not because the man is cruel or evil; it is because he expects obedience, honor, and reverence, and is not getting it. He reacts badly.

Start today practicing these things:

- ♥ Be in subjection to those in authority over you.
- ♥ Practice every day serving with a cheerful heart.
- ♥ Look for ways to serve your family.
- ♥ Ask your pastor if there is a place for you to serve in the church, and don't ask for the fun job. Do the job everyone else passes by.

HOMEWORK:

In Chapter 6 we will learn the female types and how our types match with men's. In readiness for next week's lesson, read Chapter 6 and type yourself, and do a word study on the word *example*.

Let's close in prayer and thank God for allowing us (in our future) to be our man's help meet.

TEACHER'S GUIDE FOR CHAPTER 6:
THREE TYPES OF WOMEN

OPENING:

After reading chapter 6 we should all know what type we are! In this class we will discuss what type of man each of us would best complement.

PRAYER:

▶ Ask one of the girls to open the class by asking God's blessing and direction on the class.

ICE BREAKER:

Is your Dad a Prophet, Priest or King?

ASK AND DISCUSS:

Start this session by having the girls discuss what type they are.

- ❤ What type are you?
- ❤ Do you have a friend that is a Dreamer?
- ❤ Have you ever been irritated at some other girl because of her type?
- ❤ From what you have read, what type of man would you complement the most with your gifts?

SERVANT MARRIES A KING:

Let's all think about this: If you are a servant type girl and you marry a King, you must learn to be strong and confident. This type of man will need a Queen to stand with him to help lead the people.

We read an example of this in the story of Esther. Queen Esther served the king three special meals. As queen, she had many servants to do her bidding. That she chose to serve him showed her humility and gave him honor. She did this to win his favor for the sake of her people, the Jews, who were already condemned to die. She could have stood in the corner and cried, "What can I do? I am just a girl. If I speak out, then my life will be at stake because I am secretly a Jew. Why did God put me here with such a cruel man?"

Queen Esther used her position as his wife to win his heart, then she begged for mercy. Instead of blaming the king for his lack of mercy and wisdom, she appealed to him as her lord. When the king had heard her humble yet bold appeal, he realized that he had been listening to evil men that had intentionally counseled him in such a way that would have resulted in the death of many innocent people, including his own wife. Esther had to become a queen with a servant's heart.

ASK:

Will any of you shy girls speak up and say how you might have reacted if you had been in Esther's position?

ASK AND SHARE:

Girls, ask yourself these questions: Am I a Go-to Gal or a Dreamer gal? What will I need to better equip myself if I marry a Kingly type man?

GO-TO GAL OR DREAMER GAL MARRIES A KING:

Go-to Gals and Dreamer gals will both need to learn to wait on their man to lead them. Never try to control them. Dreamers, do not become upset when your King takes the credit for what you create. The better the people love the King, the more they will honor his Queen.

Go-to Gal: If this type of girl can learn to reverence her husband, then they will go far as a couple. His leadership with her leadership can mean a very strong team. Usually Go-to Gal females never learn to submit and reverence, so instead of being a strong team, they become competitors. Their marriage will not be happy.

SERVANT MARRIES A PROPHET:

Let's talk about the mix of a Prophet marrying a Servant. What will this girl need that might naturally be lacking?

READ:

The Prophet type will make a great boyfriend because he will focus totally on his sweetie. He will be very romantic, giving flowers and gifts. If you catch the heart of a Prophet you will be his consuming passion, his greatest challenge, his dream come true. A few weeks after marriage, though, his focus will turn to another challenge. If you are his new bride you will feel abandoned. It is important for all girls to understand this great truth regardless what type you marry. You need a vibrant life before your man comes on the scene. A clingy useless wife that lacks drives, goals, ambitions, or dreams is just that: useless.

Right now, do you have a purposeful life? If you do, then when your Prophet/Visionary new husband suddenly becomes focused on some strange new driving project, your life will go on smoothly and happily. You need to remember never to be offended that he focuses on something other than you. It is his type. He can do no other. When he does turn his attention to you all the other wives will be jealous, for you will have the most romantic man around.

ASK AND DISCUSS:
What do you girls think about that?

SHARE:
▶ Have the girls who did a word study on the word *example* tell what they learned.

LEARNING BY EXAMPLE:
Look up and read: I Timothy 4:12.

OBSERVE:
I suggest you look around at the different couples that you see who are happily raising a family and ministering to other people. What are their types? How do they function as a team? Learn from their success. Notice how they respond to each other and other little things about them that bring forth good fruit. Make notes so that you will learn by their example. Also look around at couples that you see where there doesn't seem to be a balance. Learn what you don't want from them.

HOMEWORK:
Next week you will be reading chapter 7. I want each of you to come prepared to tell the class what practical thing you plan on learning which will help you be a better help meet. Be sure to follow through with how, where, and so on concerning this schooling. Do a word study on the word *knowledge*.

CLOSE IN PRAYER

TEACHER'S GUIDE FOR CHAPTER 7:
KNOWLEDGE

OPENING:

This chapter is practical. What did you think about the Death Angel story? Does anyone have a short story they would like to tell that taught them a serious lesson?

OPEN WITH PRAYER

ICE BREAKER:

Name one practical thing you have studied that you could share your knowledge of, and one practical thing you've not studied that you would like to, in order to make yourself a better help meet.

READ:

Where It Starts

Many girls waste their youth by being entertained with movies or novels, shopping, playing the social game, yakking on the phone, texting, etc., or just waiting for one of those things to happen. When someone hands them a book like *Preparing To Be A Help Meet,* they grimace and say, "I'm not much of a reader…it's just so hard; it's boring," or "I'm just so busy, I don't have time to read books like that; besides, I've already read one like that before." And so their life stays limited for lack of knowledge, understanding, and wisdom.

Not you! You have received in this book a lifetime of knowledge, wisdom from many different ladies. What you have learned about the three kinds of men and your responsibility before God in responding to your man will, if you use this knowledge, open the door to a life that you can really live.

READ ALOUD AND DISCUSS:

▶ Have the girls share what they learned about the word *knowledge*. Then have the them look up the following verses, read them aloud and discuss.

- ❤ Exodus 31:3-5
- ❤ Proverbs 1:20-22
- ❤ Proverbs 5:1-2

- Proverbs 8:10-14
- Proverbs 21:11
- Proverbs 23:12

READ AND SHARE:

Read I Peter 4:8-10. Encourage the girls to share their plans.
Hospitality is a gift that we need to develop.
What four families are you inviting over for dinner, what will you cook, and what entertainment will you provide?

READ AND SHARE:

▶ Read Luke 12:42-43. Encourage the girls to share their reactions.
Did you ever think that stretching a dollar was a function of a good help meet? It is, and we need practice.
What family do you plan to buy for, and where are you going to shop?

READ AND SHARE:

▶ Read Matthew 20:27-28. Encourage the girls to share their reactions.
Learning responsibility is greater than just being a servant. It is learning to take charge. It is actively looking for needs and meeting them.
What family do you plan to serve for one week, and in what way will you help them?

SUMMARY:

Don't wait to be asked to help. Be constantly attentive. If a room needs cleaning, then clean it. If a child is struggling to get his shoes on, immediately offer to help the child.

As you help this family, remember that you are practicing to be a mother, not to be a helpful daughter. You can practice being a helpful daughter at home. Once you are a mother you will have to serve without direction or thanks, so practice now.

HOMEWORK:

For next week read chapter 8. Read Proverbs 31:10-31. Be prepared to match each verse with its description at next week's meeting.

TEACHER'S GUIDE FOR CHAPTER 8:
THE ITALIAN PRINCE

OPENING:

We knew the Italian Prince since he was a young man. He was very focused and highly motivated in preparing himself for the ministry. We knew he would need a help meet that would not slow him down. He would need a girl that had been busy preparing herself to be an active help meet to a true man of God. When he met Ellie, her life was as full and exciting as his. You could say he met his match.

Today we are going to talk about what you are doing to meet your match.

OPEN IN PRAYER:

ICE BREAKER:

Where do you want to be in five years? And what are you doing now to get there?

READ:

▶ Here is an additional story from Shalom (Pearl) Brand, author of the teacher's guide we're following.

THE BUTTERFLY AND THE WORKER:

A few weeks ago I attended a large, splendid wedding. While I was there I couldn't help but notice two very different girls.

One of the girls had come to the wedding as a guest, resplendent in a beautiful dress, her hair done up, looking her finest. She saw a sudden, urgent need for help in the kitchen, and didn't hesitate for a moment to pitch in—she spent the entire wedding in the back, cheerfully helping prepare and then serve the food with a smile on her face.

Now, the other girl was invited to take part in the wedding as a helper. During the wedding, and during the dinner later, she did nothing but flitter around like a butterfly that had lost its way. It was obvious she wanted to let all the guys know she was there and available.

I stepped into a back room to get something for one of my children and overheard several people talking. They were all quite taken by the hardworking, happy volunteer. She was so beautiful, so refined, so this and so that. The small crowd then shifted its gaze when the second girl walked by, still fluttering uselessly around. Their pinched up faces spoke volumes enough, but someone couldn't hold their tongue. "That one is certainly a worthless piece."

Word travels fast. Doubtlessly every mother, father, brother and sister heard about both girls. Do you think the socialite "look at me" girl will have young men looking her up? I don't think so—at least, not the kind of young men a girl should be interested in. As a rule, strong, godly men do not seek out lazy divas—but they will notice the girl that enhanced the joy and beauty of a wedding day by her cheerful hard work and servant's heart.

READ ALOUD:

▶ Ask the girls to read aloud together I Corinthians 7:34.

READ:

▶ Read each verse of Proverbs 31:10-31. Have each girl call out words to describe the lady in the verse. These words are included for you to help guide the girls.

Verse 10: **Who can find a virtuous woman? For her price is far above rubies.** (key words: rare, uncommon, unusually excellent, unique, precious, matchless.)

Verse 11: **The heart of her husband doth safely trust in her, so that he shall have no need of spoil.** (key words: honorable, faithful, chaste, trustworthy, inspires confidence, honest.)

Verse 12: **She will do him good and not evil all the days of her life.** (key words: enduring, unchanging, loyal, permanent.)

Verse 13: **She seeketh wool and flax, and worketh willingly with her hands.** (key words: industrious, hardworking, diligent, patient.)

Verse 14: **She is like the merchants' ships; she bringeth her food from afar.** (key words: frugal, not wasteful, wise shopper.)

Verse 15: **She riseth also while it is yet night, and giveth meat to her**

household, and a portion to her maidens. (key words: motivated, self-starter, energetic, proactive)

Verse 16: **She considereth a field, and buyeth it: with the fruit of her hands she planteth a vineyard.** (key words: enterprising, resourceful, active in business, frugal.)

Verse 17: **She girdeth her loins with strength, and strengtheneth her arms.** (key words: hardworking, physically fit, diligent laborer.)

Verse 18: **She perceiveth that her merchandise is good: her candle goeth not out by night.** (key words: consistent, always available, considers value, wise.)

Verse 19: **She layeth her hands to the spindle, and her hands hold the distaff.** (key words: diligent, dependable, willing to do repetitive work)

Verse 20: **She stretcheth out her hand to the poor; yea, she reacheth forth her hands to the needy.** (key words: compassionate, merciful, generous, hospitable, actively seeking those in need.)

Verse 21: **She is not afraid of the snow for her household: for all her household are clothed with scarlet.** (key words: prepared, watch-care, dependable.)

Verse 22: **She maketh herself coverings of tapestry; her clothing is silk and purple.** (key words: self-sufficient, masters skills of sewing, crafts and weaving.)

Verse 23: **Her husband is known in the gates, when he sitteth among the elders of the land.** (key words: respected, supporter, encourager, brings honor.)

Verse 24: **She maketh fine linen, and selleth it; and delivereth girdles unto the merchants.** (key words: organized, managerial, creative, makes and keeps contracts)

Verse 25: **Strength and honour are her clothing; and she shall rejoice in time to come.** (key words: strong, confident, capable, cheerful, stable.)

Verse 26: **She openeth her mouth with wisdom; and in her tongue is the law of kindness.** (key words: discerning, kind, gentle, thoughtful.)

Verse 27: **She looketh well to the ways of her household, and eateth not the bread of idleness.** (key words: reliable, hardworking, responsible.)

Verse 28: **Her children arise up, and call her blessed; her husband also, and he praiseth her.** (key words: rewarded, reapeth, joyous.)

Verse 29: **Many daughters have done virtuously, but thou excellest them all.** (key thought: virtue means acting power. She earned her place.)

Verse 30: **Favour is deceitful, and beauty is vain: but a woman that feareth the LORD, she shall be praised.** (key thought: fear of God is the beginning of wisdom.)

Verse 31: **Give her of the fruit of her hands; and let her own works praise her in the gates.** (key words: complimented, deserving, admired, applauded, worthy.)

God's estimation of a virtuous woman?

She is one hard working, creative, frugal, cheerful, kind and pleasant lady.

HOMEWORK:

Read chapter 9. Do a word study on the word *virtue*. Make a list of qualities you want in your Prince and find verses to describe each one. Come dressed in the perfect outfit for your first date.

CLOSE IN PRAYER

TEACHER'S GUIDE FOR CHAPTER 9:
FINDING BALANCE

OPENING:

How many felt a tiny bit embarrassed as you read about Grabbers and Hidden Flowers? Did you see how important it is to be balanced in how we live our lives? This was a good wake-up call.

PRAYER:

Call on someone to open in prayer.

ICE BREAKER:

Describe the perfect first date with the man you are going to marry. Stand up and show us your outfit for your first date.

DISCUSS:

Share your homework list of what you admire in a man and the verses you have found.

ASK AND DISCUSS:

Ask the girls the following questions. Encourage them to discuss the subjects. Keep it light and fun.

A GRABBER:

- ♥ What is a Grabber?
- ♥ Why do girls become Grabbers?
- ♥ Have any of you ever acted like a Grabber?
- ♥ Would your friends think you are a Grabber?
- ♥ Have you ever seen a girl that was acting like a Grabber and you became jealous that she was getting all the attention? The Bible has a chapter warning young men against Grabbers.

Have all the girls open their Bibles to Proverbs chapter 5. Take turns reading a verse and discussing it.

ASK AND DISCUSS:

Ask questions and encourage the girls to talk.

- What is a Hidden Flower?
- Why do girls become Hidden Flowers?
- Have any of you ever acted overly spiritual or tried to appear better than others?
- Would your friends say you are a Hidden Flower?

Encourage the girls to share: Who did a study on the word *virtue*? Read these verses to add to any that the girls share:

- II Peter 1:3
- II Peter 1:5

READ, DISCUSS AND MEMORIZE:

These are two passages on virtue that I encourage you to commit to memory.

- Philippians 4:8
- II Peter 1:5-8

HOMEWORK:

Read Chapter 10 and do a word study on the word *patience*.

CLOSE IN PRAYER

TEACHER'S GUIDE FOR CHAPTER 10:
ANTSY BABES

OPENING:

We all get antsy when things seem to be sitting still. We saw in this chapter that there are ways to get around this problem. Our word study was on patience, so we will be hearing from those of you who studied what God says about patience.

OPEN IN PRAYER

ICE BREAKER:

What was your most embarrassing moment?

ASK AND DISCUSS:

Now let's get started. Who did a study on patience? Share with us what you learned. This is a list of synonyms for patient. Call out an antonym beside each word that will help you resist reacting in this way.

- ❤ Enduring
- ❤ Tolerant
- ❤ Unwearied
- ❤ Uncomplaining
- ❤ Longsuffering
- ❤ Serene

READ AND DISCUSS:

▶ Have the girls read these verses and discuss them.

- ❤ Romans 15: 4-5
- ❤ I Thessalonians 1:3
- ❤ Hebrews 12:1
- ❤ James 1:4
- ❤ What is the most important lesson you have learned in this section?
- ❤ What is the most important lesson you have learned so far in this book?
- ❤ Read these questions and let the girls think about them.
- ❤ In the past, have you been antsy? How?

- Have you ever been guilty of being just a little bit of a Grabber?
- Are you a Hidden Flower? Describe how.
- What good opportunities to serve will you seek now that you recognize yourself as a Hidden Flower?
- Have you been just a little lazy and not aggressive enough to look for opportunities to serve? What are you going to start seeking?
- Are you willing to do the less "cool" jobs and serve more as a real servant? Name some small serving jobs that you could do.
- Have you ever demanded, even nicely, an answer from a guy? How would you approach the situation now?
- What was Ellie doing with her life while she waited?
- What verse kept her focused?
- Do you think staying busy helps keep your mind and heart patient? What are you going to do to get busy?

For next week's meeting read Chapter 11. Review the word study you did on *conversation* and be ready to share some new ideas on the subject.

CLOSE IN PRAYER

TEACHER'S GUIDE FOR CHAPTER 11:
PIE IN THE SKY

OPENING:

This was the hardest hitting chapter yet. It is a new kind of sin that the Devil is now using to destroy lives. We need to ask God to give us open hearts and ears to hear so that we can learn this lesson and avoid disgracing ourselves, our parents and God.

PRAYER:

Someone open us up in prayer to this end.

ICE BREAKER:

Write on a slip of paper how many pairs of shoes, counting boots, you have in your closet. (Draw out and let the girls guess who is the greatest shoe diva.)

OPENING QUESTION:

What was the most monumental text or email that you have ever written or received?

READ:

So this week you read some sad stories about love made in the imagination of our hearts. It is easy for a girl to fall victim to this kind of love. But the Lord has given us a clear way to keep our hearts safe. Here is what the Bible says about imagination, "The imagination of the heart is wicked."

READ AND DISCUSS:

▶ Have the girls read and discuss these verses.

- ♥ Genesis 6:5
- ♥ Genesis 8:21
- ♥ Deuteronomy 5:29
- ♥ Deuteronomy 28:47
- ♥ Proverbs 16:9, 21-23

READ AND DISCUSS:

With new technology comes new challenges in relationships. This instant access to every trivial detail of our lives can quickly create emotional intimacy and dependency.

ASK:

Girls, ask yourself: would you share on the same level if that man were in your presence, observing your real self in daily life?

A man is captured by physical appeal. Man's temptation is sexual lust. A man taking a whorish woman doesn't get to know her and wouldn't recognize her on the street three days later.

A woman is hooked by emotional openness. The woman's temptation is to be physically admired. Some girls unknowingly cross the line into intimacy with men who are not their husbands…they do it texting. When we feel lonely and know John Doe is always sympathetic, we are tempted to chat with him online. Our lust is just as evil as the man's lust; just different.

READ ALOUD:

Let's read a few verses on where our hearts as single girls should be.
Proverbs 3:5: **"Trust in the Lord with all thine heart; and lean not unto thine own understanding."**

LOOK UP AND DISCUSS:

▶ Have the girls look up and discuss:
- ♥ Deuteronomy 13:3-5
- ♥ Deuteronomy 6:5
- ♥ Deuteronomy 30:14-17
- ♥ Psalms 24:4
- ♥ Psalms 27:14
- ♥ Psalms 37:4
- ♥ Psalms 111:10
- ♥ Proverbs 4:23
- ♥ Proverbs 1:7

HOMEWORK:

Look up the following verses and be prepared to talk about them next week. Do any word chases that come to mind from these verses. Read Chapter 12 for next week.

- II Corinthians 11:2-3
- Titus 2:5
- I Peter 3:2-3

CLOSE IN PRAYER

TEACHER'S GUIDE FOR CHAPTER 12:
CINDERELLA

OPENING:

Last week was Pie in the Sky. Did any of you change your habits on texting this week? Any wise person would have given it grave consideration. This week was about a modern day Cinderella. This chapter had some very salient statements in it. We are going to recap a few of those this week and let you talk about them.

PRAYER:

Let's open in prayer. Who would like to pray for us?

ICE BREAKER:

Who was the first guy you ever had a crush on?

Tell the girls about yours first, then let girls give their answers.

DISCUSS:

▶ Talk about these verses: II Corinthians 11: 2-3, Titus 2:5, and I Peter 3: 2-3.

❤ What does chaste mean?

❤ What is a modern day word for chaste?

❤ Explain three ways that you can show that you are a chaste woman?

READ AND DISCUSS:

▶ Read each quote below, then read the question. Give your own answer or get one of the girls to answer each question and discuss it as a group.

Quotes from Cinderella:

❤ I realized that I was building my reputation as someone's future wife. Someday my husband would either be honored or dishonored by my conduct as a single woman. **"She does her husband good and not evil all the days of her life."**

Did you realize that during your single years you are building your reputation as a wife? What have you learned that will change the way you conduct yourself?

♥   Most girls tote a fat list of credentials and want to marry a sold-out, godly man, but few of us have taken the beam out of our own eye.

Think about what kind of girl the man of your dreams will want to marry.

♥   You are building faith and character to take into your marriage to bless your husband and future children.

What are some character traits that you can be strengthening now?

♥   Each "first" was like a special present I had saved for him. Once you realize a man is going to be your husband, you wish you had never given any guy in your past even the time of day.

Tell us a simple first you will present to your prince.

♥   My advice is to love the Lord your God with all your heart, soul and mind, to seek Him in everything, no matter what trials come. If you are seeking the Lord, He will direct your steps and lead you. Don't have a fairytale mentality of sitting at home waiting for your prince. Anytime God did something in the Bible, it required action.

We have discussed getting involved in activities of serving others in previous chapters. After reading this story, do you have further ideas of what you could be involved in?

♥   One thought always helped me weed out potentials: Is this the kind of guy I want to bring home to Thanksgiving dinner to meet all my family? Is this the kind of guy that I want to be seen or known to be with?

Tell us one thing that you see in men that you know you would not want to introduce to Grandma. (For instance, a purple-haired, smoker, etc.)

♥   I grew frustrated and complained to my parents, "He never says he likes me. What kind of girl does he think I am? I don't continue a relationship with a guy if it is not going anywhere." My praying mama soothed, "Honey, he is studying you right now to make an informed decision."

Mom might have saved her from being Antsy or even a Grabber! Think of a time when you wanted to grab. Tell us about it.

♥   I tried to think ten years into our marriage—if I felt like leaving, what would keep me in? The thought kept coming back that God called David and me into this marriage. I leaned on this reflection heavily as it was confirmed through parents, friends and prayer.

Notice her list of how she felt confirmed. What would your list be?

♥   Girls, don't give up and don't settle for less. Become the girl of a godly man's dreams. And don't mess around with any guys that aren't your godly prince.

Think about how what you are doing now will affect your future.

♥   We purposed to never seek marital advice from our parents or friends after marriage. We wanted to honor and respect one another publicaly. We do, however, believe in mentoring and accountability. I started meeting for marriage mentoring with an older, godly woman once a month after we got married. Titus 2:2-5: **"The aged women likewise…That they may teach the young women to be sober, to love their husbands, to love their children, To be discreet, chaste, keepers at home, good, obedient to their own husbands, that the word of God be not blasphemed."**

Think of someone you might be able to seek out for counsel.

♥   Pick a quiet, unassuming lady who others might pass by. Remember that when you seek counsel you will be actually helping the older woman stay focused on God's will in her marriage. Start praying for God's blessing and wisdom for that lady. She will need plenty of God's understanding to be a good counselor.

HOMEWORK:

The next chapter is an interview with a new bride about her beautiful wedding. Write down things you know you want for your wedding. Also, as you read the next chapter write down your weekly, yearly and life goals. We will read some of them next week.

TEACHER'S GUIDE FOR CHAPTER 13:
THE WEDDING

OPENING:

At this meeting we are going to be talking about our dreams and plans for our weddings. It will be fun to hear from all of you.

PRAYER:

Let's start by thanking God for all that we have learned concerning becoming a good help meet.

ICE BREAKER:

What was the funniest thing you have ever seen or heard about that happened at a wedding?

READ:

This is Shalom (Pearl) Brand's story of a funny moment at her wedding.

My funniest moment came when I had only been married for about thirty minutes. My Prince Charming and I were cutting our wedding cake together. He sweetly fed me a bite of cake. Then, beaming, I picked up some cake to put in his mouth. You need to understand that he is not one for old traditions! Instead of closing his mouth like a normal, polite guy, he blew that big mouthful of cake out all over me. I had cake all over my dress, hair and face. The ladies watching gasped in horror, but the men burst into laughter. My new husband and I both started laughing as we rubbed cake off my hair. This might make you say, "How dare he!" but when we are 70 we will tell our grandkids and we will still be laughing. I am laughing as I write. You have to know my man to really appreciate just how funny it was.

DISCUSS:

▶ Have the girls talk about the kind of wedding they are planning and let each girl say how their plans have changed since reading the book.

▶ Have the girls talk about the weekly, yearly and life goals each girl wrote. Then ask, "If you only had $500 to spend on your wedding, how would you spend it?" "How would you spend $50,000?"

READ:

Another note from Shalom:

I have seen some fun weddings and some stressful ones. It is easy to assess what makes one wedding joyful and the next wedding tense. I have summed the difference into one word: Thankfulness. An unthankful bride gets personally offended if everything doesn't go her way. In her mind, it is her day and it better be to her liking. It is a poor way to feel, especially on your wedding day.

Some brides radiate profound joy. People want to help when they see a thankful, joyous bride. Here is a good example of how thankfulness can make a wedding special. Once I went to a wedding that had really nice flowers and decorations. I'll call this bride "Bride A." I had another friend marrying just four days later. I'll call her "Bride B." Anyway, I knew that Bride B would have very few flowers due to lack of funds. While at the first wedding I asked Bride A if after everyone left I could get some of the decorations for Bride B. The now married Bride A was delighted to share her used flowers. The colors of the new decorations and flowers were not the colors Bride B had chosen, yet when she saw what I had brought she was so thankful. Everyone helping at the wedding was smiling as they quickly began rearranging the unexpected bounty, creating the most beautiful, exotic outdoor wedding I have ever seen.

Believe me when I say this: if a bride is not controlling and uptight, but obviously just happy to be marrying the man of her dreams, then everyone will want her wedding to be beautiful and will do all they can to make that happen for her. It is a day to be remembered, not for its beauty, extravagance, or grandeur, but for the joy and happiness of the occasion. Learn to be thankful. Learn to be flexible. Learn <u>what</u> to value and <u>what not</u> to value.

SUMMARY:

The sentence, "**O give thanks unto the LORD, for he is good: for his mercy endureth for ever**" appears four times in Scripture. Look them up and mark them in your Bible. (Psalms 107:1, 118:1, 118:29, 136:1) The words "give thanks" appear 80 times in Scripture. It is remarkable that God tells us 80 times to give thanks. It is important that we obey.

Also look up and discuss Psalms 92:1 and 105:1.

HOMEWORK:

Next week we will be reading Chapter 13. This chapter is asking us the big question: do you really know Jesus? Each of you needs to look up and read the scripture for each question. I will randomly ask the questions, so be prepared to answer.

CLOSE IN PRAYER

TEACHERS GUIDE FOR CHAPTER 14:
ALL THINGS NEW & BEAUTIFUL

ICE BREAKER:

Have any of you ever had a déjà vu? This is when you experience an event that you feel like you have already experienced before. It is a creepy feeling that you feel your life has already happened. Encourage the girls to share.

OPENING:

The chapter we are covering today could be the most important one for you. It is easy to get caught up into what is going on around us. It used to be called jumping on the bandwagon. When you grow up in church it is easy to just get on the bandwagon because all our friends are there and never really come to know and love the Savior. This is why we must take this time to examine ourselves and our walk with the Savior. Personalities are different. One girl can be sure she is saved and never have a doubt simply because it is her personality to not give over to self-doubt. Another girl might often question her relationship with God. God gives us a directive regardless of our confidence level: **"Examine yourselves, whether ye be in the faith; prove your own selves. Know ye not your own selves, how that Jesus Christ is in you, except ye be reprobates?"** Today's class will be a sober time of doing just that.

PRAYER:

Pray that God will open our hearts to truth.

READ AND DISCUSS:

▶ Read each question and ask the girls to look up the verses and take turns reading one aloud. Discuss each one.

- ❤ How much righteousness does it take to get to heaven? Matthew 5:20
- ❤ Will any be turned away who believe they are saved? Luke 13:24, Matthew 7:13, Matthew 7:22-23
- ❤ Is it enough to believe in God? James 2:19
- ❤ How many sins does one have to commit to be lost? James 2:10

- ♥ Paul gives a list of sins in Romans 1:21-22 that are worthy of death. What are the two first sins?
- ♥ Are you guilty of not glorifying God or of being unthankful?
- ♥ How many times must you lie to your friends for them to think of you as a liar?
- ♥ How many times could you steal from someone before they thought you to be a thief?
- ♥ Have you ever said of someone, "She is a liar"? Matthew 7:2
- ♥ Is there anything you can do that will make you acceptable to God? Romans 3:10-12
- ♥ What is the penalty of sin? Roman 6:23, Hebrews 9:27

READ ALOUD AND ASK:

▶ Read Luke 16:19-31 and give a summary

- ♥ How many people are lost and in need of forgiveness?
- ♥ Are you one?

READ:

God wants you to know him. He gave everything that your sins might be washed away and he could receive you as his own. His salvation comes from understanding and receiving his forgiveness. It is a choice...your choice.

- ♥ What work do I need to do to be saved? Ephesians 2:8-9
- ♥ Why did Jesus have to die? Romans 3:23, I Corinthians 15:1-4, Hebrews 9:22B, Ephesians 1:7
- ♥ How did God obtain forgiveness for you? Isaiah 53:10
- ♥ Can you be perfect before God? II Corinthians 5:21
- ♥ God looks on the heart. He knows if you are turning to him.
- ♥ Is salvation by works or grace? Romans 4:3-4, Romans 11:6
- ♥ How can you know you are saved? Romans 8:16, John 3:18, I John 5:13
- ♥ God says, **"For the preaching of the cross is to them that perish foolishness; but unto us which are saved it is the power of God."** I Corinthians 1:18
- ♥ Have you enjoyed reading the Scriptures that teach what Christ has done for you? God says that if you know him then simply reading these verses will fill you with the power of God.

♥ Ephesians 1:18-20

HOMEWORK:

Next week we will be reading chapter 15. Do a word study on either *reverence* or *honor*. Come prepared to share your study in class.

CLOSE IN PRAYER:

Thank God for his wonderful mercy and grace.

TEACHER'S GUIDE FOR CHAPTER 15:
A LESSON ON FLEAS

OPENING:

Today we are going to learn how you can start right now in learning how to reverence and honor your husband.

PRAYER:

Ask a girl to open in prayer.

ICE BREAKER:

What animal, insect or creature do you *not* want God to use to get your attention?

SHARE AND READ:

▶ Ask the girls if one of them wants to share her word study on *reverence*.

▶ Fill in what the girls miss:

Reverence means: respect, admiration, worship, awe, veneration, astonishment, amazement and fear.

READ:

The antonym to reverence is *contempt*. The word contempt means: distain, disrespect, disapproval, scorn and condescension.

God puts things in our life so that we will learn to honor and fear him, so that we will obey. Ephesians 5:33, "and the wife see that she reverence her husband". Remember how God taught the lady from the flea story to honor him as well as her husband.

SHARE:

▶ Call on a girl to give her word study on honor.

READ:

Read the following quote and remind the girls that this is how God taught Patricia to honor her husband. She felt contempt for her husband.

Several days later my dear husband suggested, "I'm beginning to get itchy. The plant must have fleas; you'd better get rid of it."

I gave him a look signifying how stupid he was, "Plants don't have fleas!" I conveniently forgot his suggestion to throw the plant out. Days passed, and he warned me again, "You need to get rid of that plant, because the fleas are getting worse."

♥ Has your dad or mom ever given a suggestion that you thought was stupid?

♥ Did you ignore it because it was not a direct command and because you thought you were smarter than they are?

LOOK UP AND READ ALOUD:

▶ Read the following and have the girls look up the verses and read them aloud:

♥ The word *reverence* that is found in Ephesians 5:33 is also translated in other verses as fear and obedience. Let's read a few of them. Revelation 19:5, Rev.14:7, 1 Peter 3:6.

♥ The Bible tells us that the beginning of wisdom is the fear of God. Read Psalms 111:10.

The book of Proverbs has many verses that teach us to fear the Lord. Let's look up a few of these verses and read together. Look up any verses we don't get to this week for homework.

♥ Proverbs 1:7, 29

♥ Proverbs 8:13

♥ Proverbs 9:10

♥ Proverbs 10:27

♥ Proverbs 14:26-27

♥ Proverbs 15:16, 33

♥ Proverbs 19:23

♥ Proverbs 22:4

♥ Proverbs 23:17

READ:

"This is a great mystery: but I speak concerning Christ and the church... and the wife see that she reverence her husband" (Eph. 5:32-33).

There are twelve mysteries in God's Word, but only the seventh is listed as the great mystery. Each mystery is a strange, beautiful truth which is hard for us to understand. The old Webster's dictionary defines mystery as "something hidden from human knowledge and fitted to inspire a sense of awe; especially something incomprehensible through being above human intelligence. An enigma; anything artfully made difficult."

Jesus wants us for a friend. He wants a companion, someone with whom to discuss ideas. He wants a playmate, someone with whom to laugh and enjoy life. He wants a buddy with whom to spend time. He wants a lover, someone to care about and someone to care about him. He wants a help meet, someone to share in his work of creation and management. He wants to be a groom, and he wants the church to be his bride. This is the great mystery. He seeks to create in me and my relationship to my husband a working scale model of his relationship with the church throughout eternity.

Amazing as it sounds, marriage between a man and a woman is what God chose as the closest example of Christ's relationship to his bride, the church. You are part of eternity when you submit to your husband. Submission, reverence, and honor are virtues God seeks to establish in his Son's bride. Your marriage to your husband is preparing you for your marriage to Christ. You may say, "But it would be easy being married to Christ." Then you don't know your Bible. What if your husband required you to offer your son upon an altar as a burnt sacrifice? That is what God required of Abraham.

For a woman to usurp authority over a man is an affront to God Almighty, like treason in the camp. It would be like a man taking authority over Christ, or like the church becoming jealous of Jesus' leadership and taking authority unto itself. It would be doing just what Lucifer did when he said in Isaiah 14:13-14, **"I will ascend into heaven, I will exalt my throne above the stars of God: I will sit also upon the mount of the congregation, in the sides of the north...I will be like the most High."** Lucifer, like Eve, was not satisfied with his station in God's eternal program. He tried to jump rank and ascend higher on the chain of command. God cast him down, as he will do with men and women who attempt to live beyond their created positions.

Knowing that my role as a wife typifies the church's relationship to Christ has molded my life. As I reverence my husband, I am creating a picture of how we, the church, should reverence Christ. You have wondered why God would tell us to do such a thing as to reverence our husbands. Now you know.

"This is a great mystery: but I speak concerning Christ and the church... and the wife see that she reverence her husband" (Eph. 5:32). Reverence: to revere, to be in awe; fear mingled with respect and esteem.

1. Obedience is doing what you know the other person wants you to do.
2. Submission is your heart giving over to the other person's will.
3. Reverence is more than just doing what a man expects or demands. It is an act of the woman's will to treat him with a high degree of regard and awe.

Obedience, submission, and reverence are all acts of the will and are not based on feelings. Showing deference toward one's husband is an act of reverence toward the God who placed you in that role.

HOMEWORK:

This week think of one person you have been thinking negatively about lately, and commit to loving that person in your thoughts and praying for him/her. Keep a diary of how you are praying for him/her and how it has been changing your attitude.

CLOSE IN PRAYER

TEACHER'S GUIDE FOR CHAPTER 16:
THE POWER OF STINKING THINKING

OPENING:

This chapter, "Stinking Thinking," is key in marriage. It is really key in all walks of the Christian life. If you marry a Prophet-type man, it will be the single most important lesson in your life. If you are a Dreamer type of girl it is paramount. I Corinthians 13:7 says this in reference to active love, which is called charity: **"Beareth all things, believeth all things, hopeth all things, endureth all things."** You must learn to practice thinking well of others.

Your thought life <u>now</u> is a reflection on how you will think once you are married. If you have a bad attitude toward a friend, if you have been think-ing negative thoughts about someone you know, if you just avoid someone because you think they are _____, then you are already giving yourself over to the fiery darts that destroy relationships and wreak chaos in the body of Christ. If you practice carrying grudges now then it will be easy for Satan to use your habits to destroy your future marriage. As you have practiced, so you will be. The chapter you read this week is written for you to learn how to put down negativity and your critical thinking and to purpose to stop having an accusing heart. It is time for God's peace to reign. Defeating this problem now could save your future marriage.

PRAYER:

Call on several girls to open in prayer. Ask them to ask God to open their minds and hearts to hear him speaking to them today.

READ:

▶ Start the meeting reading a true story about a bride who lost her hus-band's love. He ended up divorcing her for the sake of his kingdom. Here is her story.

STORY OF A QUEEN WHO TREATED HER KING WITH CONTEMPT:

The Bible records a story of a king who was very powerful and had many riches. He threw a huge party, inviting his subjects to come and look upon all his wealth and honor him. The celebration went on for 100 days. Then the king prepared a great seven day feast for all the men of his country, great and small. The palace was amazing. The Bible records its splendor in Esther chapter 1 verse 6-7: **"where were white, green, and blue, hangings, fastened with cords of fine linen and purple to silver rings and pillars of marble: the beds were of gold and silver, upon a pavement of red, and blue, and white, and black, marble. And they gave them drink in vessels of gold, (the vessels being diverse one from another,) and royal wine in abundance, according to the state of the king."** Such glory was great to behold. On the last day of the feast the king decided to show off his beautiful queen to cap the wonders of his great kingdom. He sent his servants to go get her, but she was disgusted that he would expect her to stand before such lowly people, especially a bunch of drinking men. She refused to obey.

What good was all the king's glory and honor when his own wife publicly held him in contempt? All the men at the feast felt his shame. These simple men knew that if the king's wife dishonored him, how could they expect their wives to obey them? Her contempt would weaken the nation because it would destroy the relationship of the family. The Bible tells us in Chapter 1 verses 16-17 how the men were thinking, **"For this deed of the queen shall come abroad unto all the women, so that they shall despise their husbands in their eyes, when it shall be reported, The king Ahasuerus commanded Vashti the queen to be brought in before him, but she came not. Likewise shall the ladies of Persia and Media say this day unto all the king's princes, which have heard of the deed of the queen. Thus shall there arise too much contempt and wrath."**

All the king's men requested for the sake of the rest of the families that the king divorce his wife, and so it was done. She could have shown him honor at that feast day, and in doing so she would have been revered as a great queen, but instead the once coddled and loved queen was cast out like a nobody, **"... and let the king give her royal estate unto another that is better than she."** The Scripture records in verses 20-22 that a document was published: **"...all the wives shall give to their husbands honour, both great and small...For he sent letters into all the king's provinces, into every province according to the writing thereof, and to every people after their**

language, that every man should bear rule in his own house, and that it should be published according to the language of every people."

God made a statement. Order in the family must be maintained. A leader's wife can cause a whole kingdom, church or family line to falter and fail. The Bible says in James 3:1, **"Brethren, be not many masters, knowing that we shall receive the greater condemnation."** The wife of a man who is seeking to lead others needs to understand that her honor to her husband can affect many people's lives. It is a position not to be taken lightly. Vashti demonstrated this lesson.

Within a few years Esther sat on the throne as the queen. Even though Esther's marriage was arranged with neither her nor her family having a say in the matter, and even though the king was a divorced heathen, she still honored him as her husband. God's plan for the headship of the household in marriage was from the beginning for all people.

LOOK UP AND DISCUSS:

▶ Have the girls look these verses up and read together. Encourage discussion.

PURE THOUGHTS:
- ♥ Proverbs 16:3
- ♥ Proverbs 19:20 & 21
- ♥ Matthew 5:8
- ♥ I Timothy 1:5
- ♥ Titus 1:15
- ♥ James 3:17

HOMEWORK:

The next chapter is opinions from married men. Read the chapter then go and ask a married man (like your father or a married brother) what he appreciates best in a woman. Be prepared to relate his answer to the class. Also, prepare to share three verses or passages that God has used in your life while you went through this class.

CLOSE IN PRAYER

TEACHER'S GUIDE FOR CHAPTER 17:
WHAT SAY THE MEN?

OPENING:

Today we will hear from the men in your life. What do they value in a woman? What do you need to become that kind of woman? It will be interesting to learn.

PRAYER:

Have several girls pray God will grant us wisdom as we learn from these men.

ICE BREAKER:

Which of the following statements are true?

- ♥ Guys love girls who can cook.
- ♥ Guys hate it when girls overreact.
- ♥ Guys love all perfume.

(Shhh, this is wrong: Most guys do not like all perfume. All other statements are generally true.)

- ♥ Guys like femininity, not feebleness.
- ♥ The first sign a guy likes you is when he starts teasing you.

LOOK UP AND READ:

The Scriptures say 148 times, "is better." What is better than what?

Write down a proverb that says, "_____ is better than _____."

Look up and read these verses in Proverbs on "is better":

Proverbs 8:11, 8:19, 12:9, 15:16, 15:17, 16:8, 16:16, 16:19, 16:32, 17:1, 19:1, 21:9, 25:7, 25:24, 28:6

DISCUSS:

▶ Have the girls take turns reading what the men in their lives said is important. Also have them tell what scripture has influenced them the most.

READ AND DISCUSS:

▶ Read over what the Farmer had to say about attraction feeling like *falling in love*. Ask the girls to talk about this subject.

HOMEWORK:

Read the last chapter. Read and record I Corinthians 13 as you will find at the end of the book. Bring your book and we will reread the last chapter together and go over your answers. Come to our meeting wearing something pink and we will have tea and fellowship.

CLOSE IN PRAYER

TEACHER'S GUIDE FOR CHAPTER 18:
REFLECTIONS

OPENING:

We have covered a lot of ground in this class. We have learned together and grown in the Lord. Today we will review and share with each other what we have learned.

PRAYER:

▶ Teacher, pray for the girls by name. Ask God's blessings on them as they go out to honor him. Ask God to lead them to the man they will be best at serving. Ask God to cause each girl to be the kind of woman God would have her to be.

READ AND DISCUSS:

Read each chapter's review and have the girls go around the room sharing their thoughts.

READ:

Note from Debi Pearl

I have enjoyed writing this book. In my mind's eye I can see you, a fresh, young bunch of eager faces and shining eyes filled with the hopes and dreams of love. There is nothing so fulfilling, rewarding and just wonderfully exhilarating as being loved, really, really loved. I pray God blesses each of you with this wonderful gift of being a loved woman.

There is one more thing I would like to share with you before we part. Every year I have chosen special verses from God's word. These verses were committed to memory and recorded onto pretty cards which I put up over my dresser. They were my compass for that year. Over the years these verses have marked my growth in the Lord. One such verse was II Peter 3:18 **"But grow in grace, and in the knowledge of our Lord and Savior Jesus Christ. To him be the glory both now and for ever. Amen."**

One year I chose Isaiah 12. It is a great passage of victory. When I was 18 years-old, I chose Philippians 3:10. I encourage you to begin right now claiming a verse for each year. Mark your Bible, and when it wears out, record your list of verses in your new Bible.

I will close with the verses I chose the year I married: Philippians 4:8-9 **"Finally brethren, whatsoever things are true, whatsoever things are honest, whatsoever things are just, whatsoever things are pure, whatsoever things are lovely, whatsoever things are of good report; if there be any virtue, and if there be any praise, think on these things. Those things, which ye have both learned, and received, and heard, and seen in me, do: and the God of peace shall be with you."**

CLOSE IN PRAYER

Chapter 12

WARNINGS – Cheyenne's attention was abruptly captured by the silence as her dad jumped to his feet. Malachi's tall, lanky frame moved quickly toward the front, speaking as he walked, "Take your Bible and turn with me, if you will, to the sixth chapter of Ephesians, verse 10." He seemed tense.

Before anyone had a chance to find the passage, and just as Malachi's long legs bypassed the steps to jump up on the two and a half foot high stage to step behind the podium, he was praying, "Lord, give us a heart to see the fields are white unto harvest. Grant us a vision of the best way to reap the crop. Guide my words. Amen … Amen … in Jesus' precious name … Amen."

A small group of people sat in the humble country church building. A request had been made for church members and TLP workers to make every effort to attend. It was a low key request. Most had opted to stay home.

Through the open windows a soft breeze lifted Cheyenne's dark hair from around her face. She pushed it back as she leaned forward to where Asher usually sat. His seat was, of course, empty. She looked down at her fingers, mentally counting the days until he returned. Prayer for him came to her mind as automatically as breathing. "God, give him wisdom and grace. Help him reach those whose hearts you have prepared for the gospel."

The off-balance rocking of the ceiling fan clanged against its pull chain. *Tick, tick, tick.* A small child stirred restlessly and was soothed by his mother. Old Louise's popping gum seemed to be keeping time with the fan. Everyone wondered and waited for Malachi to unveil the reasons for this special meeting.

Malachi stroked his long gray beard and looked at his text. His bushy brows hid his eyes. He seemed to be waiting on God to move him. He looked up, scanning the many empty seats. His face radiated spiritual insight. His searching examination of the room caused others to turn and mentally note the others who were present … and absent. It suddenly seemed to matter who was there.

Finally his strong, authoritative voice addressed their anticipation. "You are aware of the failed attempt to burn out TLP Ministries over the weekend. God has sent his angels to encamp around about us this time." Then he looked up, and as if addressing God he said, "May he continue to be our shield."

Searching the faces again, Malachi continued, "Most of you who are here have chosen to commit yourself to sowing the seed of the Word of God. Some of you have sacrificed much, but, I fear, not as much as you will sacrifice before we have completed this journey.

∽

Even as the old minister poured out his heart, eight Muslim men huddled in the small storage room in the back of the tobacco shop, reading the latest email from an imam in New York City. "He is due to arrive in two days. He is bringing the explosives with him. Allah Akbar!"

∽

"If we leave the devil alone, he will leave us alone, but if we go into his territory with the gospel of truth, he will come after us. As long as we stand in faith we have nothing to fear. I tell you, Jesus has *bound the strong man* and I intend to *spoil his goods*. I cannot do this alone. Are you with me? Will you pay the price? Will you take up your cross every morning, saying, 'Lord, if it please you today, I am ready to die for you'?"

Malachi paused and looked from face to face. Even the fan seemed to have temporarily gone silent. The room was as still as midnight. A challenge lay in front of everyone.

"This meeting has a dual purpose: One, to encourage those of you who do not want to be on the front lines to depart in peace. The second reason we are here tonight is to teach those of you who are ready to go forward what you must do to prepare yourself for this spiritual war.

"It is possible—I guess I should say likely—that if you continue with me in the publishing ministry, you will be risking your life, and maybe the lives of your loved ones. No, no one will think any less of you if you leave. This is what God has called me to do, not necessarily what he has called you to do.

"I have had a dream, a vision, if you will. I believe God has given me the privilege of publishing the gospel to the Muslim people—a vast multitude of Muslim people."

Malachi was overcome with inexpressible emotion. He leaned over the podium and began to weep in earnest.

Both Julie and Cheyenne, sitting three rows back, broke into sobs, although neither could have explained why. Cheyenne had never seen her daddy really cry, and now he wept like a baby. Even Bobbie Jo's eyes swam with tears at the sight of the strong man weeping.

For a full minute sobs echoed in the church. The small group looked around in mute wonder at the enormity of what they had heard. Cheyenne suddenly thought of how alone Louise must feel, being in a strange new place and now listening to everyone fall apart. She glanced over to the older woman but saw that the old face was full of peace.

From the corner of her eye Cheyenne saw Omar slowly moving to the front of the room. When he reached Malachi he placed his arm across the older man's shoulder, tenderly directing him to his seat. His gentleness toward Malachi and their oneness of heart spoke of a shared vision.

For a long moment Omar thoughtfully looked down at his beloved teacher. Then he, too, searched the countenances of the people before he slowly began to speak. "I think I know what Malachi wants to tell you."

Taking a deep breath, Omar's dark eyes searched the ceiling. Focused, he leveled his gaze on the gathering. "We have spent many hours praying, seeking God on this matter of safety. It is a grave decision, not just for us, but you as well."

THE DREAM – "As you know, Malachi is not a dreamer. He says dreams are the products of too much spicy supper, but he had a dream a few months ago that left him shaken. He believes it is from God. Remember, Acts 2:17 says,

> *And it shall come to pass in the last days, saith God, I will pour out of my Spirit upon all flesh: and your sons and your daughters shall prophesy, and your young men shall see visions, and your old men shall dream dreams:*

"In his dream he saw Muslim people crowded into a tight group. Then, as a camera began moving out for a wider angle, the picture revealed the group was bigger and bigger until he could not see any end to the people, and each one was reaching out his hand trying to receive a copy of *God's Story*. It was almost within their reach.

"Even as the people reached for this book of truth, other Muslims came with swords and began to slay men, women and children until they all lay dead. Hundreds of thousands of precious Muslims fell beneath the sword of their own leaders. Until that time, Malachi—none of us really—had any idea just how big Islam had grown and just how terribly violent it was in its growth.

"That dream awakened in Malachi a vision for reaching the Muslim people with the gospel. Malachi began asking God to provide the necessary funds to mass produce and distribute the *God's Story* book, and to make it available through multiple sites on the web, free of charge, in the Arabic language.

"Just think, Saudi Arabia is closed up airtight against the gospel. Anyone caught with a Bible or Christian literature would be subject to death. No missionary can go there and share his message, but we can go there, directly into the private rooms of everyone who has access to the web. The rulers of Saudi Arabia will be able to secretly read *God's Story* and understand fully the message of salvation. Our little digital missionaries cannot be arrested. If they block one website we will open ten more. As long as a Muslim has access to the web, he will have the gospel at his fingertips. Terrorists hiding in the caves of Afghanistan who have satellite web access will be able to see the gospel in a beautiful presentation. Many will be saved and the mullahs will not like it. We will be targeted. Apparently we are already in their sights, and our book is not even posted yet.

"The reason Malachi invited you here tonight is to help you understand that this coming ministry is both glorious and dreadful. He has received several phone calls and emails warning him against making this book available in Arabic.

"One-fourth of the world is now Muslim. If you add all the Christian religions together, we are not even close to their number. We are overwhelmingly outnumbered by a people residing in every nation, taught to conquer or destroy non-Muslims. There is no place for us to flee.

"Malachi wants you to know his vision and the danger that comes with it. Tonight will be the last meeting in this building. For those of you willing to spend your lives in this great cause, contact us. We will continue to have Bible studies for new believers in private homes, but we will move around a lot, never being in the same place two times in a row."

Without further comment, Omar dropped his head and began to pray. "Lord, make us wise. Cause us to daily put on the whole armour of God. Give us courage for the days to come. In the power of the precious blood of Jesus … Amen."

Omar stood while the people quietly filed out. Then he walked back to where Ben and Dusty were now standing, quietly talking with Cheyenne and Bobbie Jo. He gave them a searching gaze.

Magdalene's whisper caused all of them to jump. "The car was here. I saw him. Only this time there were three men with him."

"Well," Omar said as he knelt to pick up his youngest son, "This is the beginning."

EXCERPT FROM AMAZON'S TOP-SELLER,
CREATED TO BE HIS HELP MEET
BY DEBI PEARL

Chapter 8

THREE KINDS OF MEN

Men are not all the same. I have become aware that there are basically three types of men. The different types are just as marked in one-year-olds as they are in adult men. It seems that God made each male to express one side of his triad nature. No single man completely expresses the well-rounded image of God. If a man were all three types at the same time, he would be the perfect man, but I have never met, heard of, or read in a book of history or fiction of a man who is the proper balance of all three. Certainly Jesus was the perfect balance. Most men are a little of all three, but tend to be dominant in one. And all the training and experiences of life will never successfully make a man into a different type of man. There is nothing clumsier and more pathetic than a man trying to act differently from who he is. As we review the types, you will probably readily identify your husband and be able to see where you have been a curse or a blessing to him.

By the time a young woman gets married, she has developed a composite image of what her husband ought to be like. The men she has known and the characters in books and movies provide each woman with a concept of the perfect man. Poor guys! Our preconceived ideas make it tough on them. They are never perfect–far from it. God gave each one a nature that in part is like himself, but never complete. When you add in the factor that all men are fallen creatures, it makes a girl wonder why she would ever want to tie her life to one of these sons of Adam. But God made us ladies to have this unreasonable desire to be needed by a man, and our hormones are working strenuously to bring us together.

When a girl suddenly finds herself permanently wed to a man who is not like she thinks he ought to be, rather than adapt to him, she usually spends the rest of their marriage–which may not be very long–trying to change him into what she thinks her man ought to be. Most young girls are married only a short time when they make the awful discovery that they may have gotten a lemon. Rather than bemoan your "fate," ask God for wisdom.

Wisdom is knowing what you "bought" when you married that man, and learning to adapt to him as he is, not as you want him to be.

Men are not alike. Your husband most likely will not be like your father or brother or the man in your favorite romance novel. Our husbands are created in the image of God, and it takes all kinds of men to even come close to completing that image. No man is a perfect balance; if he were, he would be too divine to need you. God gives imperfect women to imperfect men so they can be heirs together of the grace of life and become something more together than either one of them would ever be alone. If you fight your husband's inadequacies or seek to be dominant where he is not, both of you will fail. If you love him and support him with his inadequacies and without taking charge, both of you will succeed and grow.

MR. COMMAND MAN

God is dominant–a sovereign and all-powerful God. He is also visionary–omniscient and desirous of carrying out his plans. And, God is steady–the same yesterday, and today, and forever, our faithful High Priest. Most men epitomize one of these three aspects of God.

A few men are born with more than their share of dominance and, on the surface, a deficit in gentleness. They often end up in positions that command other men. We will call them Command Men. They are born leaders. They are often chosen by other men to be military commanders, politicians, preachers and heads of corporations. Winston Churchill, George Patton, and Ronald Reagan are examples of dominant men. Since our world needs only a few leaders, God seems to limit the number of these Command Men. Throughout history, men created in God the Father's image have all surrounded themselves with good men to help get big jobs completed. Command Men usually do more than is required of them.

They are known for expecting their wives to wait on them hand and foot. A Command Man does not want his wife involved in any project that prevents her from serving him. If you are blessed to be married to a strong, forceful, bossy man, as I am, then it is very important for you to learn how to make an appeal without challenging his authority. We will discuss how to make an appeal later in this book.

Command Men have less tolerance, so they will often walk off and leave their clamoring wife before she has a chance to realize that she is even close to losing her marriage. By the time she realizes that there is a serious problem, she is already a divorced mother seeking help in how to raise her children alone. A woman can fight until she is blue in the face, yet the Command Man will not yield. He is not as intimate or vulnerable as are other men in sharing his personal feelings or vocation with his wife. He seems to be sufficient unto himself. It is awful being shut out. A woman married to a Command Man has to earn her place in his heart by proving that she will stand by her man, faithful, loyal, and obedient. When she has won his confidence, he will treasure her to the extreme.

She is on call every minute of her day. Her man wants to know where she is, what she is doing, and why she is doing it. He corrects her without thought. For better or for worse, it is his nature to control.

A woman married to a Command Man wears a heavier yoke than most women, but it can be a very rewarding yoke. In a way, her walk as his help meet is easier because there is never any possibility of her being in control. There are no gray areas; she always knows exactly what is required of her, therefore she has a calm sense of safety and rest.

The Command Man feels it his duty and responsibility to lead people, and so he does, whether they think they want him to lead or not. Amazingly, this is what the public is most comfortable with. Very few people have enough confidence to strike out on their own; plus, the feeling of being blamed for mistakes holds them back. The Command Man is willing to take the chance, and for that purpose God created these king-like men. Their road is not easy, for James said, "My brethren, be not many masters, knowing that we shall receive the greater condemnation" (James 3:1).

On 9-11, when the World Trade Center was destroyed, another plane flying over Pennsylvania was being highjacked by other terrorists. Mr. Todd Beamer was on that plane. It was his voice we all heard saying the now famous line, "Let's roll." He must have been a strong Mr. Command Man. He, and others like him, took control of a desperate situation and saved many other lives while sacrificing their own. It could have been a terrible mistake, but Mr. Beamer evaluated the situation, made a decision, and then acted upon it. He knew the lives of all those people were in his hands. It was a heavy responsibility, yet he was "willing to do what a man's gotta do." You will remember how strong and queenly his young widow seemed when we watched her on TV after the attacks. A good Mr. Command sees the bigger picture and strives to help the greatest number, even if it costs him his life and the lives of those he loves. If he is an honest man, he will take financial loss in order to help lead those who need him, but in the end he will usually come out on top. If he is not an honest man, he will be selfish and use the resources of others to further his own interests.

A King wants a Queen, which is why a man in command wants a faithful wife to share his fame and glory. Without a woman's admiration, his victories are muted. If a wife learns early to enjoy the benefits of taking the second seat, and if she does not take offense to his headstrong aggressiveness, she will be the one sitting at his right side being adored, because this kind of man will totally adore his woman and exalt her. She will be his closest, and sometimes his only, confidante. Over the years, the Command Man can become more yielding and gentle. His wife will discover secret portals to his heart.

If you are married to a king, honor and reverence is something you must give him on a daily basis if you want him to be a benevolent, honest, strong, and fulfilled man of God. He has the potential to become an amazing leader. Never shame him, and do not belittle him or ignore his accomplishments.

If the wife of a Command Man resists his control, he will readily move forward without her. If he is not a principled Christian, he will allow the marriage to come to divorce. Like King Ahasuerus of Persia, if she defies him, he will replace her and not look back. If his Christian convictions prevent him from divorcing, he will remain stubbornly in command, and she will be known as a miserable old wretch.

If a Command Man has not developed working skills, and thus accomplishes little, he will have the tendency to tell stories about himself and brag until people are sick of him. If he has left his wife and lost his children, thus having no legitimate "kingdom" of his own, he will be obnoxiously garrulous.

A Command Man who has gone bad is likely to be abusive. It is important to remember that much of how a Command Man reacts depends on his wife's reverence toward him. When a Command Man (lost or saved) is treated with honor and reverence, a good help meet will find that her man will be wonderfully protective and supportive. In most marriages, the strife is not because the man is cruel or evil; it is because he expects obedience, honor, and reverence, and is not getting it. Thus, he reacts badly. When a wife plays her part as a help meet, the Command Man will respond differently. Of course, there are a few men who are so cruel and violent that even when the wife is a proper help meet, he will still physically abuse her or the children. In such cases, it would be the duty of the wife to alert the authorities so that they might become the arm of the Lord to do justice.

• Mr. Command will not take the trash out, as a general rule, and he will not clean up the mess at the trash area. He may organize and command someone else to do it. Any woman trying to force Mr. Command into becoming a nice trash man will likely end up alone, trashed by her man.

• Mr. Command will want to talk about his plans, ideas, and finished projects. He will be very objective, very unemotional, and he will not enjoy small talk. His vision is like a man looking from a high mountain; he sees the distant goal. He will expect his wife to help him remember individuals' needs.

• Mr. Command Man will be most uncomfortable and at a loss when dealing with the sick, helpless, and dying. Where there is no hope, there will be no need for a Command Man.

• A born leader is a man who can, when necessary, adapt principles or rules to circumstances for the greater good of the greatest number of people.

MR. VISIONARY

God is a Visionary as seen in his person, the Holy Spirit. He made some men in the image of that part of his nature. Prophets, be they true or false, are usually of this type. Some of you are married to men who are shakers, changers, and dreamers. These men get the entire family upset about peripheral issues, such as: do we believe in Christmas? Should we use state marriage licenses? Should a Christian opt out of the Social Security system? The issues may be serious and worthy of one's commitment, but, in varying degrees, these men have tunnel vision, tenaciously focusing on single issues. They will easily pick up and relocate without any idea of what they are going to do for a living at their new location. They are often the church splitters and the ones who demand doctrinal purity and proper dress and conduct. Like a prophet, they call people to task for their inconsistencies. If they are not wise, they can be real fools who push their agendas, forcing others to go their way. One Visionary will campaign for the legalization of pot, while another will be an activist to make abortions illegal. Most will just sit around the house and complain, but in their souls they are Visionaries.

Visionaries are often gifted men or inventors, and I am sure it was men of this caliber who conquered the Wild West, though they would not have been the farmers who settled it. Today, Visionary men are street preachers, political activists, organizers and instigators of any front-line social issue. They love confrontation, and hate the status quo. "Why leave it the way it is when you can change it?" They are the men who keep the rest of the world from getting stagnant or dull. The Visionary is consumed with a need to communicate with his words, music, writing, voice, art, or actions. He is the "voice crying out in the wilderness" striving to change the way humanity is behaving or thinking. Good intentions don't always keep Visionaries from causing great harm. They can stir up pudding and end up with toxic waste, if they are not wise. An unwise wife can add to the poison with negative words, or she can, with simple words of caution, bring attention to the goodness of the pudding and the wisdom in leaving it alone. Every Mr. Visionary needs a good, wise, prudent, stable wife who has a positive outlook on life.

If you are married to one of these fellows, expect to be rich or poor, rarely middle class. He may invest everything in a chance and lose it all or make a fortune, but he will not do well working 8 to 5 in the same place for thirty years, and then retiring to live the good life. If he works a regular job, he may either not show up half the time or he will work like a maniac 80 hours a week and love every minute. He may purchase an alligator farm in Florida or a ski resort in Colorado, or he may buy an old house trailer for $150 with hopes of fixing it up and selling it for

$10,000, only to find out that it is so deteriorated that it can't be moved. He will then have his wife and all the kids help him tear the top off and carry the scraps to the dump, (saving the appliances in the already crowded garage), so he can make a farm trailer out of the axles. Now that he has a farm trailer and no animals, expect him to get a deal on three, old, sick cows, and... He may never be rich in money, but he will be rich in experience.

Come to think of it, maybe my husband is not a 100% Mr. Command Man, because he seems quite a bit like this Mr. Visionary. I remember, on more than one occasion, helping him tear down someone's old barn in order to drag the junk home to fill up our old barn. Remember, most men are a mixture of types, but usually stronger in one.

The wife of Mr. Visionary should be just a little bit reckless and blind in one eye if she is going to enjoy the ride. If this is your man, you need to learn two very important things (beyond how to make an appeal). Learn how to be flexible, and learn how to always be loyal to your man. You will be amazed at how much happier you will be and how much fun life can be if you learn to just go with the flow–his flow. Life will become an adventure. You will actually begin to feel sorry for the gals married to the stick-in-the-mud, steady type. And once you get it into your head that your husband does not have to be "right" for you to follow him, you will FINALLY be able to say "bye-bye" to your overwrought parents, even when they are screaming that you are married to a crazy man. People looking on will marvel that you are able to love and appreciate your husband, but you will know better because you will see his greatness.

Greatness is a state of soul, not certain accomplishments. Thomas Edison, though not recognized as such, was great after his 999th failure to make a light bulb. The Wright brothers were great when they neglected their lucrative occupation of fixing bicycles and "wasted time" trying to make one of them fly. If the light bulb had never worked and the plane had never flown, and no one remembered their names today, they would have been the same men, and their lives would have still been just as full and their days just as challenging. Did Edison's wife think him great when he used his last dime on another failed idea? If she didn't, just think what she missed.

The Visionary man needs his woman's support, and he will appreciate it when it is freely given. Without her, he feels alone. This guy will be a little hard to live with at first. Big, wild fights are the usual beginnings if a nice, normal girl (who had a Mr. Steady daddy) marries one of "the weird ones." They will either have a bitter divorce (she divorces him) in the first few years, or she will decide to learn to appreciate him, because he is really rather lovable. I get very few letters from wives married to these high-strung, going-to-reinvent-the-wheel men. I do get lots of letters from their mothers-in-law, asking us to write and straighten out their sons-in-law.

Some of these guys talk with glowing enthusiasm and animation. Usually, they enjoy hashing over ideas, plans and dreams. If you are married to one, he loves to tell you about his newest idea, and he wants your enthusiastic support, not a critique of his idea. He will look at his idea more critically later, but for the moment, the idea itself is invigorating to him. He will have a thousand ideas for every project he attempts, and he will try many that he will never finish, and he will finish some that are worthless, and you "knew it all along." Remind him of that the next time he has an idea, and you will destroy your marriage–but you won't change him. He will share his "dumb ideas" with someone else.

LEARN TO ENJOY THE TRIP

Several years back, a newlywed couple decided to take a bicycle road trip for their honeymoon. They had the map all worked out and the bikes and camping gear ready. After riding for a couple days, the young wife noticed that her good husband was going the wrong way. She stopped him and tried to show him on the map that he had veered off the course. She had always been endowed with a natural ability to read maps and knew exactly where they were. He was not so gifted and argued that she was dead wrong and insisted that they were headed the right way. Later that day, when he did discover that he had indeed taken the wrong road, he brushed it off and blamed the signs or gave some plausible reason. Again he took the wrong road, and she argued with him. He kept correcting their course, but they were not getting anywhere by its shortest route. She let him know his error. That part of the honeymoon was not very "honeyed." Nothing would change his mind. He knew he was right, and if not exactly right, then he was as right as could be expected under the circumstances, and criticism was not welcomed.

What could she do? The young wife was not pleased with the way they were relating, and she reasoned to herself that this could become the pattern for the rest of their lives. As she brooded on the matter, it occurred to her that it was very important to him to be right and to be in charge, and it really didn't matter which road they took. They were taking this trip to be together, not to get somewhere in particular. God in his mercy and grace gave this sweet young wife a new heart. She decided to follow her husband down any road he chose, without question or second-guessing. So she cheerfully began to enjoy the beautiful day and the glory of being young and in love as she continued to pedal her bike down a road that was taking them to where every marriage ought to go, even though it was not according to the map.

This little lady is married to a 100% Visionary Man. She started her marriage right, following him wherever he led, regardless of whether she thought it was the right direction or not. She has been flexible and is enjoying her ride. Someday, when her husband is assured that he can trust her with his heart, he will let her be his navigator—and still take the credit for it. The moral to this story is: the way you think determines how you will feel, and how you feel influences the way you will act.

If you are married to the Visionary Man, learn to enjoy the trip, for if he ever does make a better light bulb, he will want you to be the one who turns it on for the first time in public. It will be your face he looks into to see the marvel of what a great thing he has done. You are his most important fan. When you know your man really needs you, you can be happy with just about anything.

Over time, this type of man will become more practical. If you are a young wife married to a man whom your mama thinks is totally crazy—then you may be married to Mr. Visionary. Right now, purpose in your heart to be loyal to him, and to be flexible; then, let your dreamer dream. Lean back and enjoy the ride; it should prove interesting.

The world needs the Visionary Man, for he is the one who seeks out hypocrisy and injustice and slays the dragons. He calls himself and those around him to a higher standard. He knows how to do nearly everything and is readily willing to advise others. In time, he will be quite accomplished in more than one thing.

• Visionary Man will take the trash out if he remembers it. But, he may also end up inventing a way whereby the trash takes itself out or is turned into an energy source, or he may just waste a lot of time building a cart for you to take it out. He will not mind cleaning up if he notices it needs doing, but he may get so deeply involved that he decides to paint while he is sweeping, and then switch projects before he gets finished painting. And he will likely be irritated when his wife nags him about it.

• Visionary Man will talk and talk and talk to his honey if she approves of him. He will be subjective, thinking about feelings, moods, and spiritual insights. One of his greatest needs will be for his wife to think objectively (proven truth) and use common sense, which will help keep his feet from flying too far from solid ground. He spends his life looking through a telescope or microscope, and he will be stunned that what he sees (or thinks he sees), others do not seem to notice or care about. Every small issue will become mind-consuming, and he will need his wife to casually talk about the big picture and the possible end results of relation-ships, finances, or health if he continues to totally focus on his present interest. His sweetheart needs to stay in a positive state of mind, yet never jump into his make-believe world, trying to be too much of a cheerleader on dead-end issues. Let him burn out on things that are not wise. But don't throw water on his fire. Let him find his own balance through bumping into hard realities. The Old Testament prophets of God must surely have been the Visionary types. Remember Elijah, Jeremiah, and Ezekiel and all their trials?

• Visionary Man is an initiator and provoker. He is a point man, trailblazer, and a voice to get things done. He will start and keep the party going until the Command Man gets there to lead on.

• Visionary Man's focus is so intense that matters can easily be blown out of proportion. A wife must guard against negative conversation about people. An idle conversation by her can bring about the end of a life-long friendship. This is true with all men, but especially so with Mr. Visionary. Search your heart and discover your motive in what you say about people. What is your intent when you speak? To build him up and give him joy, or to build up yourself and make him think that you alone are perfect? If you mention people and make them look a little bad and yourself a little "taken for granted," your husband may get the idea that friends and family are treating you unfairly, and he may become withdrawn and suspicious. You could unwittingly render your husband unteachable. If you want your husband to grow into a confident, outgoing man of God, then he needs to have a clear conscience toward his friends and family. God says a woman's conversation can win her lost husband. In the same vein, a woman's idle, negative conversation can cripple a strong man and cause him to become an angry, confrontational, divisive man. "Likewise, ye wives, be in subjection to your own husbands; that, if any obey not the word, they also may without the word be won by the conversation of the wives; While they behold your chaste conversation coupled with fear" (1 Peter 3:1-2).

• Mr. Visionary needs a lady who does not take offense easily. She needs to be tough. He needs his lady to be full of life and joy. A Visionary Man is not equipped to be a comforter–for himself or anyone else. His lady will need to learn to tuck in that quivering lip, square those shoulders, and put on that smile.

• Mr. Visionary can be a leader, but because he has tunnel vision his leadership will have a more narrow focus.

MR. STEADY

God is as steady as an eternal rock, caring, providing, and faithful, like a priest–like Jesus Christ. He created many men in that image. We will call him Mr. Steady–"in the middle, not given to extremes." The Steady Man does not make snap decisions or spend his last dime on a new idea, and he doesn't try to tell other people what to do. He avoids controversy. He doesn't invent the light bulb like

Mr. Visionary, but he will be the one to build the factory and manage the assembly line that produces the light bulb and the airplane. He does not jump to the front of the plane to take a razor knife away from a terrorist, unless he is encouraged to do so by Mr. Command. He would never lead a revolution against the government or the church. He will quietly ignore hypocrisy in others. He will selflessly fight the wars that Mr. Visionary starts and Mr. Command leads. He builds the oil tankers, farms the soil, and quietly raises his family. As a general rule, he will be faithful till the day he dies in the same bed he has slept in for the last 40 or 50 years. Older women who are divorced and have learned by their mistakes know the value of peace and safety, and they will long for a nice steady man of his stature, but such a man is rarely available—unless his foolish wife has left him. This man is content with the wife of his youth.

JOYS AND TRIBULATIONS

Being married to a Steady Man has its rewards and its trials. On the good side, your husband never puts undue pressure on you to perform miracles. He doesn't expect you to be his servant. You do not spend your days putting out emotional fires, because he doesn't create tension in the family. You rarely feel hurried, pushed, pressured, or forced. The women married to Visionary Men look at you in wonder that your husband seems so balanced and stable. The wife of Command Man marvels at the free time you seem to have. If your dad happened to be a Steady Man, then chances are you will appreciate your husband's down-to-earth, practical life for the wonderful treasure it is.

When you are married to a man who is steady and cautious, and you have a bit of the impatient romantic in you, you may not see his worth and readily honor him. You may be discontent because he is slow and cautious to take authority or make quick decisions. A bossy woman sees her husband's lack of hasty judgment and calls her Steady husband "wishy-washy." His steadiness makes him the last to change, so he seems to be a follower because he is seldom out front forming up the troops. There is no exciting rush in him, just a slow, steady climb with no bells or whistles. You wish he would just make up his mind, and that he would take a stand in the church. He seems to just let people use him. There are times you wish he would boldly tell you what to do so you would not have to carry all the burden of decision-making.

Some women equate their husband's wise caution and lack of open passion as being unspiritual. His lack of spontaneity and open boldness may look like indifference to spiritual things. However, he is like deep, deep water. The very depth makes the movement almost imperceptible, but it is, nevertheless, very strong.

He will be confused with your unhappiness and try to serve you more, which may further diminish your respect for his masculinity. Disappointment and unthankfulness can make you wearier than any amount of duties. The trials he seems to cause you are really your discontented responses to what you consider to be his shortcomings. If you didn't attempt to change him into something other than what God created him to be, he would not cause you any grief. His very steadiness keeps him on his middle-of-the-road course, and it will drive a controlling woman crazy.

This is why many disgruntled ladies married to Mr. Steadys fall victim to hormonal imbalance, physical illness, or emotional problems.

When a woman is married to a bossy, dominant man, people marvel that she is willing to serve him without complaint, so she comes out looking like a wonderful woman of great patience and sacrifice. A woman married to the impulsive Visionary Man, who puts the family through hardships, will stir amazement in everyone. "How can she tolerate his weird ideas with such peace and joy?" She comes out being a real saint, maybe even a martyr. But if you are married to a wonderful, kind, loving, serving man, and you are just a little bit selfish, then you are likely to end up looking like an unthankful shrew. He helps you, adores you, protects you, and is careful to provide for you, and you are still not satisfied. Shame on you!

KNOW YOUR MAN

Wives are very much flesh and blood, and as young women, we don't come to marriage with all the skills needed to make it start out good, let alone perfect. When you come to know your man for whom God created him to be, you will stop trying to change him into what you think he should be. The key is to know your man. If he is Mr. Steady, you need to learn to be thankful and to honor him as the one created for you in the image of God. God's Word says in Hebrews 13:8, "Jesus Christ the same yesterday, and to day, and for ever." A man who is created steady brings peace and safety to a woman's soul. Your husband's gentleness is not a weakness; it is his strength. Your husband's hesitation is not indecision; it is cautious wisdom. Your husband's lack of deep spiritual conversation is not a lack of caring; it is simply the cap on a mountain of intense emotions.

To order the book:
call 1-866-292-9936 (orders only)
8 a.m. - 5 p.m. C.S.T.,
or visit our online store at www.NoGreaterJoy.org

For other materials by Michael and Debi Pearl contact:
No Greater Joy, 1000 Pearl Road, Pleasantville, TN 37033
1-866-292-9936 (<u>orders only</u>) 8 a.m. - 5 p.m. C.S.T., or visit
our online store at www.NoGreaterJoy.org
Subscribe to the free No Greater Joy Magazine and email notifications.

THE VISION

What do you get when Islamic terrorists and White Supremacists go up against a small group of Bible believers in the hills of East Tennessee? Get your hands on a copy of this intensely exciting, informative novel!

GOOD AND EVIL COLOR

Award winning, illustrated novel, 330 pages of dazzling full color art work telling the Bible story chronologically from Genesis to Revelation. Written by Michael Pearl and drawn by Danny Bulanadi, a retired Marvel Comic Book artist. Now in over 30 languages, popular with missionaries and youth workers, this book has tremendous appeal to all ages and cultures–great as Sunday School curriculum. ***330-page book.***

CREATED TO BE HIS HELP MEET

What God is doing through this book is amazing. Has it provoked you to want to be the help meet God created you to be? We pray so. If it has blessed you (and your beloved) then consider passing the blessing on to someone you love by purchasing *Created To Be His Help Meet* for them. ***296-page book. English or Spanish. Available in MP3.***

THE HELP MEET'S JOURNEY

The Journey is a 184-page year-long companion journal for Created To Be His Help Meet. There are extra pages for your stories, doodlings, studies, and pictures where you will create a lasting memory of the miracle God is doing in you. This is a perfect study guide for individuals or women's study groups. ***Workbook journal.***

MARRIAGE GOD'S WAY VIDEO

A perfect marriage is 100/100. It is a man and a woman giving 100% to the other. What if he or she won't give 100%? Then you can match their 10% with your 10% and continue in an unfulfilling relationship, or, by the grace of God and the power of the Holy Spirit, you can give 100% to your spouse for their sake and watch their 10% grow into 100%.

Michael takes the viewer through the Word of God to uncover the Divine plan for husbands and wives. ***2 DVD set.***

TO TRAIN UP A CHILD
OVER 650,000 SOLD

From successful parents, learn how to train up your children rather than discipline them up. With humor and real-life examples, this book shows you how to train your children before the need to discipline arises. Be done with corrective discipline; make them allies rather than adversaries. The stress will be gone and your obedient children will praise you. ***122-page book.***

ONLY MEN

Michael Pearl speaks directly and frankly to men about their responsibilities as husbands. Wives should not listen to this tape. We don't want you taking advantage of your man. *Available on 1 CD.*

HOLY SEX

Michael Pearl takes his readers through a refreshing journey of Biblical texts, centered in the Song of Solomon. This sanctifying look at the most powerful passion God ever created will free the reader from false guilt and inhibition. Michael Pearl says, "It is time for Christian couples to take back this sacred ground and enjoy the holy gift of sexual pleasure." *82-page Book.*

NO GREATER JOY

No Greater Joy Vol. 1
Reprints of the first two years of No Greater Joy articles. Covers the subjects of sibling rivalry, pouting, bad attitudes, and much more. *110-page book.*

No Greater Joy Vol. 2
Let your children listen to great bedtime stories. Covers the subjects of rowdy boys, homeschooling, grief, and much more.
110-page book.

No Greater Joy Vol. 3
Children learn wisdom and enjoy listening to the stories as you read to them. Covers the subjects of marriage relationships and how they affect children, joy, much more. *110-page book.*

PORNOGRAPHY ROAD TO HELL

While most ministers avoid the subject, Michael Pearl addresses the deadly scourge of pornography head-on. He shows how repentance toward God and the power of the gospel of Jesus Christ can break the bondage of this wicked perversion through the abundant mercy and grace of a loving God. There is hope for the man caught in the snare of pornography and hope for the helpless, angry wife who finds it difficult to honor him. ***Booklet.***

RIGHTEOUSNESS

This set contains four messages on salvation and righteousness: The Man Christ Jesus, Saving Righteousness, Imputed Righteousness, and The Blood. The messages explore intriguing topics such as the humanity of Christ and why he referred to himself as "The Son of Man", why man's blood is required when he spills the blood of another man, God's clearly defined method of making a person righteous enough to get to heaven, and how the blood of Jesus washes away our sins. ***MP3 CD.***

FREE MAGAZINE SUBSCRIPTION

Go to the No Greater Joy website at www. nogreaterjoy.org and click "subscribe." While you are there subscribe to the weekly email notifications for information on seminars, specials, discounts and extra articles.

"Who can find a
virtuous woman?
for her price is far
above rubies."

Proverbs 31:10